THE REFERENCE SHELF   VOLUME 38 NUMBER 4

REPRESENTATIVE
AMERICAN SPEECHES:
1965-1966

EDITED BY LESTER THONSSEN

Professor of Speech
Metropolitan State College of Colorado at Denver

THE H. W. WILSON COMPANY
NEW YORK   **1966**

THE REFERENCE SHELF

The books in this series contain reprints of articles, excerpts from books, and addresses on current issues and social trends in the United States and other countries. There are six separately bound numbers in each volume, all of which are generally published in the same calendar year. One number is a collection of recent speeches; each of the others is devoted to a single subject and gives background information and discussion from various points of view, concluding with a comprehensive bibliography.

Subscribers to the current volume receive the books as issued. The subscription rate is $12 ($15 foreign) for a volume of six numbers. Single numbers are $3 each.

Copyright © 1966
By The H. W. Wilson Company
Library of Congress Catalog Card No. (38-27962)

PRINTED IN THE UNITED STATES OF AMERICA

PREFACE

J. Donald Adams, retired editor of the New York *Times Book Review,* once remarked that "words are almost on a par with the weather in their universality of appeal." Reflecting on the use and abuse of our common tongue, he said that "words remain one of the most living things of man's creation; indeed, one might argue that they have more vitality than anything else we have fashioned." The measure of their vitality and power has varied from age to age. So has the recognition of verbal competence as a standard of a man's worth. In the area of public address, for example, we continue to speculate whether high skill in speaking is a requirement for effective leadership. Must the public man be an orator? Is oratory influential in our time? In his well-known lecture on rhetoric, British Prime Minister Stanley Baldwin asserted that "it is not necessarily the man most fluent of speech to whom we should entrust the destinies of the country." But reporter Tom Wicker of the New York *Times,* conceding that eloquence and greatness in public figures were not the same, yet concluded that "in politics the former is almost always the indispensable tool of the latter." The noted French author André Maurois went even further, declaring that "the worth of a statesman's character is often equivalent to the excellence of his prose." As notable instances in support of his judgment, Maurois mentioned Charles de Gaulle, Winston Churchill, Franklin D. Roosevelt, and John F. Kennedy.

Perhaps the inquiry is not of cosmic concern; and indeed the mere mention of names to confirm the conflicting views will not be decisive. During his senatorial years, Vice President Hubert H. Humphrey used public address importantly and influentially; so do Senators Wayne Morse, J. W. Fulbright, and Everett Dirksen, to name but a few. On the other hand, Senator Carl Hayden of Arizona, who has spent some fifty years in Washington, "is said to wield more influence with less oratory than any other member of

3

Congress." After delivering a long speech in 1927 against certain features of the proposed Boulder Dam, he allegedly did not engage in further oratory for the next twenty years. "When you've got the votes," he once remarked, "you don't have to talk."

Some of the most powerful leaders in history, however, have not shared this view. With shocking irresponsibility, dictators and demagogues have occasionally used oratory—hypnotically incessant oratory—as an adjunct of authority. But it is perhaps mildly naïve to conclude that their speechmaking demonstrated the ultimate power of the spoken word. To attribute influence to words when the leader has a huge army behind him is a bit short of realistic. The amount of force supporting the rants and raves makes a significant difference in the response of the listeners.

A half century ago, Arthur Twining Hadley, then President of Yale University, reflected on the power of national leaders in shaping public opinion. He concluded that men such as Henry Clay, John C. Calhoun, Daniel Webster, and Abraham Lincoln exercised great influence through speech, largely because they appealed "to something higher than personal interest" and they created "something with more cohesive power than a mere enlightened selfishness. . . ." Each "was inspired by a lofty ideal of the public conscience, and helped the whole American people to realize that ideal." Nowadays, however, Dr. Hadley continued, "it is almost proverbial that the effective speeches are those which voice a prepossession already felt, and give a rallying cry to partisan or personal interests." I trust that the addresses included in this twenty-ninth edition of REPRESENTATIVE AMERICAN SPEECHES transcend the purely partisan commitments that incurred Dr. Hadley's displeasure, and that they give voice to ideas and ideals befitting man at his higher levels of private and public duty.

I express thanks to the contributors for permission to reprint their addresses. For assistance at various stages in the preparation of this volume, I gratefully acknowledge my obligation to John Jamieson, Ethel A. Crockford, and Ruth Ulman of The H. W. Wilson Company, Dean Keats R. McKinney of the Metropolitan State College of Colorado, Mary Margaret Robb of the University of Colorado, Dorothea Thonssen, Marva McKinney, Ruth Taylor, Sandi Schloffman, and Dr. E. S. Taylor of the University of Colorado Medical School at Denver.

LESTER THONSSEN

Denver, Colorado
June 1966

CONTENTS

THE UNRESOLVED CRISIS

VIETNAM: THE STRUGGLE TO BE FREE [1]

LYNDON B. JOHNSON [2]

In his George Huntington Williams Memorial Lecture at Johns Hopkins University on October 16, 1965, Secretary of State Dean Rusk called the search for peace the "paramount imperative of our time." He was but voicing the conviction of President Lyndon B. Johnson that the search was in fact the "assignment of the century." It remains a stern and unyielding assignment.

Secretary Rusk has remarked that the President and he enjoy "the dubious advantage" of knowing about ten or twelve trouble spots where crises might develop momentarily. But all others aside, the distant land of Vietnam, comprising little more than 125,000 square miles, continues to be the area of most anxious concern and tragic happening.

During the past year, the world community has witnessed a succession of fast-breaking events in the Vietnamese conflict. For the Americans particularly there was the military escalation, the mounting fear of confrontation with the Chinese Communists, the cessation and subsequent resumption of bombing of North Vietnam military targets, the build-up of American forces, and the sobering casualty lists from air strikes and guerrilla engagements. Moreover, broadcast journalism brought at least a fractional part of the face of war into public view. Speaking in New York City on January 28, 1966, Frank Stanton, president of the Columbia Broadcasting System, remarked that the desperation of Vietnam

> is witnessed every day by the vast majority of Americans in their own homes. Very possibly before it is over, it will be brought directly by satellite. War has ceased to be a far-off thing of cold casualty statistics, unpronounceable geographical names, and unread speeches by unknown statesmen. The misery of war, the pain, the death, the fear, the drudgery, the intensely felt convictions, the troubled dissents, the shrill protests, the deep determination—all these are brought full-scale to the people with whom the final responsibility for national commitments in a democratic society rests.

[1] Text furnished by Bill Moyers, special assistant to President Johnson.
[2] For biographical note, see Appendix.

Many public documents and statements outlined proposals to deal with the conflict. On January 3, 1966, the Mansfield Report was filed with the Senate Committee on Foreign Relations. Among its conclusions was the prediction that "the longer the war continues in its present pattern and the more it expands in scope, the greater will become the strain placed upon the relations of the United States with Allies both in the Far East and in Europe." With President Johnson's announcement on January 31, 1966, of the resumption of bombing of military installations in North Vietnam came the transmittal through Ambassador Arthur Goldberg of a letter to the United Nations, asking that the Security Council be called into session to consider the Vietnam question. By a vote of 9 to 2, with 4 abstentions, the Council voted to discuss the United States' "bid for a negotiated settlement." No direct debate on the proposed terms of negotiation has taken place. On February 6-8, 1966, President Johnson, together with several Cabinet members and advisers, met with South Vietnamese leaders in Honolulu to review economic and military plans leading, it was hoped, to an early end of the war and to the social reconstruction of the country. At the President's request, Vice President Hubert H. Humphrey flew to Southeast Asia "to dramatize," as the New York *Times* put it, "United States support for the projected reforms." Then came the widely publicized testimony of a panel of distinguished authorities—including Secretary Rusk, George F. Kennan, and General Maxwell D. Taylor—before the Senate Foreign Relations Committee. These hearings, in turn, prompted spirited debates in the Senate—debates that dealt not only with the justification and conduct of the war, but also with the relation and extent of presidential power to congressional authority.

Against this backdrop, which is only a partial picture, President Johnson delivered the following address on February 23, 1966, to a Freedom House audience in New York City on the occasion of his receiving the National Freedom Award.

Some observers in Washington doubt that the President really likes debate. He would rather work backstage. But circumstances sometimes require open acknowledgment of opposition. So in the Freedom Award speech, as James Reston properly remarked, "he was angry with his critics but eloquent about the right of dissent."

In a recent report in the London *Observer*, Michael Davie said President Johnson resembles "his only hero, Franklin Roosevelt, more than he resembles his immediate predecessors." But James Reston thinks "Roosevelt was a cautious and even cynical man compared with his protégé, Lyndon Johnson." Moreover, Johnson "is bolder and far more melodramatic." In this televised address, the President invoked the spirit and import of Roosevelt's four freedoms of mankind; and he joined in Wendell Willkie's belief that "freedom is an indivisible word." "If we want to enjoy it and fight for it, we must be prepared to extend it to everyone, whether they are rich or poor, whether they agree with us or not, no matter what their race or the color of their skin." "We know," said the President, "that the Four Freedoms are not secure in America when they are violently denied elsewhere in the world."

The opening sections of the address were not a little eloquent. Permeated with idealism and a laudable concern for the happiness of men everywhere, they reaffirmed the best dreams and visions of our time. But, as a newsman once remarked, there is always Vietnam. Perhaps James Reston was right in calling the speech a "symbol of the tragedy of his Administration." The greater part of the address was given over to ten questions, asked and answered by the President, about the war. The burden of the answers was, in effect, a call to Americans "to keep the faith for freedom." This was a partial answer to the critics of his Vietnam policy. Some wondered, however, whether he was not resorting "to the idealistic idiom of the American past" and applying it to today's disordered world.

To be honored with this award by this organization is a very proud moment for me. I accept it with the gratitude of my heart and with renewed commitment to the cause that it represents, the cause of freedom at home and the cause of freedom abroad.

Twenty-five years ago, to a world that was darkened by war, President Franklin Roosevelt described the Four Freedoms of mankind: freedom of speech and expression; freedom of every person to worship God in his own way; freedom from want; freedom from fear. Franklin Roosevelt knew that these freedoms could not be the province of one people alone. He called on all his countrymen to assist those who endured the tyrant's bombs and suffered his opposition and oppression. He called for courage and for generosity, and for resolution in the face of terror. And then he said, "Freedom means the supremacy of human rights everywhere. Our support goes to those who struggle to gain those rights—or keep them."

Wendell Willkie, Franklin Roosevelt's opponent in the campaign of 1940, shared his belief that freedom could not be founded only on American shores or only for those whose skin is white. "Freedom is an indivisible word," Wendell Willkie said. "If we want to enjoy it and fight for it we must be prepared to extend it to everyone, whether they are rich or poor, whether they agree with us or not, no matter what their race or the color of their skin."

That was Republican policy twenty-five years ago. It was Democratic policy twenty-five years ago. It is American policy here tonight.

Then how well have we done in our time in making the Four Freedoms real for our people and for the other people of the world? Here in America we accord every man the right to worship as he wills. I believe we are more tolerant of sectional and religious and racial differences than we were a quarter of a century ago. The majority of our people believe that a qualified man or woman, of any race, of any religion, of any section, could hold any office in our land. This was not so, not very clear at all in 1940. We are committed now, however great the trial and tension, to protecting the right of free expression and peaceful dissent.

We have learned to despise the witch-hunt, the unprincipled harassment of a man's integrity and his right to be different. We have gained in tolerance, and I am determined to use the high office I hold to protect and to encourage that tolerance. I do not mean to say that I will remain altogether silent on the critical issues of our day. For just as strongly as I believe in other men's freedom to disagree, so do I also believe in the President's freedom to attempt to persuade.

So let me assure you and my fellow Americans tonight that I will do everything in my power to defend both.

Twenty-five years ago freedom from want had the ring of urgency for our people. The unemployment rate stood at 14.5 per cent. Millions of Americans had spent the last decade in the breadlines or on farms where the winds howled away any chance for a decent life. Tonight there are still millions whose poverty haunts our conscience. There are still fathers without jobs, and there are still children without hope. Yet for the vast majority of Americans these are times when the hand of plenty has replaced the grip of want. And for the first time in almost nine years, tonight the unemployment rate has fallen to 4 per cent. This liberation from want, for which we thank God, is a testimony to the enduring vitality of the American competitive system, the American free enterprise economy. It is a testimony also to an enlightened public policy, established by Franklin Roosevelt and strengthened by every Administration since his death. That policy has freed Americans for more hopeful and more productive lives.

It has relieved their fears of growing old—by Social Security and by Medicare. It has inspired them with hope for their children, by aid to elementary and higher education. It has helped to create economic opportunity by enlightened fiscal policies. It has granted to millions, born into hopelessness, the chance of a new start in life by public works, by private incentive, by poverty programs. For the Negro American, it has opened the door after centuries of enslavement and discrimination—opened the doors to the blessings that America offers to those that are willing and able to earn them.

Thus we address the spirit of Franklin Roosevelt, twenty-five years after his message to America and the world, with confidence and with an unflagging determination. We have served his vision of the Four Freedoms essential to mankind—here, in America.

Yet we know that he did not speak only for America. We know that the Four Freedoms are not secure in America when they are violently denied elsewhere in the world. We know, too, that it requires more than speeches to resist the international enemies of freedom. We know that men respond to deeds when they are deaf to words. Even the precious word *freedom* may become empty to those without the means to use it. For what does freedom mean when famine cloaks the land, when new millions crowd upon already strained resources, when narrow privilege is entrenched behind law and custom, when all conspires to teach men that they cannot change the conditions of their lives?

I do not need to tell you how five Administrations have labored to give real meaning to *Freedom*, in a world where it is often merely a phrase that conceals oppression and neglect. Men in this room, men throughout America, have given their skills and their treasure to that work. You have warned our people how insatiable is aggression and how it thrives on human misery. You have carried the word that, without the sense that we can change the conditions of their lives, nothing can avail the oppressed of this earth—neither good will, nor national sovereignty, nor massive grants of aid from their more fortunate brothers. You have known, too, that men who believe they can change their destinies will change their destinies. Armed with that belief, they will be willing—yes, they will be eager—to make the sacrifices that freedom demands. They will be anxious to shoulder the responsibilities that are inseparably bound to freedom. They will be able to look beyond the four essential freedoms—beyond to the freedom to learn, to master new skills, to acquaint themselves with the lore of man and nature; to the freedom to grow, to become the best that is within them to become, to cast off the yoke of discrimination and disease; to the freedom to hope, and to build on that hope lives of integrity and well-being.

This is what our struggle in Vietnam is about tonight. This is what our struggle for equal rights in this country is all about tonight. We seek to create that climate, at home and abroad, where unlettered men can learn, where deprived children can grow, where hopeless millions can be inspired to change the terms of their existence for the better. That climate cannot be created where terror fills the air. Children cannot learn, and men cannot earn their bread, and women cannot heal the sick where the night of violence has blotted out the sun. Whether in the cities and hamlets of Vietnam or in the ghettoes of our own cities, the struggle is the same. That struggle is to end the violence against the human mind and body—so that the work of peace may be done and the fruits of freedom may be won.

We are pitting the resources of the law, of education and training, of our vision and our compassion against that violence here in America. And we shall end it in our time.

On the other side of the earth we are no less committed to ending violence against men who are struggling tonight to be free. It is about that commitment that I have come here to speak now.

Tonight in Vietnam more than 200,000 of your young Americans stand there fighting for your freedom. Tonight our people are determined that these men shall have whatever help they need and that their cause, which is our cause, shall be sustained. But in these last days there have been questions about what we are doing in Vietnam, and these questions have been answered loudly and clearly for every citizen to see and to hear. The strength of America can never be sapped by discussion, and we have no better nor stronger tradition than open debate, free debate, in hours of danger. We believe, with Macaulay, that men are never so likely to settle a question rightly as when they discuss it freely. We are united in our commitment to free discussion. So also we are united in our determination that no foe anywhere should ever mistake our arguments for indecision, nor our debates for weakness.

So what are the questions that are still being asked?

First, some ask if this is a war for unlimited objectives. The answer is plain. The answer is No.

Our purpose in Vietnam is to prevent the success of aggression. It is not conquest; it is not empire; it is not foreign bases; it is not domination. It is, simply put, just to prevent the forceful conquest of South Vietnam by North Vietnam.

Second, some people ask if we are caught in a blind escalation of force that is putting us headlong toward a wider war that no one wants. The answer, again, is a simple No. We are using that force and only that force that is necessary to stop this aggression. Our fighting men are in Vietnam because tens of thousands of invaders came south before them. Our numbers have increased in Vietnam because the aggression of others has increased in Vietnam. The high hopes of the aggressor have been dimmed and the tide of the battle has been turned—and our measured use of force will and must be continued. But this is prudent firmness, under what I believe is careful control. There is not, and there will not be, a mindless escalation.

Third, others ask if our fighting men are to be denied the help they need. The answer, again, is and will be a resounding No. Our great military establishment has moved 200,000 men across ten thousand miles since last spring. These men have, and will have, all they need to fight the aggressor. They have already performed miracles in combat. The men behind them have worked miracles of supply—building new ports, transporting new equipment, opening new roads. The American forces of freedom are strong tonight in South Vietnam, and we plan to keep them so. As you know, they are led there by a brilliant and resourceful commander, General William C. Westmoreland. He knows the needs of war and he supports the works of peace. And when he asks for more Americans to help the men that he has, his requests will be immediately studied, and, as I promised the nation last July, his needs will be immediately met.

Fourth, some ask if our men go alone to Vietnam, if we alone respect our great commitment in the Southeast Asia Treaty. Still again the answer is a simple No. We have seven allies in SEATO, and we have seen five of them give us vital support, each with his own strength and in his own way, to the cause of freedom in Southeast Asia.

Fifth, some ask about the risks of a wider war, perhaps against the vast land armies of Red China. And again the answer is No, never by any act of ours—and not if there is any reason left behind the wild words from Peiping.

We have threatened no one, and we will not. We seek the end of no regime, and we will not. Our purpose is solely to defend against aggression. To any armed attack, we will reply. We have measured the strength and the weakness of others, and we think we know our own. We observe in ourselves, and we applaud in others, a careful restraint in action. We can live with anger in word as long as it is matched by caution in deed.

Sixth, men ask if we rely on guns alone. Still again the answer is No. From our Honolulu meeting, from the clear pledge which joins us with our allies, there has emerged a common dedication to the peaceful progress of the people of Vietnam—to schools for their children, to care for their health, to hope and bounty for their land.

The Vice President returned tonight from his constructive and very highly successful visit to Saigon and to other capitals, and he tells me that he and Ambassador Lodge have found a new conviction and purpose in South Vietnam—for the battle against want and injustice as well as the battle against aggression.

So the pledge of Honolulu will be kept, and the pledge of Baltimore stands open—to help the men of the North when they have the wisdom to be ready.

We Americans must understand how fundamental is the meaning of this second war, the war on want. I talked on my ranch last fall with Secretary Freeman, the Secretary of Agriculture, and in my office last week with Secretary Gardner, Secretary of Health, Education, and Welfare, making over and over again the same central point: The breeding ground of war is human misery. If we are not to fight forever in faraway places—in Europe, or the far Pacific, or the jungles of Africa, or the suburbs of Santo Domingo—then we just must learn to get at the roots of violence. As a nation we must magnify our struggle against world hunger and illiteracy and disease. We must bring hope to men whose lives now end at two score or less—because without that hope, without progress in this war on want, we will be called on again to fight, again and again, as we are fighting tonight.

Seventh, men ask who has a right to rule in South Vietnam. Our answer there is what it has been for two hundred years. The people must have this right, the South Vietnamese people, and no one else. Washington will not impose upon the people of South Vietnam a government not of their choice. Hanoi shall not impose upon the people of South Vietnam a government not of their choice. So we will insist for ourselves on what we require from Hanoi: Respect for the principle of government by the consent of the governed. We stand for self-determination—for free elections—and we will honor their result.

Eighth, men ask if we are neglecting any hopeful chance of peace. And the answer is No. A great servant of peace, Secretary Dean Rusk, has sent the message of peace on every wire and by every hand to every continent. A great pleader for peace here with us tonight, Ambassador Arthur Goldberg, has worked at home and abroad in this same cause. Their undiscouraged efforts will continue. How much wiser it would have been, how much more compassionate towards its own people, if Hanoi had only come to the bargaining table at the close of the year. Then the seven thousand Communist troops who have died in battle since January the first, and the many thousands who have been wounded in that same period, would have lived in peace with their fellow men.

Today, as then, Hanoi has the opportunity to end the increasing toll the war is taking on those under its command.

Ninth, some ask how long we must bear this burden. To that question, in all honesty, I can give you no answer tonight. During the Battle of Britain when that nation stood alone, in 1940, Winston Churchill gave no answer to that question. When the forces of freedom were driven from the Philippines, President Roosevelt could not and did not name the date that we would return. If the aggressor persists in Vietnam, the struggle may well be long. Our men in battle know and they accept this hard fact. We who are at home can do as much, because there is no computer that can tell the hour and the day of peace, but we do know that it will come only to the steadfast and never to the weak in heart.

Tenth, and finally, men ask if it is worth it. I think you know that answer. It is the answer that Americans have given for a quarter of a century, wherever American strength has been pledged to prevent aggression. The contest in Vietnam is confused and hard, and many of its forms are new. Yet our American purpose and policy are unchanged. Our men in Vietnam are there. They are there, as Secretary Dillon told you, to keep a promise that was made twelve years ago. The Southeast Asia Treaty promised, as Secretary John Foster Dulles said for the United States, "that an attack upon the treaty area would occasion a reaction so united, and so strong, and so well placed that the aggressor would lose more than it could hope to gain."

But we keep more than a specific treaty promise in Vietnam tonight. We keep the faith for freedom.

Four Presidents have pledged to keep that faith.

The first was Franklin D. Roosevelt, in his State of the Union Message twenty-five years ago. He said:

We are committed to the proposition that principles of morality and considerations for our own security will never permit us to acquiesce in a peace dictated by aggressors and sponsored by appeasers. We know that enduring peace cannot be bought at the cost of other people's freedom.

The second was Harry S. Truman, in 1947, at a historic turning point in the history of guerrilla warfare—and of Greece, Turkey, and the United States. These were his words then:

I believe that it must be the policy of the United States to support free peoples who are resisting attempted subjugation by armed minorities or by outside pressures.

I believe that we must assist free peoples to work out their own destinies in their own way.

The third was Dwight D. Eisenhower, in his first Inaugural Address. He promised this:

Realizing that common sense and common decency alike dictate the futility of appeasement, we shall never try to placate an aggressor by the false and wicked bargain of trading honor for security. Americans, indeed, all free men, remember that in the final choice a soldier's pack is not so heavy a burden as a prisoner's chains.

And then five years ago, John F. Kennedy, on the cold bright noon of his first day in office, proclaimed:

Let the word go forth from this time and place, to friend and foe alike, that the torch has been passed to a new generation of Americans —born in this century, tempered by war, disciplined by a hard and bitter peace, proud of our ancient heritage, and unwilling to witness or permit the slow undoing of those human rights to which this nation has always been committed and to which we are committed today at home and around the world.

Let every nation know, whether it wishes us well or ill, that we shall pay any price, bear any burden, meet any hardship, support any friend, oppose any foe to assure the survival and the success of liberty.

This is the American tradition. Built in free discussion, proven on a hundred battlefields, rewarded by a progress at home that

has no match in history, it beckons us forward tonight to the
work of peace in Vietnam. We will build freedom while we
fight, and we will seek peace every day by every honorable means.
But we will persevere along the high hard road of freedom. We
are too old to be foolhardy and we are too young to be tired. We
are too strong for fear and too determined for retreat.

Each evening when I retire, I take up—from a bedside table—
reports from the battlefront and reports from the capitals around
the world. They tell me how our men have fared that day in the
hills and the valleys of Vietnam. They tell me what hope there
seems to be that the message of peace will be heard and that this
tragic war may be ended. I have read of individual acts of hero-
ism—of dedicated men and women whose valor matches that of
any generation that has ever gone before. I read of men risking
their lives to save others—of men giving their lives to save freedom. Always among these reports are a few letters from the men
out there themselves. If there is any doubt among some here at
home about our purposes in Vietnam, I never find it reflected in
those letters from Vietnam.

Our soldiers, our marines, our airmen and our sailors know
why they are in Vietnam. They know, as five Presidents have
known, how inseparably bound together are America's freedom
and the freedom of her friends around the world.

So tonight let me read you from a letter that I received from
an American father, a warm friend of mine of many years, about
his son, a young Army captain. He said:

   I have never known a man at war who showed less bravado in his
communications with home. When he was not flying missions in his
helicopter or working out of the battalion headquarters, he and some of
his buddies on their own visited the orphanages as individuals and
played with the kids. He was deeply interested in the Vietnamese people,
particularly the peasants, and he told me how sorely they wanted,
more than anything else, to just be left alone in some semblance
of freedom to grow their rice and to raise their families. This good
young American, as thousands like him, was not on the other side of
the world fighting specifically for you or for me, Mr. President. He was
fighting in perhaps our oldest American tradition, taking up for people
who are being pushed around.

The young captain described in this letter is dead tonight, but his spirit lives in the 200,000 young Americans who stand out there on freedom's frontier in Vietnam. It lives in their mothers and in their fathers here in America, who have proudly watched them leave their homes for their distant struggle.

So tonight I ask each citizen to join me, to join me in the homes and the meeting places our men are fighting to keep free, in a prayer for their safety.

I ask you to join me in a pledge to the cause for which they fight, the cause of human freedom to which this organization is dedicated. I ask you for your help, for your understanding, and for your commitment so that this united people may show forth to all the world that America has not ended the only struggle that is worthy of man's unceasing sacrifice—the struggle to be free.

UNITED STATES POLICY AND ACTIONS IN VIETNAM [3]

Ernest Gruening [4]

Near the year's end in 1965, Emmet John Hughes, writing in *Newsweek*, spoke of the "striking fact that no United States military venture in a generation has distressed or disheartened so many responsible and vocal citizens" as the war in Vietnam. The reasons for the distress are numerous, and the explanations, cutting across party lines, are varied. Among the most outspoken critics of the policy in Southeast Asia, however, there is a feeling, eloquently voiced by Senator Wayne Morse, Democrat of Oregon, that the Administration has "sought to reduce all our difficulties . . . to the neat and understandable pattern of the 1930's." "It is they [the State Department, Defense Department, and the White House]," he said in a speech to the Senate on January 19, 1966, "who have tried to equate all of Asia with the analogy of Munich, and who have used a too-pat 'devil' theory to arouse passions into a warlike stance against both North Vietnam and China."

In theory, practically everyone seems to believe in the right of dissent. But when it is practiced on delicate issues, it often finds detractors where before it had friends. The continuing debates, both in and out of the Senate, attest to this circumstance. At the end of a CBS television discussion on February 13, 1966, Eric Sevareid remarked that public debate "about the validity in the conduct of a war in which thousands of Americans are already risking their lives" involves some danger. But, he concluded, "we have to remember that life in the free society is not supposed to be safe. It is supposed to be free in the belief that only in this free conflict of ideas do you ultimately find the way to the final safety." Moreover, the belief that our open debates on the issue of war give comfort to the enemy is only a partial truth. Doubtless, as Walter Lippmann remarked, what is done in Hanoi and Peking "will be determined by the realities as they see them in Asia, and not by how they read the Gallup poll in the United States."

Senator Ernest Gruening, Democrat of Alaska, is one of the vigorous proponents of free debate on the sensitive issue of Vietnam. For many months he has taken part in this vital dialogue on college and university campuses, at public meetings, and on the floor of the Senate. An opponent of the Administration policy, he has given leadership to open inquiry into our actions in Southeast Asia.

[3] Text furnished by Senator Gruening, with permission for this reprint.
[4] For biographical note, see Appendix.

Deeply interested and highly knowledgeable in the antecedents of what he calls "our military plunge into the quagmire," Senator Gruening has developed detailed reports of the history of our alleged commitment in Vietnam. One such statement was the speech reprinted here, delivered on December 9, 1965, at Cambridge, Massachusetts, to the graduate students of the Harvard Law School. Believing it impossible to appraise realistically "what should have been our course of action and what it should be now and in the future without a presentation of that other side of how we got into this mess," he traced certain historical facts leading up to our involvement in the war. "We are now at war," he remarked, "and in my judgment, and that of Wayne Morse, who is a constitutional lawyer, we are . . . in violation of the Constitution." For a development of the contrary view, students are invited to read the legal memorandum prepared by Leonard C. Meeker, legal adviser of the State Department. The statement was submitted on March 8, 1966, to the Senate Committee on Foreign Relations and was published under the title of "The Legality of United States Participation in the Defense of Vietnam" in *The Department of State Bulletin* of March 28, 1966.

Turning then to the "realm of personal opinion," Senator Gruening expressed no confidence in the so-called domino theory which holds "that had we not gone in, these nations of Southeast Asia would have fallen into the hands of the Communist Chinese." "Nothing," he declared, "that happens in South Vietnam jeopardizes the security of the United States." Moreover,

> there is a question of whether that would justify our invading Vietnam and bombing it any more than we can justify the seizure by Stalin of the formerly independent countries surrounding Russia—Latvia, Lithuania, Estonia, Poland, Czechoslovakia, Hungary—on the grounds that their control was essential to the security of Soviet Russia.

I have been asked to address you on the subject of the United States policies and actions in Vietnam. As you know, for reasons which I will discuss in detail, I am not in agreement with those policies and actions.

Recently those who have publicly criticized those policies have come under increasing attack. This is a surprising development. I would assume that in this land of freedom, the right to speak out openly on behalf of peace would be taken for granted. I would consider it not only a right but a duty, an imperative duty.

As the St. Louis *Post Dispatch,* one of the nation's finest newspapers, stated editorially on December 2:

One of the striking things about the criticism of Vietnam policy is its persistent refusal to be silenced. We hope that continues to be the case. Every citizen shares the moral responsibility for his country's conduct. If he believes his country's conduct to be wrong, but fails to speak out, he is betraying his own obligations as a citizen. . . . Just as public criticism of a no-negotiation policy brought about a policy of pro-negotiation, so criticism of mistaken objectives in Asia can bring about adoption of the right objectives. It is vital that discussion of the nation's Asian objectives be free and vigorous.

Since the Bill of Rights, the first ten amendments to the Constitution, prohibits the Congress, and by implication all other legislative and executive authorities in the nation and state, from abridging freedom of speech, the burden of proof should rest heavily on any who would deny or seek to impair such freedom. I know of no right more precious or more inherent in our nation's philosophy and its often reiterated professions.

But our nation is now at war—an undeclared war, to be sure —and many of our fellow citizens hold the view that it is our duty as patriotic Americans to support the Administration, which has assumed the responsibility for our course of action in Southeast Asia and is conducting the war. When our men are dying in combat deep passions are naturally aroused, the martial spirit becomes rampant, and dissent and protest become increasingly perilous.

Yet it is just at such a time that speaking out is more than ever essential.

Earlier this week I received a letter from a professor in a large western state university, asking me to come there and address the student body and faculty on Vietnam and related matters. I quote from his letter: "We have had a small protest demonstration . . . and this has produced a most violent reaction which has assumed chilling proportions, creating a climate extremely unfavorable to rational discussion of these problems."

There in a brief sentence you have what is going on all over the country, and it emphasizes the need for presentation on both sides of the case, for and against the United States policies in Southeast Asia and our armed intervention there.

So, whatever the consequences, I agree with the *Post-Dispatch* editorial that he who dissents from his country's policy but fails to speak out, is indeed betraying his obligations as a citizen.

Clearly it is not easy to oppose the publicly expressed and reiterated declaration of policy and related action by the President of the United States, policies largely supported by the press —with some honorable and courageous exceptions—and in behalf of which the powerful machinery of Government is militantly mobilized.

Yet those who disagree with our national policy in this area can support President Johnson's statement in his April 27th news conference, which is pertinent to recall.

Asked: "Mr. President, do you think any of the participants in the national discussion on Vietnam could appropriately be likened to the appeasers of twenty-five or thirty years ago?"

He replied:

I don't believe in characterizing people with labels. I think you do a great disservice when you engage in name calling. We want honest, forthright discussion in this country, and that will be discussion with differences of views, and we welcome what our friends have to say, whether they agree with us or not. I would not want to label people who agree with me or disagree with me.

It is not a secret that I have been one of those who have disagreed. I began voicing my disagreement in a full-length speech on the floor of the Senate on March 10, 1964, just twenty-one months ago. It was entitled: "The United States Should Get Out of Vietnam." That was before our country had committed a single soldier to combat or dropped a bomb. It would have been far easier to negotiate an honorable settlement at that time and to obviate much of the slaughter and all else that has happened since and the grim prospect that now lies before us.

Among the imperative reasons for full public discussion and disclosure is because, in my view, the justification for the course which has now so deeply and tragically involved our country in Vietnam and in Southeast Asia, with apparently only a prospect for further and deeper involvement, is that the basis—the alleged basis—as I have studied it differs very materially from the actual historic record. And it is not possible realistically to appraise what should have been our course of action and what it should be now and in the future without a presentation of that other side of how we got into this mess.

During World War II the French colony of Indochina was overrun by the Japanese. Fighting to liberate this area were Vietnamese and the Allied forces at war with Japan. The native aspirations—part of the world-wide revolt against foreign domination, against colonialism—were for independence. But the French wanted to regain their colonial possessions. Because of the fear that Communist China would take over this area, the Eisenhower Administration was urged to assist the French in reconquering their former colony. Certain voices in the United States urged all-out military assistance. Others advised against it. President Eisenhower declined to send our troops into combat to aid the French although we did give the French substantial financial assistance and some cooperation in military training through a military mission established in Saigon. But lacking this all-out support, the French were defeated by the local forces, the Vietminh, suffering staggering losses and surrender at Dien Bien Phu.

In consequence, there was a meeting at Geneva of representatives of fourteen nations, where accords were drawn up which provided that three new nations should be born out of the former French colony—namely Laos, Cambodia, and Vietnam. The accords provided that Vietnam was to be temporarily, but only temporarily, divided into North and South Vietnam for reasons of demobilization, but that within two years an election would be held to choose the officials who would govern the reunited Vietnamese.

The United States was in South Vietnam with its military mission at Saigon, and with the political demise of the French, was in charge. It was the United States that brought Ngo Dien Diem back from monastic life in the United States, . . . installed by us as President of the Cabinet, and in a subsequent plebiscite backed him against the playboy Emperor Bao Dai.

Now we come to what I consider the pertinent part of the history of United States involvement.

The United States did not sign the Geneva Accords, but it expressed support of them in a unilateral statement.

This statement was by Under Secretary of State Walter Bedell Smith, dated July 21, 1954, was declared by him to be a unilateral declaration of United States position in these matters, and it stated:

The Government of the United States being resolved to devote its efforts to the strengthening of peace in accordance with the principles and purposes of the United Nations takes note of the agreements concluded at Geneva on July 20 and 21, 1954.

The statement declared its support of Paragraphs 1-12 inclusive of the Geneva agreements and that

it will refrain from the threat or the use of force to disturb them in accordance with Article 2 (4) of the Charter of the United Nations dealing with the obligation of members to refrain in their international relations from the threat or use of force [and second it] would view any renewal of the aggression in violation with grave concern and as seriously threatening international peace and security.

In connection with the statement in the declaration concerning free elections in Vietnam my Government wishes to make clear its position which it has expressed in a declaration made in Washington on June 29, 1954, as follows:

"In the case of nations now divided against their will, we shall continue to seek to achieve unity through free elections supervised by the United Nations to insure that they are conducted fairly."

With respect to the statement made by the representative of the State of Vietnam, the United States reiterates its traditional position that peoples are entitled to determine their own future and that it will not join in an arrangement which would hinder this. Nothing in its declaration just made is intended to or does indicate any departure from this traditional position.

We share the hope that the agreements will permit Cambodia, Laos, and Vietnam to play their part, in full independence and sovereignty, in the peaceful community of nations, and will enable the peoples of that area to determine their own future.

You will note that in this declaration by the United States we speak only of Vietnam, not of South Vietnam or North Vietnam, but Vietnam, and we reiterate our traditional position that its people are entitled to determine their own future.

On the same day, July 21, 1954, President Eisenhower issued a statement confirming Under Secretary Bedell Smith's declarations.

Now the official justification for our subsequent and present military involvement there and our steadily increasing involvement in South Vietnam was stated as follows:

In the State of the Union message in January 1965 President Johnson said:

> We are there, first, because a friendly nation has asked us for help against Communist aggression. Ten years ago we pledged our help. Three Presidents have supported that pledge. We will not break it.

He elaborated on this statement in his Johns Hopkins speech on April 7, 1965, saying:

> Why are we in South Vietnam?
>
> We are there because we have a promise to keep. Since 1954 every American President has offered support to the people of South Vietnam. We have helped to build, and we have helped to defend. Thus, over many years, we have made a national pledge to help South Vietnam defend its independence.
>
> I intend to keep that promise. To dishonor that pledge . . . would be an unforgivable wrong.

Now let us go back and see what that first pledge was—the pledge by the first of the three Presidents President Johnson refers to, namely President Eisenhower.

It was contained in a letter to President Diem as President of the Council of Ministers of Vietnam on October 23, 1954. I will read it.

Dear Mr. President:

> I have been following with great interest the course of developments in Vietnam, particularly since the conclusion of the conference at Geneva. The implications of the agreement concerning Vietnam have caused grave concern regarding the future of a country temporarily divided by an artificial military grouping weakened by a long and ex-

hausting war and faced with enemies without and by their subversive collaborators within.

Your recent requests for aid to assist in the formidable project of the movement of several hundred thousand loyal Vietnamese citizens away from areas which are passing under a de facto rule and political ideology which they abhor, are being fulfilled. I am glad that the United States is able to assist in this humanitarian effort.

You will note that what I shall read now, which follows those first two paragraphs of President Eisenhower's letter to Diem, says nothing about a further request by President Diem for assistance. The only request of record was limited to assistance in moving several hundred thousand Vietnamese from the north to the south. There is nothing to indicate that Diem was asking and that President Eisenhower was responding to a request "for help against Communist aggression."

I now resume the quoting of Eisenhower's letter:

We have been exploring ways and means to permit our aid to Vietnam to be more effective and to make a greater contribution to the welfare and stability of the government of Vietnam. I am, accordingly, instructing the American Ambassador to Vietnam to examine with you, in your capacity as chief of government, how an intelligent program of American aid given directly to your government can serve to assist Vietnam in its present hour of trial, provided that your government is prepared to give assurances as to the standards of performance it would be able to maintain in the event such aid were supplied.

Consider now this language. "*We*," namely the Government of the United States, "have been exploring ways and means" of aiding Vietnam. But that aid is to be given only "provided that your government is prepared to give assurances as to standards of performance it would be able to maintain in the event such aid were supplied."

Now to continue President Eisenhower's letter:

The purpose of this offer is to assist the government of Vietnam in developing and maintaining a strong, viable state, capable of resisting attempted subversion or aggression through military means. The Government of the United States expects that this aid will be met by performance on the part of the government of Vietnam in undertaking needed reforms.

I continue to quote from President Eisenhower's letter:

It [namely the Government of the United States] hopes that such aid, combined with your own continuing efforts, will contribute effectively toward an independent Vietnam endowed with a strong government. Such a government would, I hope, be so responsive to the nationalist aspirations of its people, so enlightened in purpose and effective in performance, that it will be respected both at home and abroad and discourage any who might wish to impose a foreign ideology on your free people.

So here we have a third pre-condition for United States aid. The Viet government was to be a government respected both at home and abroad. We know how responsive it was to the aspirations of its people, how enlightened its purpose, how much respected at home—since a civil war broke out against it. And it was not respected abroad, as evidenced by the fact that Ambassador Lodge supported the removal of Diem and the Nhus. Of course, those conditions prescribed by President Eisenhower were not fulfilled by the Diem regime. But in any event nothing was said about sending in our troops. There was no promise or pledge of military aid.

This is further confirmed by a White House statement of November 3, 1954, which states that President Eisenhower had instructed General J. Lawton Collins as his special representative "to explore" with President Diem and his government how "to help them with their critical problems and to supplement measures adopted by the Vietnamese themselves." Again, no mention of any request by Diem for that aid. Had there been, it is hardly likely that such a request would not have been mentioned. That is why I believe that *we asked ourselves in.* The most that was implied was economic aid, which was given, and President Eisenhower himself declared a few months ago that he had only offered economic aid. During the remaining six years of the Eisenhower Administration, we had a military mission which did not exceed some six hundred officers and men; not one of these were engaging in combat, no American lives were risked or lost during that period. So much for the first of the three Presidents.

Now we come to the second President, John F. Kennedy, who was persuaded by his Secretary of Defense, Robert McNamara, to escalate our commitment to the extent of sending military advisers whose number rose before the end of his presidency to some fifteen thousand. But as late as September 2, 1963, less than three months before his death, in an interview with CBS newscaster, Walter Cronkite, President Kennedy said: "I don't think that unless a greater effort is made by the government to win popular support that the war can be won out there."

So, President Kennedy had reached the conclusion that Diem had not fulfilled Eisenhower's conditions although he had had nine years to do so from 1954 to 1963. And then President Kennedy goes on to say:

In the final analysis, it is their war. They are the ones who have to win it or lose it. We can give them equipment, we can send our men out there as advisers, but they have to win it—the people of Vietnam —against the Communists. We are prepared to continue to assist them, but I don't think that the war can be won unless the people support the effort, and, in my opinion, in the last two months the government has gotten out of touch with the people.

I believe this record shows that we did not make a solemn pledge to support that government. And in any event that government ceased to exist after its failure was manifest. One of the reasons why civil war broke out against Diem in addition to his own oppressive tactics of jailing hundreds of people without trial, some of them being tortured in prison, was the repudiation of the provision to hold general elections in July 1956. This was the most basic item in the Geneva Accord and you will recall our unilateral commitment to it by Walter Bedell Smith, Under Secretary of State, when he stated that "in the case of nations now divided against their will, we shall continue to seek to achieve unity through free elections. . . ."

Yet, the United States, which dominated the situation of South Vietnam, approved and ratified that government's refusal to hold the elections. We and they refused to hold them for the reason, frankly stated, that it was felt that Ho Chi Minh would be elected President. But what principles are we espousing when we agree to go to an election and then call it off because we feel we are going to lose it? That is the unquestionable record on this issue. How do we square that with our national conscience and a tradition that would be inviolate under our standards?

Now, some deny that this is a civil war and one of the partial myths on which we base our actions is that the whole trouble stems from aggression from Hanoi. Well, no one could have been better informed on this issue than John F. Kennedy who was in the Senate since 1954 and who, in his news conference of July 18, 1963, referred to "the civil war which has gone on for ten years."

Chapter 3, Article 16, of the agreement on the cessation of hostilities provides:

With effect from the date of entry into force of the present agreement, the introduction into Vietnam of any troop reinforcements and additional military personnel is prohibited.

And, further,

With effect from the date of entry into force of the present agreement, the introduction into Vietnam of any reinforcements in the form of all types of arms, munitions and other war matériel such as combat aircraft, naval craft, pieces of ordnance, jet engines and jet weapons and armored vehicles, is prohibited.

The Geneva Agreement provided for an International Commission to supervise the carrying out of the Geneva Accord and to see that its provisions were carried out in Vietnam. The Commission consisted of three representatives, one from Canada, one from India, and one from Poland. They made various reports which indicated increasing violations of the agreements by *both* parties. When one reads them objectively one gains the impression that the violations by the South Vietnamese under United States tutelage were far more serious and far more extensive. A special report by the Commission in Paragraph 12 states:

Since December 1961 the Commission's Teams in South Vietnam have been persistently denied the right to control and inspect, which are part of the mandatory tasks. Thus, these Teams, though they were able to observe the steady and continuous arrival of war matériel, including aircraft carriers with helicopters on board, were unable, in view of the denial of controls, to determine precisely the quantum and nature of war matériel unloaded and introduced into South Vietnam.

And it continues in Paragraph 17:

As the Commission has been denied mandatory controls, as pointed out earlier in Paragraph 12 above, it has not been able to make a precise assessment of the number of military personnel and the quantum of war matériel brought in. However, from 3rd December, 1961, up to 5th May, 1962, the Commission's Teams have controlled the entry of 72 military personnel, and observed but not controlled 173 military personnel, 62 helicopters, 6 reconnaissance aircraft, 5 jet aircraft, 57 fighters/fighter bombers, 25 transport aircraft, 26 unspecified types of aircraft, 102 jeeps, 8 tractors, 8 105-mm. howitzers, 3 armoured carriers (tracked), 29 armoured fighting vehicle trailers, 404 other trailers, and radar equipment and crates, 5 warships, 9 LST's (including 4 visiting LST's), 3 LCT's, 5 visiting aircraft carriers and spares of various kinds. . . .

In the case of North Vietnam, the Commission (the Polish delegate dissenting, which is not surprising since he represented a country behind the iron curtain) concluded that

in specific instances there was evidence to show that armed and unarmed personnel, arms and other supplies had been sent from the North to the South with the purpose of supporting, organizing and carrying out hostile activities including armed attacks, directed against the Armed Forces and Administration of the Zone in the South. These activities are in violation of Articles 10, 19, 24 and 27 of the agreement of cessation of hostilities in Vietnam.

Obviously, both sides, North and South, were violating the Geneva Agreement. It would appear that those of the South were far larger and they had the support and approval of the United States. The violations on both sides were charged by the Canadian and Indian Representatives who may well be credited with impartiality. The Polish delegate, whose report may not be accepted as unbiased, refused to join in the indictment of the charges against North Vietnam but joined with his colleagues against those of the South.

We now come to further United States violations. The United States is a signatory to the United Nations Charter. In fact, the United States was largely instrumental in creating the United Nations.

Article 2, of Chapter 1, Paragraph 4, provides:

1. All Members shall refrain in their international relations from the threat or use of force against the territorial integrity or political in-

dependence of any state, or in any other manner inconsistent with the purposes of the United Nations.

Article 33, of Chapter 6, provides:

1. The parties to any dispute, the continuance of which is likely to endanger the maintenance of international peace and security, shall first of all, seek a solution by negotiation, enquiry, mediation, conciliation, arbitration, judicial settlement, resort to regional agencies or arrangements, or other peaceful means of their own choice.

Now you notice that this Article does not say that they may do this but that they *shall* do it, and lists eight alternative methods which should be used "first of all." Now we may well ask, did we, the United States, when there were violations of the Geneva agreements, seek a solution by negotiation? We did not. Did we seek a solution by enquiry? We did not. Did we seek a solution by mediation? We did not. Did we seek a solution by conciliation? We did not. Did we seek a solution by arbitration? We did not. Did we seek a solution by judicial settlement? We did not. Did we seek a solution by resorting to regional agencies or arrangements? We did not. Or did we seek a solution by "other peaceful means of our (their) own choice?" We did not.

One of the "regional agencies or arrangements" whose aid we might have invoked for a peaceful solution was the Southeast Asia Treaty Organization which was created at the instance and by the leadership of Secretary of State John Foster Dulles and whose signatories were the United States, Australia, France, New Zealand, Pakistan, the Philippines, Thailand, and the United Kingdom. It reaffirms in Article I the agreement to settle international disputes by peaceful means, and, to quote it exactly:

The Parties undertake, as set forth in the Charter of the United Nations, to settle any international disputes in which they may be involved by peaceful means in such a manner that international peace and security and justice are not endangered, and to refrain in their international relations from the threat or use of force in any manner inconsistent with the purposes of the United Nations.

Thus having used force the United States was also violating the SEATO treaty. I have spoken of the violation of Article 2,

Paragraph 4, Chapter 1 (which was specifically mentioned by Under Secretary Walter Bedell Smith's declaration of United States policy which we would adhere to), and the violation of Article 33, Chapter 6, of the United Nations Charter that provides for the settlement of disputes by peaceful means. Another violation was that of Article 37 which provides that if parties to a dispute of the matters referred to in Article 33 fail to settle it by the means indicated in that Article they shall refer it to the Security Council. Again not *may* but *shall.* The United States has not done that.

So when those in authority in Washington speak of "a national pledge" as a justification for our course of action in Vietnam, I find it difficult not to contrast that dubious conditional, qualified, tentative offer of help to a vanished South Vietnamese chief of state, who did not fulfill the conditions, with our violation of the unqualified treaty commitments, of which there could be no more solemn category—the United Nations Charter, the Southeast Asia Treaty—and the violations of the unilateral statement by Under Secretary Walter Bedell Smith, reiterated on the same day by President Eisenhower, that we would support Vietnam supervised elections in 1956.

To review briefly what has happened in the Congress: In August of 1964 it was reported that two, or possibly three, PT boats had attacked our Seventh Fleet in the Tonkin Gulf. But if, as reported (although it is questionable whether the full facts have been revealed to the American people), this was an act of aggression—although perhaps as unimportant as an attack by a fourteen-year-old boy with a beanshooter against Cassius Clay—the President was wholly within his rights to order a retaliatory attack by airplanes from the fleet on the base from which these PT boats emerged. However, the next day a resolution drafted in the White House was submitted to the Congress not merely approving everything that had been done before in Southeast Asia, but giving the President unlimited power in his own discretion to use the armed forces of the United States anywhere in Southeast Asia. It passed the House unanimously and in the Senate there were two opposing votes—those of Senator Wayne

Morse and mine. I could not justify giving the President this unlimited, unrestricted power out of which our steadily escalating military commitment stems. For one thing, the Constitution of the United States is specific that only Congress can declare war. We are now at war, and in my judgment and that of Wayne Morse, who is a constitutional lawyer, we are thereby in violation of the Constitution.

In February last we started bombing North Vietnam. The justification for this drastic change of policy was that there had been an attack on one of our outposts at Pleiku. Pleiku is about two hundred miles south of the seventeenth parallel, the boundary between North and South Vietnam. At night a group of Vietcong passed through the lines of the South Vietnamese troops who were either too inert or uninterested to alert our men in the barracks. The Vietcong opened fire with a mortar of American make, which they had apparently secured from the South Vietnamese forces, and killed eight American soldiers. There was no direct relation between this incident and North Vietnamese infiltration, but it was made the justification for the bombing which has now continued for ten months with no appreciable result. It appears rather to have hardened the determination of the North Vietnamese to continue what they have been doing and rather to increase their aid to the South Vietnamese National Army of Liberation.

Last May the President sent to the Congress an appropriation request of $700 million to conduct this undeclared war in Vietnam. President Johnson frankly stated that this request was being made not because monies were needed to supply our armed forces in Vietnam, for he could transfer money needed from other sources, but rather as a vehicle to secure additional congressional approval of his carrying on the undeclared war in Vietnam and anywhere else in Southeast Asia that he saw fit. This the President made clear at the outset of his message, when he stated:

This is not a routine appropriation. For each member of Congress who supports this request is also voting to persist in our effort to halt Communist aggression in South Vietnam. Each is saying that the Congress and the President stand united before the world in joint determination that the independence of South Vietnam shall be preserved and Communist attack will not succeed.

Since this money was not needed and was to be used merely as a symbol of support for our policy, I found myself unable to vote for it, as likewise did Wayne Morse, and we were joined by another Senator, Gaylord Nelson, of Wisconsin. In the House, seven members voted against it.

Going from these factual presentations to the realm of personal opinion, it is my deep-seated belief that we made a very serious mistake in getting involved militarily because first, in my view, nothing that happens in South Vietnam jeopardizes the security of the United States. And even if it did so, there is a question of whether that would justify our invading Vietnam and bombing it any more than we can justify the seizure by Stalin of the formerly independent countries surrounding Russia—Latvia, Lithuania, Estonia, Poland, Czechoslovakia, Hungary—on the grounds that their control was essential to the security of Soviet Russia. Nor do I subscribe to the domino theory which is that had we not gone in, these nations of Southeast Asia would have fallen into the hands of the Communist Chinese. And then we are told in sequent flights of fancy that—after Southeast Asia—the Philippines, Australia, New Zealand would fall and we would have to be fighting the Communists on the beaches of California. That to me is arrant nonsense. Certainly our control of the Pacific by sea and air renders that absurd. Moreover, I am not a pacifist and I do not like and am utterly opposed to the advance of totalitarianism anywhere. If a situation should arise whereby a free government such as that of Australia or New Zealand were threatened by attack and invasion by the forces of imperial communism and there was a request from those governments for our aid, I would be for giving that aid without stint or limit. The situation in South Vietnam is quite different. I am confident, and this is further in the realm of opinion, that had we stayed out entirely we would have three independent countries formed out of French Indochina, that they would have installed their own social and political ideology, which they would have had every right to do, and that a united Vietnam would have adopted communism as its social and economic system. But it would have been a Communist regime independent of Peking and there is evidence that many non-Communists are enlisted in the civil war against the South Vietnam government. The history of Vietnam shows conclusively their people's dislike and fear of the Chinese, and their war is largely motivated by a desire to get rid of all foreign rule. They want independence, and that should be a cause that ought to appeal to Americans. They did not want the French in. They did not want the Chinese, and I doubt whether a majority want us in. In Europe, to achieve a corresponding situation, namely in Yugoslavia, a Communist state independent of Moscow, the United States invested two billion dollars in aid for Tito, and our policy makers considered that, and now consider it, a sound and profitable investment.

I need not detain you longer to point out what has happened and what is happening. I consider our bombing of North Vietnam totally without justification morally, legally, or otherwise. It is the sort of thing we condemned scathingly when done by totalitarian powers in past years; and as we have seen now after ten months of such bombing, it has merely stiffened the resistance of those whom we are fighting. We are getting in deeper and deeper; not only are our casualty lists growing, but the toll not merely of those fighting but of civilian noncombatants mounts daily. It is my reasoned view that in our effort to stop the advance of imperialist communism, we are actually aiding it. So far, at least, the situation must be to the liking of the Communist rulers of China, for to date they have not committed a single soldier to this war. And yet there we are—a great Western power, the greatest in the world—engaging in a desperate, bitter, and horrible struggle on the continent of Asia with a small Asiatic nation, sacrificing the lives of our youth and spending billions of dollars.

The situation is different even from that of Korea. First, there was overt aggression from the North there. Second, we were there under a United Nations mandate. Third, the South Koreans wanted to fight. These factors are not present, at least not in the same degree, in Vietnam. There was no overt initial aggression from the North at the start. There has been infiltration, subsequent infiltration, but paralleling the United States support of South Vietnam, and at least not appreciably until our and Diem's refusal to hold elections. The United States went in unilaterally and until very recently, and only in response to great pressure from us, we had little support from our SEATO allies—none from Pakistan, none (to speak of) from Britain, none from France— and when Administration spokesmen cite the total number of nations that are allegedly with us, in a kind of numbers game, we find that they have come in late—and largely with only token assistance. In the November 29 issue of *Newsweek* there was a little item in its Periscope column entitled "Spain Lends a Hand" which reads:

Spain is the latest country to lend a hand in Vietnam. After much prodding from LBJ, the Franco government hopes to ship in four ambulances with medical crews. Actually the ambulances will have little significance (the helicopters do their work now) but the medics are wanted and the Spanish contingent will be welcomed as evidence of support for the United States and Saigon.

When I was in South America last January I found that every American ambassador had received orders to go to the president of the country to which he was accredited to request support for our efforts in Vietnam. Many of them were reluctant to do this and in many cases their pleas were unheeded, while in others there was the same kind of token compliance which we now see we have coming from Spain. These countries are all recipients of lavish American aid and the United States is, in effect, paying for these tokens and is in a position to apply pressure.

I could only wish there could be a ready and quick answer to and a way out of the tragic dilemma that the President, his advisers, and the people of the United States find themselves in. We are now so deeply committed that a way out is extremely difficult to find. There have been numerous suggestions made and we should explore them all actively. Our so-called unconditional discussions are not unconditional as long as we do not firmly pledge willingness to negotiate also with the people who are doing the fighting, the National Liberation Front, or Vietcong; guarantee the carrying out of the general agreements to which we once pledged support, namely supervised elections in all Vietnam, but whose violation we approved; and make every effort for a cease-fire and simultaneous phasing out of the combatants of both sides. Unless we make such modifications in our attempts at negotiation and stop the bombing of North Vietnam—because no people will yield under those circumstances—this senseless war will go on and get steadily more disastrous.

What the United States should do, in sum, is to return to the rule of law. We should have invoked the United Nations at the very beginning when we felt that treaty commitments were violated, and we have not used the United Nations as we should have.

In this connection, the disclosures by Adlai Stevenson to Eric Sevareid, which appeared in the November 30th issue of *Look* magazine, that both McNamara and Rusk turned a deaf ear to the efforts of U Thant to secure negotiations which were then possible, are very disturbing.

Because I strongly value adherence to law, I cannot approve the action of a few of our draftees in burning up their draft cards. They are in violation of the law and must take the consequences, however one may sympathize with their feelings that we should never have been in Vietnam and that what we are doing there is morally wrong and self-defeating. But peaceful protests and freedom of speech should remain inviolate and we should continue to urge almost any sensible solution that would put an end to the killing. It would be much better than the dark prospect of more and more slaughter which lies ahead and which ultimately, in my judgment, will result in a solution which could have been achieved bloodlessly a few years ago. The sad fact is that we cannot win this war. When I say "win," I do not necessarily mean in a strict military sense. If we continue to pour troops into Southeast Asia, blast its villages from the air with bombs and napalm, kill more tens of thousands, we may in time impose a military domination, although even that is by no means certain. But even if we did, what then? Sooner or later the problems of Asia will be settled by Asians, as they should be. We should have learned that the white man cannot settle them for the Asians. We will be told that there are some Asians fighting on our side, as in the case of the Koreans, but they are beholden to us, and in general it appears to me that we have very little spontaneous enthusiastic support from almost any source.

I cannot conceive that it is desirable or wise for us to throw our young men into every cockpit in the world where Communist totalitarianism rears its ugly head. And why should we assume the role of self-appointed "citizen fixit," of world policemen, all over the globe? If the cause is sufficiently good and urgent, an approach should always be made under the United Nations on a basis of international legality and with the support, from the very beginning, of others who believe that freedom is truly at stake and that those for whom we fight also know and value freedom and are prepared to do their share. This is far from the reality in Vietnam.

There are still other impending grave casualties of our military plunge into the quagmire of Southeast Asia. To date over 1,500 fine young Americans have been killed in action. Several hundred more have died in noncombat fatalities. Ten thousand have been wounded, many crippled for life, and that ghastly toll is just beginning. Meanwhile, the great achievements on the domestic front of President Johnson and the Eighty-ninth Congress in its first session— and they were great—will be largely nullified. They will be nullified just as their implementation was to begin. The inspiring vision of the "Great Society" will be blurred if not blacked out. There will not be the means for both the construction of that society at home and the destruction of war ahead. Most tragic of all, apart from the human sacrifices and the blighting of countless homes, is the fading of the national image of our beloved country, which despite some of its failings, we have had every right to be proud of, to cherish, and to wish to maintain.

I can only express the fervent hope that we can, somehow, soon, call a halt before that image and that vision of this great land become a memory. Let us all do our utmost to bring that about.

THE ISSUE IN VIETNAM [5]

George W. Ball [6]

Late January 1966 was a time of diplomatic climax in world councils, if indeed any period in this uneasy era can be labeled more dramatic than another. The debate over Vietnam had brought the so-called hawks and doves (those who insisted that the military offensive should be stepped up and those who urged renewed efforts to end the strife through negotiations) into sharp conflict. After a 37-day lull in the military offensive, however, President Johnson announced the resumption on January 31 of the bombing of North Vietnamese targets. Although he indicated in his radio-television address to the nation that "the end of the pause does not mean the end of our own pursuit of peace," the reaction throughout the nation and the world was prompt and determined. It soon resulted in the sweeping inquiry by the Senate Foreign Relations Committee into the purpose and means of achieving our goals in the Southest Asia conflict.

On January 30—the evening preceding the President's announcement on the resumption of bombing—Under Secretary of State George W. Ball addressed the Northwestern University Alumni Association at Evanston, Illinois. Just as Senator Gruening's address was designed to show through historical data why we should not be in Vietnam, so Secretary Ball's intent was to indicate "how we got there and why we must stay." The central issue in the controversy, said Mr. Ball, is to determine whether "the war in South Vietnam is an external aggression from the North, or . . . an indigenous revolt." If the latter, "then the United States would have no business taking sides in the conflict and helping one side to defeat the other by force of arms." (The printed version of this address, not quite complete, in the *Congressional Record* on February 7, 1966, is entitled "The Hanoi Myth of an Indigenous Rebellion.") However, "the North Vietnamese regime in Hanoi systematically created the Vietcong forces; it provides their equipment; it mounted the guerrilla war—and it controls that war from Hanoi on a day-to-day basis." Accordingly, the National Liberation Front, which the North Vietnam Communist Party announced in 1960, is "what its name implies—a Communist front organization created to mask the activities of Hanoi and to further the illusion of an indigenous revolt."

[5] Text furnished by Mary T. Kennedy, Office of Media Services, Department of State, with permission for this reprint.

[6] For biographical note, see Appendix.

Incidentally, when Senator Robert F. Kennedy of New York allegedly suggested in late February that the Vietcong be given a role in a coalition government in South Vietnam, Mr. Ball reportedly said that such a coalition would promptly become a Communist government.

Mr. Ball is a highly accomplished speaker with a fine sense of language and very considerable facility for bringing ideas into sharp focus. A respected administrator and legal authority upon whose talents the late President Kennedy relied and upon whom President Johnson now relies heavily, Mr. Ball was recently named executive chairman of an interdepartmental committee to administer many of the nation's nonmilitary agencies abroad. Although he does not share all of the President's and the State Department's views on deeper involvement in Vietnam, he remains one of the most articulate, thoughtful, and dedicated servants of the Administration.

Students of political oratory may wish to supplement their inquiries into Mr. Ball's rhetorical skills by examining "The Practice of Foreign Policy," delivered in Chicago on May 9, 1962; and "The Reallocation of World Responsibilities," given before the New York Bar Association in New York City on January 31, 1964. The latter was reprinted in REPRESENTATIVE AMERICAN SPEECHES: 1963-1964, pages 77-90.

Sooner or later the time will come when each of you will experience my sense of shock when your generous invitation led me to count up the years since I first became an alumnus of Northwestern University. I took my degree from the undergraduate school in 1930. More than a third of a century has passed since that time.

That period of more than one third of a century has been a fortunate time in which to live, an exciting time of change and ferment—particularly for an American. For during that third of a century our country ceased to be a voice offstage and moved to the center of world affairs.

When I received my first degree from Northwestern University, many Americans pretended that the rest of the world did not exist. We were still bemused by isolationism as we had been ever since we rejected the League of Nations in the early twenties. We were self-centered and self-deluding—so much so that when we faced the spectacle of the Western world in flames from Hitler's lunatic ambitions, many Americans quite solemnly contended that this was none of our affair.

But history has forced us to grow up. We have faced the harsh realities of danger and responsibility—and acquitted ourselves with honor and courage, as befits a great power.

For we are indubitably a great power today—a very different country from what we were in 1930—a wiser, more mature, and more responsible country. Our economy is four times as large—our role in world affairs many times as great.

Most of the Western European nations—which in the thirties controlled vast areas of the globe—are today largely preoccupied with their own affairs. Today we garrison the distant outposts of the world—not in support of colonial interests but in fulfillment of world responsibilities. Six hundred thousand of our countrymen are in uniform overseas. We are providing some form of economic assistance to more than ninety-five countries. And an America once determined to keep out of entangling alliances now has more than forty allies on five continents.

Today also we are fighting a shooting war in a country that until recently for most Americans was only an exotic place-name on the map of a distant continent.

Our engagement in Vietnam is but one aspect of the world role we are playing. But because we are spending both lives and resources in that faraway land and because the issue being decided profoundly affects our fortunes and our future, I should like to talk with you today about how we got there and why we must stay.

The beginning of wisdom with regard to Vietnam is to recognize that what Americans are fighting in the jungles and rice paddies of that unhappy land is not a local conflict—an isolated war that has meaning merely for one part of the world. We can properly understand the struggle in Vietnam only if we recognize it for what it is—part of a vast and continuing struggle in which we have been engaged for more than two decades.

Like most of the conflicts that have plagued the world in recent years, the conflict in Vietnam is a product of the great shifts and changes triggered by the Second World War. Out of the war, two continent-wide powers emerged—the United States and the Soviet Union. The colonial systems through which the nations of

Western Europe had governed more than a third of the people of the world were, one by one, dismantled. The Soviet Union under Stalin embarked on a reckless course of seeking to extend Communist power. An iron curtain was erected to enclose large areas of the globe. At the same time, man was learning to harness the power of the exploding sun and technology made mockery of time and distance.

The result of these vast changes, compressed within the breathless span of two decades, was to bring about a drastic rearrangement of the power structure of the world.

This rearrangement of power has resulted in a very uneasy equilibrium of forces. For even while the new national boundaries were still being marked on the map, the Soviet Union under Stalin exploited the confusion to push out the perimeter of its power and influence in an effort to extend the outer limits of Communist domination by force or the threat of force.

This process threatened the freedom of the world. It had to be checked and checked quickly. By launching the Marshall Plan to restore economic vitality to the nations of Western Europe and by forming NATO—a powerful Western alliance reinforced by United States resources and military power—America and the free nations of Europe built a dam to hold back the further encroachment of Communist ambitions.

This decisive action succeeded brilliantly. NATO, created in 1949, stopped the spread of communism over Western Europe and the northern Mediterranean.

But the world was given no time to relax. The victory of the Chinese Communists in that same year posed a new threat of Communist expansion against an Asia in ferment. Just as the Western world had mobilized its resistance against Communist force in Europe, we had to create an effective counterforce in the Far East if Communist domination were not to spread like a lava flow over the whole area.

The first test came quickly in Korea. There the United Nations forces—predominantly American—stopped the drive of Communist North Korea, supported by matériel from the Soviet Union. It stopped a vast Chinese army that followed. It brought to a halt the Communist drive to push out the line that had been drawn and to establish Communist control over the whole Korean Peninsula.

The Korean war was fought from a central conviction—that the best hope for freedom and security in the world depended on maintaining the integrity of the postwar arrangements. Stability could be achieved only by making sure that the Communist world did not expand by destroying those arrangements by force and threat—and thus upsetting the precarious power balance between the two sides of the iron curtain.

It was this conviction that led to our firm stand in Korea. It was this conviction that led America, in the years immediately after Korea, to build a barrier around the whole periphery of the Communist world by encouraging the creation of a series of alliances and commitments from the eastern edge of the NATO area to the Pacific.

The SEATO treaty that was signed in 1954 was part of that barrier, that structure of alliances. It was ratified by the Senate by a vote of 82 to 1.

Under that treaty and its protocol, the United States and other treaty partners gave their joint and several pledges to guarantee existing boundaries, including the line of demarcation between North and South Vietnam established when the French relinquished their control over Indochina. Since then three Presidents have reinforced that guarantee by further commitments given directly to the Republic of Vietnam. And on August 10, 1964, the Senate by a vote of 88 to 2 and the House by a vote of 416 to 0 adopted a joint resolution declaring their support for these commitments.

Today we are living up to those commitments by helping South Vietnam defend itself from the onslaught of Communist force, just as we helped Iran in 1946, Greece and Turkey in 1947, Formosa and Korea in 1950, and Berlin since 1948.

The bloody encounters in the highlands around Pleiku and the rice paddies of the Mekong Delta are thus in a real sense battles and skirmishes in a continuing war to prevent one Communist power after another from violating internationally recognized boundary lines fixing the outer limits of Communist dominion.

When we think of Vietnam, we think of Korea. In Vietnam, as in Korea, the Communists in one part of a divided country lying on the periphery of China have sought by force to gain dominion over the whole. But in terms of tactics on the ground, Greece is a closer analogy. For there, twenty years ago, as in South Vietnam today, the Communists sought to achieve their purpose by what is known in their lexicon as a "war of national liberation."

They chose this method of aggression both in Greece and Vietnam because tactics of terror and sabotage, of stealth and subversion, give a great advantage to a disciplined and ruthless minority—particularly where, as in those two countries, the physical terrain makes concealment easy and impedes the use of heavy weapons.

But the Communists also have a more subtle reason for favoring this type of aggression. It creates in any situation an element of confusion, a sense of ambiguity that can, they hope, so disturb and divide free men as to prevent them from making common cause against it.

This ambiguity is the central point of debate in the discussions that have surrounded the South Vietnam problem. Is the war in South Vietnam an external aggression from the North, or is it an indigenous revolt?

This is a question that Americans quite properly ask, and one to which they deserve a satisfactory answer. It is a question which we who have official responsibilities have necessarily probed in great depth. For if the Vietnam war were merely what the Communists say it is—an indigenous rebellion—then the United States would have no business taking sides in the conflict and helping one side to defeat the other by force of arms.

The evidence on the character of the Vietnam war is voluminous. Its meaning seems clear enough: The North Vietnamese regime in Hanoi systematically created the Vietcong forces; it provides their equipment; it mounted the guerrilla war—and it controls that war from Hanoi on a day-to-day basis.

The evidence shows clearly enough that, at the time of French withdrawal, when Vietnam was divided in the settlement of 1954, the Communist regime in Hanoi never intended that South Vietnam should develop in freedom. Many Communists fighting with the Vietminh army were directed to stay in the South, to cache away their arms, and to do everything possible to undermine the South Vietnamese government. Others—eighty thousand in all—were ordered to the North for training in the North Vietnamese army.

The evidence is clear enough also that the Communist rulers of the North resorted to guerrilla warfare in South Vietnam only when the success of the South Vietnam government persuaded them that they could not achieve their designs by subversion alone.

In September 1960, the Lao Dong party—the Communist party in North Vietnam—held its Third Party Congress in Hanoi. That congress called for the creation of a front organization to undertake the subversion of South Vietnam. Within two or three months thereafter, the National Liberation Front was established to provide a political facade for the conduct of an active guerrilla war. Beginning early that year the Hanoi regime began to infiltrate across the demarcation line the disciplined Communists whom the party had ordered north at the time of the settlement. In the intervening period since 1954 those men had been trained in the arts of proselytizing, sabotage, and subversion. Now they were ordered to conscript young men from the villages by force or persuasion and to form cadres around which guerrilla units could be built.

Beginning over a year ago, the Communists apparently exhausted their reservoir of Southerners who had gone north. Since then the greater number of men infiltrated into the South have been native-born North Vietnamese. Most recently, Hanoi has begun to infiltrate elements of the North Vietnamese army in increasingly larger numbers. Today there is evidence that nine regiments of regular North Vietnamese forces are fighting in organized units in the South.

I mention these facts, which are familiar enough to most of you, because they are fundamental to our policy with regard to Vietnam. These facts, it seems to us, make it clear beyond question that the war in South Vietnam has few of the attributes of an indigenous revolt. It is a cynical and systematic aggression by the North Vietnamese regime against the people of South Vietnam. It is one further chapter in the long and brutal chronicle of Communist efforts to extend the periphery of Communist power by force and terror.

This point is at the heart of our determination to stay the course in the bloody contest now under way in South Vietnam. It also necessarily shapes our position with regard to negotiations.

The President, Secretary Rusk, and all spokesmen for the Administration have stated again and again that the United States is prepared to join in unconditional discussions of the Vietnamese problem in an effort to bring about a satisfactory political solution. But so far the regime in Hanoi has refused to come to the bargaining table except on the basis of quite unacceptable conditions. One among several such conditions—but one that has been widely debated in the United States—is that we must recognize the National Liberation Front as the representative—indeed, as the sole representative—of the South Vietnamese people.

Yet to recognize the National Liberation Front in such a capacity would do violence to the truth and betray the very people whose liberty we are fighting to secure. The National Liberation Front is not a political entity expressing the will of the people of South Vietnam—or any substantial element of the South Vietnamese population. It is a facade fabricated by the Hanoi regime to confuse the issue and elaborate the myth of an indigenous revolt.

History is not obscure on this matter. As I noted earlier, the creation of the Front was announced by the North Vietnam Communist party—the Lao Dong party—in 1960, soon after the North Vietnam military leader, General [Vo Nguyen] Giap, announced that "the North is the revolutionary base for the whole country." But the Hanoi regime, while applauding its creation, has taken little pains to give the Front even the appearance of authenticity.

The individuals proclaimed as the leaders of the Front are not personalities widely known to the South Vietnamese people —or, indeed, to many members of the Vietcong. They are not revolutionary heroes or national figures. They have little meaning to the ordinary Vietcong soldier who fights and dies in the jungles and rice paddies.

Instead, the names he carries into battle are those of "Uncle Ho"—Ho Chi Minh, the President of the North Vietnamese regime—and General Giap, its military hero. When Vietcong prisoners are asked during interrogation whether they are members of the National Liberation Front, they customarily reply that they owe allegiance to the Lao Dong—the Communist party of North Vietnam—which is the equivalent of the Hanoi Communist regime.

The Front, then, is unmistakably what its name implies—a Communist front organization created to mask the activities of Hanoi and to further the illusion of an indigenous revolt.

The name of the organization was carefully chosen. It bears the same name as the National Liberation Front of Algeria. But there the resemblance ends, for the Algerian Front did, in fact, represent a substantial part of the Algerian population. It played a major role in an insurgency that was clearly an indigenous movement and not an aggression imposed from outside.

The Algerian Front, moreover, commanded the respect and, indeed, the obedience of the people. When it called a strike, the city of Algiers virtually closed down. By contrast, the Front in Vietnam has shown its fictional character by revealing its own impotence. On two occasions it has called for a general strike. These calls have been totally ignored by the people of South Vietnam.

The Algerian Front was a vital force in the Algerian community. It secured the overt allegiance of the old, established Moslem groups and leaders. As the revolt progressed, Moslems serving in the Algerian Assembly and even in the French Parliament announced their support for the Front.

But the Front in Vietnam has utterly failed in its efforts to attract the adherence of any established group within the society, whether Buddhist, Christian, or any of the sects that form substantial elements in Vietnamese life. Quite clearly, the people of South Vietnam, if they are aware of the Front at all, know it for what it is: the political cover for a North Vietnamese effort to take over the South—in practical effect, the southern arm of the North Vietnamese Communist party.

To be sure, the Vietcong military forces include a number of indigenous Southerners under Northern control. Neither the United States nor the South Vietnamese government has ever questioned that fact. But the composition of the Vietcong military forces is not the issue when one discusses the role of the Front. The issue is whether the Front has any color of claim as a political entity to represent these indigenous elements.

The evidence makes clear that it does not. It is purely and simply a factitious organization created by Hanoi to reinforce a fiction. To recognize it as the representative of the South Vietnamese population would be to give legitimacy to that fiction.

The true party in interest on the enemy side—the entity that has launched the attack on the South Vietnamese government for its own purposes, the entity that has created, controlled, and supplied the fighting forces of the Vietcong from the beginning—is the North Vietnamese regime in Hanoi. And it is the failure of that regime to come to the bargaining table that has so far frustrated every effort to move the problem of South Vietnam from a military to a political solution.

In spite of these clear realities, we have not taken, nor do we take, an obdurate or unreasoning attitude with regard to the Front. The President said in his State of the Union message, "We will meet at any conference table, we will discuss any proposals—four points or fourteen or forty—and we will consider the views of any group"—and that, of course, includes the Front along with other groups.

As the President has also said, this false issue of the Front would never prove "an insurmountable problem" if Hanoi were prepared for serious negotiations. But we cannot, to advance the political objectives of the Communist regime in Hanoi, give legitimacy to a spurious organization as though it spoke for the people of South Vietnam.

A European friend once critically observed that Americans have "a sense of mission but no sense of history." That accusation is, I think, without warrant.

We do have a sense of history, and it is that which enables us to view the war in South Vietnam for what it is. We Americans know that it is not, as I have said earlier, a local conflict; it is part of a continuing struggle to prevent the Communists from upsetting the fragile balance of power through force or the threat of force.

To succeed in that struggle we must resist every Communist effort to destroy by aggression the boundaries and demarcation lines established by the postwar arrangements. We cannot pick and choose among those boundaries. We cannot defend Berlin and yield Korea. We cannot recognize one commitment and repudiate another without tearing and weakening the entire structure on which the world's security depends.

Some thoughtful critics of our Vietnamese policy both in Europe and America challenge this. They maintain that the West should not undertake to defend the integrity of all lines of demarcation even though they may be underwritten in formal treaties. They contend that many of these lines are unnatural since they do not conform to the geopolitical realities as they see them. They contend in particular that, since the passing of colonialism, the Western Powers have no business mixing in the affairs of the Asian mainland. They imply that, regardless of our commitments, we should not try to prevent Red China from establishing its hegemony over the East Asian landmass south of the Soviet Union.

Proponents of this view advance two principal arguments to support their thesis. They contend that the very weight of Chinese power, its vast population, and its consequent ability to mobilize immense mass armies entitles it to recognition as the controlling force of Southeast Asia.

As a second reason for acknowledging the Chinese hegemony, they contend that for centuries China has maintained a dominant cultural and political influence throughout the area. They claim, therefore, that Southeast Asia lies within the Chinese sphere of influence and that we should let the Chinese redraw the lines of demarcation to suit themselves without regard to the wishes of the Southeast Asian people.

This argument, it seems to me, does not provide an acceptable basis for United States policy.

The assertion that China through hundreds of years of history has held sway over Southeast Asia is simply not accurate. Successive Chinese empires sought by force to establish such sway, but they never succeeded in doing so, except in certain sectors for limited periods. For the people of Southeast Asia have, over the centuries, shown an obstinate insistence on shaping their own destiny which the Chinese have not been able to overcome.

To adopt the sphere-of-influence approach now advocated would, therefore, not mean allowing history to repeat itself. It would mean according to China a status it had never been able to achieve by its own efforts throughout the ages. It would mean sentencing the people of Southeast Asia against their will to indefinite servitude behind the bamboo curtain. And it would mean turning our back on the principles that have formed the basis of Western policy in the whole postwar era.

Nor can one seriously insist that geographical propinquity establishes the Chinese right to dominate. At a time when man can circle the earth in ninety minutes, there is little to support such a literal commitment to nineteenth-century geopolitics. It is a dubious policy that would permit the accidents of geography to deprive peoples of their right to determine their own future free from external force. The logic of that policy has dark implications. It would rationalize the greed of great powers. It would imperil the prospects for developing and maintaining an equilibrium of power in the world.

The principles of the United Nations Charter are doctrinally more in tune with the aspirations of twentieth-century man.

This does not mean, however, that the political shape of the world should be regarded as frozen in an intractable pattern, that the boundaries established by the postwar arrangements are necessarily sacrosanct and immutable. Indeed, some of the lines of demarcation drawn after the Second World War were explicitly provisional and were to be finally determined in political settlements yet to come. This was true in Germany, in Korea, and in South Vietnam as well.

But those settlements have not yet been achieved, and we cannot permit their resolution to be preempted by force. This is the issue in Vietnam. This is what we are fighting for. This is why we are there.

We have no ambition to stay there any longer than is necessary. We have made repeatedly clear that the United States seeks no territory in Southeast Asia. We wish no military bases. We do not desire to destroy the regime in Hanoi or to remake it in a Western pattern. The United States will not retain American forces in South Vietnam once peace is assured.

The countries of Southeast Asia can be nonaligned or neutral, depending on the will of the people. We support free elections in South Vietnam as soon as violence has been eliminated and the South Vietnamese people can vote without intimidation. We look forward to free elections—and we will accept the result as a democratic people are accustomed to do. Yet we have little doubt about the outcome, for we are confident that the South Vietnamese, who have fought hard for their freedom, will not be the first people to give up that freedom to communism in a free exercise of self-determination.

Whether the peoples of the two parts of Vietnam will wish to unite is again for them to decide as soon as they are in a position to do so freely. Like other options, that of reunification must be preserved.

In the long run our hopes for the people of South Vietnam reflect our hopes for people everywhere. What we seek is a world living in peace and freedom—a world in which the cold war, with its tensions and conflicts, can recede into history. We are seeking to build a world in which men and nations will recognize and act upon a strongly shared interest in peace and in international cooperation for the common good.

We should not despair of these objectives even though at the moment they may seem rather unreal and idealistic. For we would make a mistake to regard the cold war as a permanent phenomenon. After all, it was less than two decades ago that Winston Churchill first announced in Fulton, Missouri, that "from Stettin in the Baltic to Trieste in the Adriatic an iron curtain has descended across the continent." And two decades are only a moment in the long sweep of history.

During the intervening years major changes have taken place on both sides of the iron curtain. A schism has developed within the Communist world. The Soviet Union has become the second greatest industrial power. The Soviet people have begun to acquire a stake in stability, and after the missile crisis of 1962 the Soviet Union has come face to face with the realities of power and destruction in the nuclear age and has recognized the awesome fact that in the twentieth century a war between great powers is a war without victory for anyone.

The changes taking place within the Soviet Union and among the nations of Eastern Europe are at once a reality and a promise. Over time—and in a world of rapid and pervasive change the measurement of time is difficult indeed—we may look forward to a comparable development within Communist China—a maturing process that will deflect the policies of Peiping from bellicose actions to a peaceful relation with the rest of the world.

After all, it is not the American purpose simply to preserve the status quo. That was not our history, and that is not our destiny. What we want to preserve is the freedom of choice for the peoples of the world. We will take our chances on that.

A STATEMENT ON VIETNAM [7]

George F. Kennan [8]

Under the chairmanship of J. W. Fulbright, the Senate Foreign
Relations Committee conducted a series of televised hearings in February
1966 on Vietnam. Among the participants were some of America's most
distinguished political and military authorities, including Secretary of
State Dean Rusk, General Maxwell Taylor, and George F. Kennan.
Through prepared expositions and replies to questions put by the nineteen members of the Committee, the witnesses provided what may very
well have been the most provocative and searching debate to date on the
Administration policy in Southeast Asia. Speculating on the influence of
the controversy, the New York *Times* observed:

> While there is some dispute—and no sure way of knowing—
> whether the public hearings before the Senate Foreign Relations
> Committee produced any specific shifts in public opinion on Viet-
> nam issues, there was no question in the minds of many senators
> that the hearings had stimulated harder and clearer thinking
> about those issues.

Former Ambassador to Russia and to Yugoslavia, authority on communism, and Pulitzer prize-winning historian, Mr. Kennan presents impressive credentials as a public servant. He represents a rare combination of high scholarly distinction and enormous diplomatic skill. Accordingly, his appearance before the Senate Foreign Relations Committee
attracted attention. Said the New York *Times* of his presentation:

> Speaking softly, choosing each word with care and peering
> owlishly over his [glasses] Mr. Kennan held not only the atten-
> tion but the respect of those committee members, such as Senator
> Stuart Symington, Democrat of Missouri, who plainly disagreed
> with his proposals that the United States "dig in and wait" and
> give diplomacy a chance to work before escalating the war to the
> flash point.

Mr. Kennan's statement before the Senate Foreign Relations Committee has unusual interest for the student of public address. Presented

---

[7] Text from *Supplemental Foreign Assistance Fiscal Year 1966—Vietnam;* hearings
before the Senate Committee on Foreign Relations on S. 2793 (89th Congress, 2d session) U.S. Govt. Ptg. Off. Washington, D.C. 20401. '66. p 331-6. Reprinted by
permission of Mr. Kennan.

[8] For biographical note, see Appendix.

before a highly select and concerned audience, developed as a tightly reasoned discourse in which there is a minimum of emotional detail, it is an excellent example of a closely knit argumentative pattern. Expressed with lucidity and precision, it makes its point effortlessly, economically, and with rhetorical orderliness. If as Clayton Fritchey, former Special Assistant to Secretary of Defense George Marshall, has remarked, Washington is a blasé city, not easily impressed, it is all the more remarkable that it is nonetheless "susceptible to a few well-chosen words . . . when those words are on target." Mr. Kennan's were.

The central thesis of his statement may appear at slight variance with the well-known policy of political containment of Soviet communism set forth in an article in *Foreign Affairs* in 1947. According to Marvin Kalb, Washington correspondent for CBS News, Mr. Kennan "seems to realize that one of the cruelest ironies of his life is that he conceived of the policy of containment only to see it nurture the spirit of anticommunism he finds so antithetical to what he considers the best interests of the United States." In the testimony before the Committee, Mr. Kennan asserted that our involvement in Vietnam is unfortunate— "something we would not choose deliberately if the choice were ours to make all over again today." Moreover, our aim should be "to liquidate this involvement just as soon as this can be done without inordinate damage to our own prestige or to the stability of conditions in that area." Arguing against escalation of the conflict, he regretted the harmful effects on more important questions of world affairs—such as our relations with Soviet Russia and Japan—particularly arising from our preoccupation "in a remote and secondary theatre of activity." In general, he supported the suggestion of Lieutenant General James M. Gavin, who, in an article in *Harper*'s magazine in February 1966, proposed that the United States should defend limited areas or enclaves on the Vietnamese coast, "desist in our bombing attacks in North Vietnam, and seek to find a solution through the United Nations or a conference in Geneva." In his statement before the Senate Foreign Relations Committee on February 8, 1966, Gavin warned against escalation of the conflict with its attendant risk of provoking a clash with Communist China.

Disclaiming any sympathy for the Vietcong, Mr. Kennan expressed the hope that our efforts would forestall the possibility of its gaining exclusive control of the land. On the other hand, however, he asserted that our country "should not be asked, and should not ask of itself, to shoulder the main burden of determining the political realities in any other country, and particularly not in one remote from our shores, from our culture, and from the experience of our people." The statement to the Committee helps to confirm Marvin Kalb's belief that Mr. Kennan occupies a unique position among "professional diplomats and historians in being able to synthesize giant abstractions with clarity and purpose."

Mr. Chairman, and distinguished members of the Foreign Relations Committee, the subject on which I am invited to give my views this morning is, as I understand it, the complex of problems connected with our present involvement in Vietnam. I would like to explain, in undertaking to speak on this subject, that Southeast Asia is a part of the world for which I can claim no specialized knowledge. I am not familiar with the official rationale of our policy there except as it has been revealed in the press. I cannot recall that I have ever, either during my official service in government or subsequently, been drawn by the executive branch of our Government into consultation on the problem of our policy in Southeast Asia, or even been made privy to the official discussions by which that policy was decided.

I am sure that there are many data, relevant to any thoroughly founded judgment on these matters, which are not available to me; and this being the case, I have tried in recent weeks and months not to jump to final conclusions even in my own thoughts, to remain sympathetically receptive, both to our Government's explanations of the very real difficulties it has faced and to the doubts and questions of its serious critics.

I have not been anxious to press my views on the public but I gladly give them to you for whatever they are worth, claiming no particular merit for them except perhaps that they flow from an experience with Communist affairs that runs back now for some thirty-eight years, and also from the deepest and most troubled sort of concern that we should find the proper course, the right course, at this truly crucial moment.

The first point I would like to make is that if we were not already involved as we are today in Vietnam, I would know of no reason why we should wish to become so involved, and I could think of several reasons why we should wish not to.

Vietnam is not a region of major military and industrial importance. It is difficult to believe that any decisive developments of the world situation would be determined in normal circumstances by what happens on that territory. If it were not for the considerations of prestige that arise precisely out of our present involvement, even a situation in which South Vietnam was controlled exclusively by the Vietcong, while regrettable, and no doubt morally unwarranted, would not, in my opinion, present dangers great enough to justify our direct military intervention.

Given the situation that exists today in the relations among the leading Communist powers, and by that I have, of course, in mind primarily the Soviet-Chinese conflict, there is every likelihood that a Communist regime in South Vietnam would follow a fairly independent course.

There is no reason to suspect that such a regime would find it either necessary or desirable in present circumstances to function simply as a passive puppet and instrument of Chinese power. And as for the danger that its establishment there would unleash similar tendencies in neighboring countries, this, I think, would depend largely on the manner in which it came into power. In the light of what has recently happened in Indonesia, and on the Indian subcontinent, the danger of the so-called domino effect, that is the effect that would be produced by a limited Communist success in South Vietnam, seems to me to be considerably less than it was when the main decisions were taken that have led to our present involvement.

Let me stress, I do not say that that danger does not exist, I say that it is less than it was a year or two ago when we got into this involvement.

From the long-term standpoint, therefore, and on principle, I think our military involvement in Vietnam has to be recognized as unfortunate, as something we would not choose deliberately, if the choice were ours to make all over again today, and by the same token, I think it should be our Government's aim to liquidate this involvement just as soon as this can be done without inordinate damage to our own prestige or to the stability of conditions in that area.

It is obvious on the other hand that this involvement is today a fact. It creates a new situation. It raises new questions, ulterior to the long-term problem, which have to be taken into account. A precipitate and disorderly withdrawal could represent in present circumstances a disservice to our own interests, and even to world peace, greater than any that might have been involved by our failure to engage ourselves there in the first place.

This is a reality which, if there is to be any peaceful resolution of this conflict, is going to have to be recognized both by the more critical of our friends and by our adversaries.

But at the same time, I have great misgivings about any deliberate expansion of hostilities on our part directed to the achievement of something called victory—if by the use of that term we envisage the complete disappearance of the recalcitrance with which we are now faced, the formal submission by the adversary to our will, and the complete realization of our present stated political aims.

I doubt that these things can be achieved even by the most formidable military successes.

There seems to be an impression about that if we bring sufficient military pressure to bear there will occur at some point something in the nature of a political capitulation on the other side. I think this is a most dangerous assumption. I don't say that it is absolutely impossible, but it is a dangerous assumption in the light of the experience we have had with Communist elements in the past.

The North Vietnamese and the Vietcong have between them a great deal of space and manpower to give up if they have to, and the Chinese can give them more if they need it. Fidelity to the Communist tradition would dictate that if really pressed to extremity on the military level these people should disappear entirely from the open scene and fall back exclusively on an underground political and military existence rather than to accept terms that would be openly humiliating and would represent in their eyes the betrayal of the future political prospects of the cause to which they are dedicated.

Any total rooting out of the Vietcong from the territory of South Vietnam could be achieved, if it could be achieved at all, only at the cost of a degree of damage to civilian life and of civilian suffering generally for which I would not like to see this country responsible.

And to attempt to crush North Vietnamese strength to a point where Hanoi could no longer give any support for Vietcong political activity in the South, would almost certainly, it seems to me, have the effect of bringing in Chinese forces at some point, whether formally or in the guise of volunteers, thus involving us in a military conflict with Communist China on one of the most unfavorable theatres of hostility that we could possibly choose.

This is not the only reason why I think we should do everything possible to avoid the escalation of this conflict. There is another one which is no less weighty, and this is the effect the conflict is already having on our policies and interests further afield. This involvement seems to me to represent a grievous misplacement of emphasis in our foreign policies as a whole.

Not only are great and potentially more important questions of world affairs not receiving, as a consequence of our involvement in Vietnam, the attention they should be receiving, but in some instances assets we already enjoy and hopefully possibilities we should be developing are being sacrificed to this unpromising involvement in a remote and secondary theatre. Our relations with the Soviet Union have suffered grievously as was to be expected, and this at a time when far more important things were involved in those relations than what is ultimately involved in Vietnam and when we had special reason, I think, to cultivate those relations. And more unfortunate still, in my opinion, is the damage being done to the feelings entertained for us by the Japanese people. The confidence and good disposition of the Japanese is the greatest asset we have had and the greatest asset we could have in East Asia. As the only major industrial complex in the entire Far East, and the only place where the sinews of modern war can be produced on a formidable scale, Japan is of vital importance to us and indeed to the prospects generally of peace and stability in East Asia. There is no success we could have in Vietnam that would conceivably warrant, in my opinion, the sacrifice by us of the confidence and good will of the Japanese people. Yet, I fear that we abuse that confidence and good will in the most serious way when we press the military struggle in Vietnam, and particularly when we press it by means of strategic bombing, a process to which the Japanese for historical reasons are peculiarly sensitive and averse.

I mention Japan particularly because it is an outstanding example, both in importance and in the intensity of the feelings aroused, of the psychological damage that is being done in many parts of the world by the prosecution of this conflict, and that will be done in even greater measure if the hostilities become still more bloody and tragic as a result of our deliberate effort.

It is clear that however justified our action may be in our own eyes, it has failed to win either enthusiasm or confidence even among peoples normally friendly to us.

Our motives are widely misinterpreted, and the spectacle emphasized and reproduced in thousands of press photographs and stories that appear in the press of the world, the spectacle of Americans inflicting grievous injury on the lives of a poor and helpless people, and particularly a people of different race and color, no matter how warranted by military necessity or by the excesses of the adversary, produces reactions among millions of people throughout the world profoundly detrimental to the image we would like them to hold of this country. I am not saying that this is just or right. I am saying that this is so, and that it is bound in the circumstances to be so. A victory purchased at the price of further such damage would be a hollow one in terms of our world interests, no matter what advantages it might hold from the standpoint of developments on the local scene.

Now, these are the reasons, gentlemen, why I hope that our Government will restrict our military operations in Vietnam to the minimum necessary to assure the security of our forces and to maintain our military presence there until we can achieve a satisfactory peaceful resolution of the conflict. And these are the reasons why I hope that we will continue to pursue vigorously, and I may say consistently, the quest for such a peaceful resolution of the conflict, even if this involves some moderation of our stated objectives, and even if the resulting settlement appears to us as something less than ideal.

I cannot, of course, judge the military necessities of our situation. But everything that I can learn about its political aspects suggests to me that General Gavin is on the right track in his suggestion that we should, if I understood him correctly, decide what limited areas we can safely police and defend, and restrict ourselves largely to the maintenance of our position there. I have listened with interest to the arguments that have been brought forward in opposition to his views, and I must say that I have not been much impressed with some of them. When I am told that it would be difficult to defend such enclaves it is hard for me to understand why it would be easier to defend the far greater areas to which presumably a successful escalation of our military activity would bring us.

I also find it difficult, for reasons that I won't take time to go into here, to believe that our allies, and particularly our Western European allies, most of whom themselves have given up great territories within recent years, and sometimes in a very statesmanlike way—I find it hard to believe that we would be subject to great reproach or loss of confidence at their hands simply because we followed a defensive rather than an offensive strategy in Vietnam at this time.

In matters such as this, it is not in my experience what you do that is mainly decisive. It is how you do it; and I would submit that there is more respect to be won in the opinion of this world by a resolute and courageous liquidation of unsound positions than by the most stubborn pursuit of extravagant or unpromising objectives.

And finally, when I hear it said that to adopt a defensive strategy in South Vietnam would be to rat on our commitment to the government of that territory I am a little bewildered. I would like to know what that commitment really consists of, and how and when it was incurred. What seems to be involved here is an obligation on our part not only to defend the frontiers of a certain political entity against outside attack, but to assure the internal security of its government in circumstances where that government is unable to assure that security by its own means. Now, any such obligation is one that goes obviously considerably further in its implications than the normal obligations of a military alliance.

If we did not incur such an obligation in any formal way, then I think we should not be inventing it for ourselves and assuring ourselves that we are bound by it today.

But if we did incur it, then I do fail to understand how it was possible to enter into any such commitment otherwise than through the constitutional processes which were meant to come into play when even commitments of lesser import than this were undertaken.

Now, just two concluding observations: I would like it understood that what I have said here implies nothing but the highest respect and admiration for the fighting qualities of our forces in the field. I have the greatest confidence in them, men and commanders alike. I have no doubt, in fact, that they can and will, if duty requires, produce before this thing is over military results that will surprise both our skeptical friends and our arrogant adversaries. It is not their fighting qualities. It is the purpose to which they are being employed that evokes my skepticism.

Secondly, I would like to say I am trying to look at this whole problem not from the moral standpoint but from the practical one. I see in the Vietcong a band of ruthless fanatics, many of them misled, no doubt, by the propaganda that has been drummed into them, but cruel in their methods, dictatorial, and oppressive in their aims. I am not conscious of having any sympathy for them. I think their claim to represent the people of South Vietnam is unfounded. A country which fell under this exclusive power would have my deepest sympathy; and I would hope that this eventuality at any rate would be avoided by a restrained and moderate policy on our part in South Vietnam.

But our country should not be asked, and should not ask of itself, to shoulder the main burden of determining the political realities in any other country, and particularly not in one remote from our shores, from our culture, and from the experience of our people. This is not only not our business, but I don't think we can do it successfully.

In saying this, I am only paraphrasing and very poorly the words once uttered by one who had at one time been a member of the U.S. Senate, and who, had a Foreign Relations Committee existed in his day, would unquestionably have been a member of it. This was John Quincy Adams, and I would like your permission to recall, before I close, the words of his that I have in mind. They were spoken in this city 145 years ago on the Fourth of July 1821—

Some of you may be familiar with them but they stand repeating at this moment:

Wherever the standard of freedom and independence has been or shall be unfurled, there will be America's heart, her benedictions, and her prayers. But she goes not abroad—

He went on—

in search of monsters to destroy. She is the well-wisher to the freedom and independence of all. She is the champion and vindicator only of her own. She will recommend the general cause by the countenance of her voice, and by the benignant sympathy of her example. She well knows that by once enlisting under other banners than her own, were they even the banners of foreign independence, she would involve herself beyond the power of extrication, in all the wars of interest and intrigue, of individual avarice, envy, and ambition, which assume the colors and usurp the standards of freedom. The fundamental maxims of her policy would insensibly change from liberty to force. . . . She might become the dictatress of the world. She would no longer be the ruler of her own spirit.

Now, gentlemen, I don't know exactly what John Quincy Adams had in mind when he spoke those words, but I think that without knowing it, he spoke very directly and very pertinently to us here today.

A MOMENTOUS VISIT

ADDRESS BEFORE THE UNITED NATIONS [1]

POPE PAUL VI [2]

October 4, 1965, will long remain in memory. On that day, nearly four million residents of New York City and untold millions across the land who stayed near their television sets had a vicarious role in an historic visit. Nor were the people of the United States the only participants in the event. In more than twenty other countries live coverage brought the drama of reverent anticipation to countless men and women.

This was the day Pope Paul VI came to the United States. It was an historical first, for no Pope had previously visited the New World. For fourteen hours—and they were undoubtedly hours of extreme weariness and strain—the Pontiff followed an itinerary that included streets and churches, the World's Fair, and Yankee Stadium. But the climax was of course the appearance before the United Nations to deliver a spiritual appeal for world peace. Speaking in French, the Pope addressed some 2,000 delegates and other dignitaries in the Assembly. His audience included representatives from all of the 117 member countries of the United Nations, except Albania. In respectful silence, the audience listened to the Pontiff's fervent plea: "No more war, war never again! Peace, it is peace which must guide the destinies of peoples and of all mankind." "War never again," said Ambassador Arthur J. Goldberg, voicing the Pope's words, at a press conference at the close of the twentieth session of the United Nations on December 22, 1965,

> must become the peace cry of all peoples in all lands. It must become the byword of all of us who are daily concerned with the task of making certain that "no more war" threatens our earth. For peace—a lasting peace—a just peace—is the only proper political and moral condition of a community of nations living as equals under the law.

Pope Paul revealed what Emmet John Hughes called "the sense of sanctity." The Pontiff's presence in New York and at the United Nations inspired an image of "the pure and powerful magic of candle

[1] Text furnished by the Very Rev. Msgr. Francis X. Duffy, St. Patrick's Information Center, New York City.

[2] For biographical note, see Appendix.

flame." Perhaps he demonstrated as Hughes observed "that it may not be too late, in the bloodied lives of the nations of men, for yet one more ceremony of innocence."

As we commence our address to this unique world audience, we wish to thank your Secretary General, U Thant, for the invitation which he extended to us to visit the United Nations, on the occasion of the twentieth anniversary of the foundation of this world institution for peace and for collaboration between the peoples of the entire earth.

Our thanks also to the President of the General Assembly, Mr. Amintore Fanfani, who used such kind language in our regard from the very day of his election.

We thank all of you here present for your kind welcome, and we present to each one of you our deferential and sincere salutation. In friendship you have invited us and admitted us to this meeting; and it is as a friend that we are here today.

We express to you our cordial personal homage, and we bring you that of the entire Second Vatican Ecumenical Council now meeting in Rome, and represented here by the eminent cardinals who accompany us for this purpose.

In their name and in our own, to each and every one of you, honor and greeting!

This encounter, as you all understand, marks a simple and at the same time a great moment. It is simple, because you have before you a humble man; your brother; and among you all, representatives of sovereign States, the least-invested, if you wish to think of him thus, with a minuscule, as it were symbolic, of temporal sovereignty, only as much as is necessary to be free to exercise his spiritual mission, and to assure all those who deal with him that he is independent of every other sovereignty of this world. But he, who now addresses you, has no temporal power, nor any ambition to compete with you. In fact, we have nothing to ask for, no question to raise; we have only a desire to express and a permission to request: namely, that of serving you in so far as we can, with disinterest, with humility and love.

This is our first declaration. As you can see, it is so simple as to seem insignificant to this Assembly, which always treats of most important and most difficult matters.

We said also, however, and all here today feel it, that this moment is also a great one. Great for us, great for you.

For us: You know well who we are. Whatever may be the opinion you have of the Pontiff of Rome, you know our mission. We are the bearer of a message for all mankind. And this we are, not only in our own personal name and in the name of the great Catholic family; but also in that of those Christian brethren who share the same sentiments which we express here, particularly of those who so kindly charged us explicitly to be their spokesman here. Like a messenger who, after a long journey, finally succeeds in delivering the letter which has been entrusted to him, so we appreciate the good fortune of this moment, however brief, which fulfills a desire nourished in the heart for nearly twenty centuries. For, as you will remember, we are very ancient; we here represent a long history; we here celebrate the epilogue of a wearying pilgrimage in search of a conversation with the entire world, ever since the command was given to us: Go and bring the good news to all peoples. Now, you here represent all peoples. Allow us to tell you that we have a message, a happy message, to deliver to each one of you and to all.

1. We might call our message a ratification, a solemn moral ratification of this lofty institution. This message comes from our historical experience. As "an expert in humanity," we bring to this Organization the suffrage of our recent predecessors, that of the entire Catholic episcopate and our own, convinced as we are that this Organization represents the obligatory path of modern civilization and of world peace. In saying this, we feel we are making our own the voice of the dead and of the living; of the dead, who fell in the terrible wars of the past; of the living who survived those wars, bearing in their hearts a condemnation of those who would try to renew wars; and also of those living who rise up fresh and confident, the youth of the present generation, who legitimately dream of a better human race. And we

also make our own the voice of the poor, the disinherited, the suffering, of those who hunger and thirst for justice, for the dignity of life, for freedom, for well-being and progress. The peoples of the earth turn to the United Nations as the last hope of concord and peace; we presume to present here, with their tribute of honor and of hope, our own tribute also.

That is why this moment is great for you, also.

2. We feel that you are already aware of this. Hearken now to the continuation of our message. It becomes a message of good wishes for the future. The edifice which you have constructed must never fall; it must be perfected, and made equal to the needs which world history will present. You mark a stage in the development of mankind, from which retreat must never be admitted but, from which it is necessary, that advance be made.

To the pluralism of States, which can no longer ignore one another, you offer an extremely simple and fruitful formula of coexistence. First of all, you recognize and distinguish *the ones and the others*. You do not confer existence upon States; but you qualify each single Nation as fit to sit in the orderly congress of peoples. That is, you grant recognition, of the highest ethical and juridical value, to each single sovereign national community, guaranteeing it an honored international citizenship. This in itself is a great service to the cause of humanity, namely, to define clearly and to honor the national subjects of the world community, and to classify them in a juridical condition, worthy thereby of being recognized and respected by all, and from which there may derive an orderly and stable system of international life. You give sanction to the great principle that the relations between peoples should be regulated by reason, by justice, by law, by negotiation; not by force, nor by violence, not by war, not by fear or by deceit. Thus it must be. Allow us to congratulate you for having had the wisdom to open this hall to the younger peoples, to those States which have recently attained independence and national freedom. Their presence is the proof of the universality and magnanimity which inspire the principles of this institution.

Thus it must be. This is our praise and our good wish; and, as you can see, we do not attribute these as from outside; we derive them from inside, from the very genius of your institution.

3. Your Charter goes further than this, and our message advances with it. You exist and operate to unite the Nations, to bind States together. Let us use this second formula: to bring *the ones together with the others*. You are an association. You are a bridge between peoples. You are a network of relations between States. We would almost say that your chief characteristic is a reflection, as it were, in the temporal field, of what our Catholic Church aspires to be in the spiritual field: unique and universal. In the ideological construction of mankind, there is on the natural level nothing superior to this. Your vocation is to make brothers not only of some, but of all peoples. A difficult undertaking, indeed; but this it is, your most noble undertaking. Is there anyone who does not see the necessity of coming thus progressively to the establishment of a world authority, able to act efficaciously on the juridical and political levels?

Once more we reiterate our good wish: Advance always! We will go further, and say: Strive to bring back among you any who have separated themselves, and study the right method of uniting to your pact of brotherhood, in honor and loyalty, those who do not yet share in it. Act so that those still outside will desire and merit the confidence of all; and then be generous in granting such confidence. You have the good fortune and the honor of sitting in this assembly of peaceful community; hear us as we say: Ensure that the reciprocal trust which here unites you, and enables you to do good and great things, may never be undermined or betrayed.

4. The inherent logic of this wish, which might be considered to pertain to the very structure of your Organization, leads us to complete it with other formulas. Thus, let no one, inasmuch as he is a member of your union, be superior to the others: *Never one above the other*. This is the formula of equality. We are well aware that it must be completed by the evaluation of other factors besides simple membership in this institution; but equali-

ty, too, belongs to its constitution. You are not equal, but here you make yourselves equal. For several among you, this may be an act of high virtue; allow us to say this to you, as the representative of a religion which accomplishes salvation through the humility of its divine Founder. Men cannot be brothers if they are not humble. It is pride, no matter how legitimate it may seem to be, which provokes tension and struggles for prestige, for predominance, colonialism, egoism; that is, pride disrupts brotherhood.

5. And now our message reaches its highest point, which is, at first, a negative point. You are expecting us to utter this sentence, and we are well aware of its gravity and solemnity: *Not the ones against the others,* never again, never more! It was principally for this purpose that the Organization of the United Nations arose: against war, in favor of peace! Listen to the lucid words of the great departed John Kennedy who proclaimed, four years ago: "Mankind must put an end to war, or war will put an end to mankind." Many words are not needed to proclaim this loftiest aim of your institution. It suffices to remember that the blood of millions of men, that numberless and unheard of sufferings, useless slaughter and frightful ruin, are the sanction of the pact which unites you, with an oath which must change the future history of the world: No more war, war never again! Peace, it is peace which must guide the destinies of peoples and of all mankind.

Gratitude to you, glory to you, who for twenty years have labored for peace. Gratitude and glory to you for the conflicts which you have prevented or have brought to an end. The results of your efforts in recent days in favor of peace even if not yet proved decisive, are such as to deserve that we, presuming to interpret the sentiments of the whole world, express to you both praise and thanks.

Gentlemen, you have performed and you continue to perform a great work: the education of mankind in the ways of peace. The UN is the great school where that education is imparted, and we are today in the assembly hall of that school. Everyone taking his place here becomes a pupil and also a teacher in the art of building peace. When you leave this hall, the world looks upon you as the architects and constructors of peace.

Peace, as you know, is not built up only by means of politics, by the balance of forces and of interests. It is constructed with the mind, with ideas, with works of peace. You labor in this great construction. But you are still at the beginnings. Will the world ever succeed in changing that selfish and bellicose mentality which, up to now, has been interwoven in so much of its history? It is hard to foresee; but it is easy to affirm that it is towards that new history, a peaceful, truly human, history, as promised by God to men of good will, that we must resolutely march. The roads thereto are already well marked out for you; and the first is that of disarmament.

If you wish to be brothers, let the arms fall from your hands. One cannot love while holding offensive arms. Those armaments, especially those terrible arms, which modern science has given you, long before they produce victims and ruins, nourish bad feelings, create nightmares, distrust and somber resolutions; they demand enormous expenditures; they obstruct projects of union and useful collaboration; they falsify the psychology of peoples. As long as man remains that weak, changeable and even wicked being that he often shows himself to be, defensive arms will, unfortunately, be necessary. You, however, in your courage and valiance, are studying the ways of guaranteeing the security of international life, without having recourse to arms. This is a most noble aim, this the peoples expect of you, this must be obtained! Let unanimous trust in this institution grow, let its authority increase; and this aim, we believe, will be secured. Gratitude will be expressed to you by all peoples, relieved as they will then be from the crushing expenses of armaments, and freed from the nightmare of an ever imminent war.

We rejoice in the knowledge that many of you have considered favorably our invitation, addressed to all States in the cause of peace from Bombay, last December, to divert to the benefit of the developing countries at least a part of the savings which could be realized by reducing armaments. We here renew that invitation, trusting in your sentiments of humanity and generosity.

6. In so doing, we become aware that we are echoing another principle which is structural to the United Nations, which is its positive and affirmative high point; namely, that you work here not only to avert conflicts between States, but also to make them capable of working *the ones for the others*. You are not satisfied with facilitating mere coexistence between Nations; you take a much greater step forward, one deserving of our praise and our support—you organize the brotherly collaboration of peoples. In this way a system of solidarity is set up, and its lofty civilized aims win the orderly and unanimous support of all the family of peoples for the common good and for the good of each individual. This aspect of the Organization of the United Nations is the most beautiful; it is its most truly human visage; it is the ideal of which mankind dreams on its pilgrimage through time; it is the world's greatest hope; it is, we presume to say, the reflection of the loving and transcendent design of God for the progress of the human family on earth—a reflection in which we see the message of the Gospel which is heavenly become earthly. Indeed, it seems to us that here we hear the echo of the voice of our predecessors, and particularly of that of Pope John XXIII, whose message of "Pacem in Terris" was so honorably and significantly received among you.

You proclaim here the fundamental rights and duties of man, his dignity, his freedom—and above all his religious freedom. We feel that you thus interpret the highest sphere of human wisdom and, we might add, its sacred character. For you deal here above all with human life; and the life of man is sacred; no one may dare offend it. Respect for life, even with regard to the great problem of birth, must find here in your Assembly its highest affirmation and its most reasoned defense. You must strive to multiply bread so that it suffices for the tables of mankind, and not rather favor an artificial control of birth, which would be irrational, in order to diminish the number of guests at the banquet of life.

It does not suffice, however, to feed the hungry; it is necessary also to assure to each man a life conformed to his dignity. This too you strive to perform. We may consider this the fulfillment before our very eyes, and by your efforts, of that prophetical announcement so applicable to your institution: "They will melt down their swords into ploughshares, their spears into pruningforks" (Isaiah 2:4). Are you not using the prodigious energies of the earth and the magnificent inventions of science, no longer as instruments of death but as tools of life for humanity's new era?

We know how intense and ever more efficacious are the efforts of the United Nations and its dependent world agencies to assist those governments who need help to hasten their economic and social progress.

We know how ardently you labor to overcome illiteracy and to spread good culture throughout the world; to give men adequate modern medical assistance; to employ in man's service the marvelous resources of science, of technique and of organization —all of this is magnificent, and merits the praise and support of all, including our own.

We ourself wish to give the good example, even though the smallness of our means is inadequate to the practical and quantitative needs. We intend to intensify the development of our charitable institutions to combat world hunger and fulfill world needs. It is thus, and in no other way, that peace can be built up.

7. One more word, Gentlemen, our final word: this edifice which you are constructing does not rest upon merely material and earthly foundations, for thus it would be a house built upon sand; above all, it is based on our own consciences. The hour has struck for our "conversion," for personal transformation, for interior renewal. We must get used to thinking of man in a new way; and in a new way also of men's life in common; with a new manner too of conceiving the paths of history and the destiny of the world, according to the words of Saint Paul: "You must be clothed in the new self, which is created in God's image, justified and sanctified through the truth" (Ephesians 4:23). The hour has struck for a halt, a moment of recollection, of reflection, almost of prayer. A moment to think anew of our com-

mon origin, our history, our common destiny. Today as never before, in our era so marked by human progress, there is need for an appeal to the moral conscience of man. For the danger comes, not from progress, nor from science—indeed, if properly utilized, these could rather resolve many of the grave problems which assail mankind. No, the real danger comes from man himself, wielding ever more powerful arms, which can be employed equally well for destruction or for the loftiest conquests.

In a word, then, the edifice of modern civilization must be built upon spiritual principles which alone can, not only support it, but even illuminate and animate it. To do this, such indispensable principles of superior wisdom cannot but be founded so, as you are aware, we believe upon faith in God. That unknown God of whom Saint Paul spoke to the Athenians in the Areopagus? unknown by them, although without realizing it they sought him and he was close to them, as happens also to many men of our times? To us, in any case, and to all those who accept the ineffable revelation which Christ has given us of Him, He is the living God, the Father of all men.

THE CONTINUING FERMENT

OF MOVERS AND IMMOBILISTS [1]

WILLIAM L. MARBURY [2]

Although many of the contributors to REPRESENTATIVE AMERICAN SPEECHES over the years were trained in the law, a relatively small number of so-called forensic addresses has been included. Usually the man of legal talents spoke as a businessman, or educator, or politician. The editor is always heartened, therefore, to come upon a speech which, though adapted to the wider audience, has nonetheless the flavor and substance of advocacy arising from legal context. Admittedly, the art of advocacy is not restricted to the courts, although that is its natural home. But, as the late Lord Birkett remarked in his delightful study *Six Great Advocates,* advocacy is used daily in deliberative assemblies and church pulpits and on public platforms—"and indeed everywhere that men and women meet to listen to one of their fellows expounding some subject or theme in order to win the allegiance of the particular audience." Of course, students of public address have a special interest in advocacy, particularly as it concerns discussion and debate. And critics of oratory have long been intrigued by the presumed influence of legal training upon a speaker's techniques and style of expression. Witness, for example, the essay on Lincoln ("Lincoln and the Law") by Arthur Lehman Goodhart, a distinguished Oxford University scholar, in the recently published *Lincoln and the Gettysburg Address,* edited by Allan Nevins.

Both the speaker and the critic of public address will derive profit from a study of William L. Marbury's lecture on the responsibilities which new social forces have placed upon the legal profession, an address given in Baltimore at a meeting of the Maryland Bar Association, January 14, 1966. Long associated with the firm of Piper & Marbury in Baltimore and currently president of the Maryland Bar Association, Mr. Marbury cited instances in his speech to show both the continuing and the expanding need for a sense of responsibility in the administration and practice of the law. His argument underscores the truth of Lord Birkett's *dictum* that legal advocacy "calls for the nicest sense of honour

[1] Text furnished by William L. Marbury, with permission for this reprint.
[2] For biographical note, see Appendix.

and for a complete devotion to the ideals of justice . . . vital for the maintenance of that way of life in which we have come to believe."

Forty years ago, the late Joseph C. France, thought by many to be the wisest Maryland lawyer of his generation, opened an address to this body by remarking that the speaker on such an occasion as this was expected to deliver a sermon. Now, as my children are ready to testify, my qualifications for such a task are very limited. Certainly they are not as good as those of Dr. Oliver Wendell Holmes, whose lawyer son complained that his father was forever "inculcating virtue in dull terms." Justice Holmes went on to wonder whether if he had a son, he, in his turn, would yield to the "temptation to twaddle."

It seems that even among the Olympians the inculcation of virtue has its pitfalls. But Mr. France has pointed out the path of duty in plain terms and whatever the risks, I propose to follow it. Since, then, I must preach a sermon, I have looked around for a text. I have found it in the opening paragraphs of an essay called "A Note on Progress" written by a Jesuit priest, Pierre Teilhard de Chardin. Here is the passage: [3]

The conflict dates from the day when one man, flying in the face of appearance, perceived that the forces of nature are no more unalterably fixed in their orbits than the stars themselves, but that their serene arrangement around us depicts the flow of a tremendous tide—the day on which a first voice rang out, crying to Mankind peacefully slumbering on the raft of Earth, "We are moving! We are going forward!". . .

It is a pleasant and dramatic spectacle, that of Mankind divided to its very depths into two irrevocably opposed camps—one looking towards the horizon and proclaiming with all its new-found faith, "We are moving," and the other, without shifting its position, obstinately maintaining, "Nothing changes. We are not moving at all."

These latter, the "immobilists," though they lack passion (immobility has never inspired anyone with enthusiasm!), have common sense on their side, habit of thought, inertia, pessimism and also, to some extent, morality and religion. Nothing, they argue, appears to have changed since man began to hand down the memory of the past, not the undulations of the earth, or the forms of life, or the genius of Man

[3] From: *The Future of Man*, translated from the French, *L'Avenir de l'Homme* first published by Editions du Seuil and copyright 1959 by Editions du Seuil. Copyright © 1964 in the English translation by William Collins Sons & Co. Ltd., London and Harper & Row, Inc. New York. Reprinted by permission of Harper & Row, Publishers.

or even his goodness. Thus far practical experimentation has failed to modify the fundamental characteristics of even the most humble plant. Human suffering, vice and war, although they may momentarily abate, recur from age to age with an increasing virulence. Even the striving after progress contributes to the sum of evil: to effect change is to undermine the painfully established traditional order whereby the distress of living creatures was reduced to a minimum. What innovator has not retapped the springs of blood and tears? For the sake of human tranquility, in the name of Fact, and in defence of the sacred Established Order, the immobilists forbid the earth to move. Nothing changes, they say, or can change. The raft must drift purposelessly on a shoreless sea.

But the other half of mankind, startled by the look-out's cry, has left the huddle where the rest of the crew sit with their heads together telling time-honoured tales. Gazing out over the dark sea they study for themselves the lapping of waters along the hull of the craft that bears them, breathe the scents borne to them on the breeze, gaze at the shadows cast from pole to pole by a changeless eternity. And for these all things, while remaining separately the same—the ripple of water, the scent of the air, the lights in the sky—become linked together and acquire a new sense: the fixed and random Universe is seen to move.

No one who has seen this vision can be restrained from guarding and proclaiming it. To testify to my faith in it, and to show reasons, is my purpose here.

Now that is a long text, and you may very well be wondering what possible relevance it can have to any concern of Maryland lawyers. Surely after the able addresses of my immediate predecessors in this office, we need no Galileo to tell us that the law moves. A glance at any weekly summary of important opinions will demonstrate that precedents are falling at a pace which has left the profession not exactly dumbfounded—for there has been no lack of vocal response—but certainly astonished. When Mr. France spoke, it was still possible for a lawyer to think of the law, and particularly of constitutional law, as a more or less fixed body of knowledge, the precise contours of which could be traced from a study of history and of the decided cases. To this generation such an idea is simply quaint.

But as members of the organized bar, our concern is not merely with the law. Granted that everyone recognizes that the law is moving in response to a changing society, the question remains whether the legal profession is moving with it; or are we, like

Teilhard's immobilists, still sleeping on our raft as it drifts into ever more troubled waters? That the waters are indeed getting pretty rough, stirred as they are by powerful currents and blasts of almost hurricane force, is known to everyone in this room. My purpose today is to consider whether we as a profession are meeting the responsibilities which new social forces have thrust upon us.

But first perhaps I should specify just what I mean by new social forces. That is not easy, since they take many forms, but all of them seem to me to spring from a single source, which may be identified as a drive toward equalization. All over the world inequalities between man and man, and I might add, between men and women, which used to be thought inevitable are now considered to be intolerable. In his recently published book *The Garden and the Wilderness,* Professor Mark De Wolfe Howe, who holds the Charles Warren Chair in American Legal History at the Harvard Law School, has said that "when the constitutional history of the central decades of this century comes to be written, I feel quite sure that the key to an understanding of its turbulence will be the concept of equality." This seems to me to be a wise observation which has validity well beyond the confines of American constitutional law. Is it not the concept of equality which is responsible for the ferment in Asia and Africa, and which is producing new nations every few months? Is it not the concept of equality which has made elitism a naughty word among professional educators?

Winston Churchill once remarked that the days of his youth were splendid times—for the rich and wellborn. Some of us can still remember the golden years before World War I when the family of a successful lawyer could live a life which is today quite unattainable even by the very rich. Those days have gone, of course, and while we may suffer from occasional nostalgia, I think that most of us would agree with Sir Winston that the world is better for their passing. Few are those who would now undo the great reforms of the Roosevelt era, and if we may judge by the performance of the most recent Congress, the tremendous tide of equalization is still moving in. The goals of an awakened sense of social responsibility have not yet been met.

One of the most dramatic aspects of this worldwide drive for equality is the fundamental readjustment which is taking place all over this country in the relations between the white majority and the Negro minority. This is a subject which since the earliest days of our nation has been the concern of lawyers. The basic contradiction between the institution of slavery and the principles announced in the Declaration of Independence and the Bill of Rights troubled lawyers from Thomas Jefferson to Abraham Lincoln. Maryland lawyers were among the first to seek a solution. Believing that separation of the races was impossible so long as they lived in the same country, the leaders of the Maryland bar took an important role in organizing the American Colonization Society, whose purpose was to free slaves and transport them back to Africa. This effort was, on the whole, a failure, although it left a permanent mark in the establishment of the Republic of Liberia. Even more futile and far more drastic in its consequences was the attempt of a Maryland lawyer to lay this problem to rest in the *Dred Scott* case. The tale has been told with clarity and understanding by our fellow member, Mr. Walker Lewis, in his recently published biography of Chief Justice Taney, which every Maryland lawyer will want to read.

The Emancipation Proclamation, followed shortly thereafter by the end of the Civil War, ushered in a period which a new generation of historians is even now engaged in reappraising. There were those led by Charles Sumner of Massachusetts and Thaddeus Stevens of Pennsylvania, who believed that the only proper course was to rebuild on the premise that—to paraphrase Mr. Justice Harlan's famous remark in *Plessy vs. Ferguson*—our society should be color blind. Their views did not prevail, and the struggle ended with a compromise which substituted for slavery a system of subordination in which Negroes were obliged to accept the inferior role. There was no real physical separation of the races—indeed this was believed to be entirely impracticable—and Negroes and whites continued to live and work together in intimate daily contact. True, there came to be various forms of segregation for special purposes, mostly as a result of laws passed in the last years of the nineteenth century, but these discriminations were tokens which symbolized the inferior status of the Negro. Sitting in separate seats in railroad cars, like the universal use of first names in addressing Negroes, regardless of their age or occupation, and a myriad other similar distinctions which were so familiar to us that we tended to be unconscious of them, were all intended to and for years did serve to keep the Negro "in his place."

The researches of historians have now made it clear that under the influence of Booker T. Washington the Negro leadership accepted this compromise very reluctantly and only as a temporary expedient necessary to the transition from slavery to full equality. By the end of World War I the compromise had begun to wear thin, and Adolf Hitler, with his odious persecutions based on racial theories, completely undermined it. Promptly at the end of World War II, the issues which were thought to have been settled when the period of reconstruction came to an end, were reopened.

Ironically enough, during the same period, largely as the result of the development of transportation by motor vehicle, our great urban centers began to be transformed into inner cities inhabited almost exclusively by Negroes, surrounded by white suburbs. For the first time in our history, physical separation of the races became a reality, and the word "ghetto" has become as familiar to us as it was to the people of Eastern Europe prior to World War II. Whereas before the Negro played a definite, if inferior, role in our society, he has now begun to feel excluded from it altogether except when the policeman or the tax collector or the draft official arrives at his door.

The consequences of this alienation have been analyzed in hundreds of publications ranging from studies by learned sociologists to novels, poems and plays by writers of varying talents. To the student of the history of Israel, there is little that is novel in this outpouring of words. The feelings of those who find themselves amidst the alien corn, have not changed very much.

What those feelings are, the occurrences in the Watts District of Los Angeles of last summer make all too clear.

That this great movement has had its effect on the law, no one can dispute. I will not bore you with a recital of the extensive changes in substantive and procedural law which are directly traceable to this source. What I am concerned with here is its significance to lawyers as a profession. Let me try to explain what I mean. You would agree, I am sure, that a basic tenet of our profession is that a lawyer is bound never to refuse to represent a litigant or a person charged with crime because his cause is an unpopular one. Many of you have taken or at least heard the oath administered to lawyers when they are admitted to practice before the United States District Court for the District of Maryland. I often think that if the medical profession has its Hippocratic Oath, we too can exhibit an equally lofty statement of our professional commitment. You remember what it says: "You will never reject from any consideration personal to yourself the cause of the defenseless or oppressed."

Do we as a profession live up to what we so nobly profess? In June of 1963, at the suggestion of President Kennedy, a committee of lawyers was organized to protect the civil rights of all citizens. This committee was made up of leaders of the bar from all parts of the nation, many of whom had been presidents of the American Bar Association or of their state bar associations. Under the direction of that committee a careful study was made to determine whether those involved in cases where civil rights are affected were receiving adequate representation from the legal profession. The answer, unfortunately, was all too clear. The lawyer who is willing to handle a civil rights case is a rare bird indeed.

At the meeting of the American Bar Association held in Miami last August, the chairman of the Lawyers' Committee for Civil Rights Under Law announced the opening of a law office in Jackson, Mississippi, to provide legal representation in civil rights cases. That office has a small permanent staff made up of lawyers from California, New York City, and Washington, D.C. In addition, it has the benefit of the volunteer services of young lawyers with trial experience who are associated with leading law firms throughout the country and who are willing to serve a one-month hitch in Mississippi.

Now the significant thing about this is that at the Miami meeting the president of the Mississippi Bar Association gave his warm endorsement to this work of the Lawyers' Committee and requested all members of the bar of his state to give these visiting lawyers all possible assistance. The reason for this receptive attitude on the part of the Mississippi bar may be found in a report recently made by the Civil Rights Commission after extensive investigations made by its staff in Mississippi and after considering voluminous testimony given at a public hearing held in that state. Dean Griswold, who was a member of that Commission, summarized that report in the flat statement that "there are no white lawyers in Mississippi who will ordinarily handle a civil rights case." So you see that these young lawyers from New York, Chicago, Philadelphia, Detroit and Washington—and I am happy to be able to add, from Baltimore—are upholding the honor of the profession, which has been sadly tarnished by the failure of the local bar to live up to its responsibilities.

Now, of course, the condition described by Dean Griswold is not confined to the state of Mississippi. There is, for example, the case of the young Harvard Law School student, Fred Wallace, who decided to spend his vacation in Farmville, Virginia, clerking for the only Negro lawyer in that community. Farmville is in Prince Edward County, which, as you all know, closed its public schools rather than to comply with the mandate of the Supreme Court in *Brown vs. The Board of Education*. The result was that the Negro children of the county went without schooling for many years, during which their rights were continuously in litigation. As the result, feelings in the community were aroused to a high pitch. One morning the student was sent to deliver a message to the local judge at the County Courthouse. As he approached the judge's chambers, a deputy sheriff who did not know him demanded to know what he was doing there. After what appears to have been a display of bad manners on both sides, a physical struggle took place, in the course of which the sheriff's finger was trodden upon and began to bleed. The student was promptly taken into custody and charged with assault with intent to kill.

The Dean of the Harvard Law School, believing, not without reason, that the student needed to be represented by a white lawyer of standing in the community, appealed to the head of the Lawyers' Committee for Civil Rights, who, in turn, asked the Dean of the Law School of the University of Virginia for suggestions. Dean Ribble recommended that George Allen of Richmond be asked to take the case. Mr. Allen, who was then nearly eighty years of age, is a native of Prince Edward County and is well known at that bar, although his principal reputation has been made in Richmond, where he has gained recognition as the leading plaintiffs' lawyer in the state and has been elected to the presidency of the Richmond Bar Association. He agreed to represent the student, but said that he would need the services of a member of the Prince Edward bar as local counsel. He then approached every lawyer at that bar and was turned down by every single one of them, although many of them had been associated with him in civil cases. He promptly filed a motion to transfer the case to the Federal Court and gave as one of his principal grounds the fact that no Prince Edward County lawyer could be found who was willing to appear for the defendant. Incidentally, the American College of Trial Lawyers gave its first award for fearless advocacy to George Allen at a meeting held in Miami last August, which was attended by the then president of the American Bar Association, himself a Richmond lawyer.

Let me give you one more illustration. You all remember the libel suit in which the Police Commissioner of Montgomery, Alabama, obtained a verdict of $500,000 against the New York *Times,* which was later set aside in the Supreme Court of the United States. Perhaps you may have wondered why the *Times* chose to be represented in the courts of Alabama by a New York lawyer. The answer is that New York counsel attempted unsuccessfully to obtain the services of an Alabama lawyer who was qualified to handle a case of that character. Not one of the leading law firms in that state would handle the case. This is not so surprising when you remember that a well-known Alabama lawyer was subsequently thrown out of one of the most prominent law firms in the state because he agreed to defend an FBI informer in a suit for counsel fees brought for services rendered in a case in which the agent had been indicted and had given evidence against his codefendants charged with the murder of a civil rights worker.

You may say that all these examples have arisen south of the Potomac, but I wonder whether, given a similar state of public feeling, the Maryland lawyer would be willing to pay the penalty which might be exacted from him were he to perform his plain professional duty. I do not remember that reputable members of this bar were anxious to represent persons charged with violations of the Smith Act or other allegedly communistic activities. The truth of the matter is that there are few John Adamses among us. You will recall that he gained an undying reputation for courage by defending the British soldiers who were indicted for murder as the result of the Boston Massacre. Nowadays a Massachusetts lawyer can gain a national reputation for courage simply by representing high-ranking officers of the United States Army before a congressional committee.

Here, it seems to me, is an area into which the profession should move. We simply cannot expect the individual lawyer to run the risk of social and professional ostracism which the representation of the unpopular cause sometimes brings, and we should be ashamed to try to cover the situation up by mouthing sanctimonious hypocrisies. I suggest, therefore, that it is the responsibility of each local bar association to take the necessary steps to make competent counsel available in such cases. We can, of course, help by contributing funds and services to volunteer organizations such as the Lawyers' Committee, but it seems to me that what is needed is recognition that this is a responsibility of the organized bar. When cases arise such as that which recently occurred in this state when young William Murray spent a substantial time in jail under a clearly illegal sentence, it should not have been necessary for the president of your Association to act on his own initiative in order to make sure that this young man had adequate representation. We are all deeply indebted to Mr. Charles Evans, Mr. Joseph Kaplan, and Mr. Leonard Kerpelman for upholding the reputation of the state of Maryland, but would it not have been better if a committee of the Bar Association of Baltimore City had been in existence, charged with responsibility for making legal services available under such circumstances?

Let me turn to another aspect of the subject. One very unpleasant consequence of the increasing alienation of the Negro community is the hostility of a great many decent Negro citizens toward the police. This is a very serious situation which has been recently exacerbated by the destructive tactics of some who hold positions of leadership in the Negro community, aided and abetted, I regret to say, by naïve journalists who have only a superficial knowledge of the problem. I do not for a moment suggest that there has not been fault on the side of the police, although it is certain that the charges of police brutality are exaggerated. This whole subject has received patient and sympathetic study by a representative biracial committee which recommended a plan designed to assure the community that charges against the police are not simply swept under the rug. The Complaint Evaluation Board is not and was never intended to be a review board, holding hearings and usurping the disciplinary responsibilities of the Police Commissioner. Its single responsibility is to evaluate complaints, make sure that they are thoroughly investigated, and to see that charges are brought when they should be brought. That is as far as the Board was intended to go and, in my opinion, as far as it can go without impairing the morale of a police force already buffeted by unprecedented problems of law enforcement arising out of the social forces which I have attempted to identify.

Another result of the drive for equalization is the proposal of the Office of Economic Opportunity to contribute to the support of approved plans developed by local organizations for the purpose of making legal services available to the poor. This is not the time or place to evaluate the Great Society or to compare it with its competitors. However, the upheaval in the Baltimore City Bar Association which followed upon the recent approval by the

Executive Committee of that Association of a plan for expanding the work of the Legal Aid Bureau with the aid of Federal funds, has focused attention once more on the age-old problem of legal assistance to the poor. Every lawyer recognizes an obligation to furnish legal services to those who cannot pay for it, but the time has long since gone by when the volunteer service of the individual lawyer can pretend to meet the needs of the poor for legal advice and assistance. We can, of course, contribute to the Community Chest and thus indirectly to the Legal Aid Bureau, but the plain fact is that if every dollar contributed by lawyers to the Community Chest were channeled into the work of the Legal Aid Bureau, it would still not have nearly enough money to fill the need. If we are honest with ourselves, we are bound to admit that lawyers have fallen far behind the medical profession in caring for those who cannot afford to pay for their services. Yet I venture to say that most lawyers welcomed the passage by Congress of the recent program of federally financed medical care. Certainly, very few lawyers would withhold governmental assistance to hospitals caring for the indigent sick. In the words of Chief Judge Markell, to do so would be to return to the "bow and arrow days."

Now I realize that there were at that meeting some who found fault with details of the plan which had been approved by the Executive Committee and others who felt that it should have been more thoroughly considered and explained before its approval. With them I have no quarrel, but unless I misunderstand the tenor of some of the speeches which were made on that occasion, objections were voiced to the plan which were far more deep-seated. Not only was there hostility to the use of tax money for any such purpose, but there was a suggestion that any organization engaged in supplying legal aid to the poor by making available the services of a staff of paid lawyers was in some way violating the canons of professional ethics and destroying the profession. I could not help wondering whether the speakers had ever heard of the Legal Aid Bureau or had any knowledge of what it has been doing for the past fifty-four years.

But I do not propose here to argue the merits of any particular plan. The president of the Bar Association of Baltimore City has appointed a committee to study that matter, and I am pleased to note that one of its ex officio members is also the chairman of the Committee on Legal Services of this Association. What I do suggest is that the time has come for Maryland lawyers to face facts. It is an undeniable fact that there are thousands of men and women in this state who need the services of lawyers in civil matters and who do not get them. Most of them know no lawyers and, indeed, fear them. Their contacts with the law have not been such as to make them think of the lawyer as the protector of the poor and oppressed.

Recently I got a call from a man who used to work as a servant in my mother's household. He had bought a household appliance on the installment plan under a contract which guaranteed service for a specified period. The appliance had proven to be defective, but repeated letters and telephone calls asking that the defects be corrected had been ignored. Finally he had declined to make payment of an installment and sent a letter explaining his reasons. In reply he had received a form letter from a lawyer advising him that unless the payment was made by a specified time, the appliance would be repossessed. I asked one of the young men in my office to look into the matter. He made one telephone call. The next day I got a call from my client telling me that the appliance had been fixed and expressing his profound gratitude. I replied that I had done very little—just had one of my associates put in a telephone call. "Mr. Marbury," he replied, "it all depends on who does the calling."

That man knew a lawyer to whom he could turn for help. There are thousands like him who do not and who, in like circumstances, would simply have suffered the loss of the payments which had been made on the appliance. I do not doubt that there are dozens of such occurrences every day throughout this state. Each one is a bit of social dynamite, ready to explode at the first spark. Do we not, as a profession, owe a duty to grapple effectively with this problem? Or shall we continue to "sit with our heads together, telling time-honoured tales" about our glorious profession and its readiness to serve the poor?

You will have noted that I have said nothing about the representation of the indigent charged with crime. Frankly, I think that subject has not lacked for discussion. One trouble is that we do not yet fully understand the rules of the game. There is still a heated controversy as to when counsel must be supplied to persons who are taken into custody by the police. Law journals are filled with polemics on this subject, and the interchange of letters between the Attorney General of the United States and the Chief Judge of the United States Court of Appeals for the District of Columbia has become notorious. No doubt in time the full scope of the *Gideon* and *Escobedo* cases will be determined and the profession will by necessity have to devise methods for discharging the responsibilities which will automatically fall upon the bar. In the meantime, let us take care that vested interests are not established which it will be difficult to eliminate. All history teaches us that the dispensation of patronage is a corrupting force which should as far as possible be removed from the hands of those who should be above politics. It is a cause of genuine concern that our judges now have the responsibility for dispensing such large sums in the way of compensation to counsel appointed to represent indigent defendants in criminal cases. Here again it seems to me that the profession should be moving to devise adequate methods for coping with a new situation. We have made a beginning in that direction, but much remains to be done.

There is one aspect of equality which all admit should be the special concern of lawyers. The phrase "equal justice under law" expresses the highest aspiration of our profession. It is trite to say that to be equal, justice must be speedy. Everyone knows that the financially weak litigant is obviously the greater sufferer from the law's proverbial delays. It is now sixty years since a young Nebraska lawyer named Roscoe Pound startled the members of the American Bar Association by delivering an address entitled "The Principal Causes for the Public Dissatisfaction with the Administration of Justice." One of the striking points which he made was that in England and Wales 95 judges seemed able to handle with expedition and in a manner which set a standard for the rest of the world, all the civil litigation, both at the nisi prius and appellate level, generated by a nation of thirty-two million people. I cannot help wondering what Dean Pound would think if he could be told that in Maryland in 1966 69 judges are getting far behind in the attempt to handle the litigation of a community of roughly three and one-half million people. Not more than one third of the time of our judges is devoted to criminal cases, and to offset this it must be remembered that the English courts handled bankruptcy, admiralty and probate matters as well as much other civil litigation which under our system lands in the Federal courts. So the comparison is pretty devastating.

You all know what the trouble is. Our judicial system is based on geographical divisions which make no sense today; the best available men are too often not appointed to the bench; we continue to admit to our bar men and women who have not had the necessary preparation in order to enable them to assume the responsibilities of a member of our profession, many of them graduates of schools which are not even accredited; we do not afford practicing lawyers the opportunities for continuing legal education which they need to keep abreast of a constantly changing legal system; we have failed to make full use of tested methods of expediting the disposition of cases, such as the pre-trial conference; our criminal law is a patchwork full of pitfalls for the unwary.

I could go on with this dreary rehearsal, but you have heard it all before. Indeed, it is only fair to say that lawyers as a profession and, in particular, Maryland lawyers, are struggling with these problems. The Committee on Judicial Administration of this Association has begun the task of modernizing our judicial system. Our Committee on Judicial Selection is striving to improve the method by which our judges are chosen. Our Committee on Legal Education is trying to raise the standards for admission to the bar and to eliminate the law schools which are not accredited. Our Committee on Continuing Legal Education is trying to make available to lawyers throughout the state the opportunity to keep abreast of developments in the law. I might add that we have an active Section on Criminal Law which is taking an important part in a general revision of our criminal statutes which has been undertaken by the Governor's committee headed by former Chief Judge Brune. Furthermore, your Board of Governors has recently approved the appointment of a committee representing not only this Association but also each of the county bar associations who will, it is hoped, render active assistance to the Governor's Commission on a Constitutional Convention.

In these respects, at least, we are moving forward, although, we must admit, not as rapidly or as effectively as might be hoped. The truth of the matter is that until the Maryland Bar Association speaks with the voice of the entire profession, we shall not do what we could and should be doing even in this specialized field of our own expertise. But that is another story, about which you will be hearing a good deal during the coming months from a Committee on Unifying the Bar, whose members have just been appointed by the Board of Governors.

You will think, perhaps, that I am asking too much of the organized bar to expect it to cope with all of these problems. I should point out to you, however, that the young lawyers who are now coming to the bar seem far more eager than their elders to undertake these tasks. Apparently our law schools are inculcating in their students a greater sense of social responsibility than was common a generation or more ago. These young men and women, taking them by and large, are anxious to come to grips with the vexing problems which I have attempted to present to you today. We, their elders, can, of course, surrender the task into their hands, but I suggest that our leadership is still needed, or else for what have we lived so long?

CIVIL RIGHTS AND THE PUBLIC UNIVERSITIES [4]

JOHN A. HANNAH [5]

It would be hard to conceive of a more felicitous combination of talents and experience to deal with the subject of civil rights and the responsibilities of the public institutions of higher learning than is found in Dr. John A. Hannah. He is president of Michigan State University, one of the ten largest academic institutions in the United States. Additionally, he is chairman of the United States Commission on Civil Rights, a position that he has held since its establishment in 1957.

Dr. Hannah delivered this speech on November 16, 1965, in Minneapolis, Minnesota, at the convention of the National Association of State Universities and Land-Grant Colleges. Presidents and other administrative officers from about one hundred institutions were in attendance at the meeting.

The speech was in a sense an exhortation. Using a definition of "civil rights" prepared by the Reverend Theodore M. Hesburgh, president of the University of Notre Dame, Dr. Hannah outlined the areas in which the public universities must be active if solutions are to be found to "the greatest domestic problem of our times." "Education has been cast in a leading role in this social drama," he said; the public institutions are in a favored position, because of their great resources of talent and of the confidence they enjoy, to facilitate the pursuit of happiness to which every person is entitled. While asserting that his concern was for both whites and Negroes, he asserted that the solicitude for the Negro "must be more intense and possibly more immediate for the simple reason that he labors under handicaps more severe, more humiliating, and more destructive of will and motivation, than any of the others." After setting forth specific suggestions for encouraging "our disadvantaged minority groups to make the best use of their educational opportunities," he closed with this appeal:

The primary task . . . is to prepare all of our students, regardless of race, or color, or national origin, to live comfortably, to work productively, and to serve effectively in an integrated society. Meanwhile, our universities can make enormous contributions to the solution of the complicated puzzle of human relations through

[4] Text furnished by John A. Hannah. *Journal of Higher Education*. 37:61-7. F. '66. Reprinted by permission of Dr. Hannah, the National Association of State Universities and Land-Grant Colleges, and the *Journal of Higher Education*.

[5] For biographical note, see Appendix.

encouraging the research and service programs we already have to put a high priority on work designed to advance progress in the entire field of civil rights.

Students interested in a virtual review of the activities of the Commission on Civil Rights from 1957 to date are invited to read Dr. Hannah's speech of January 27, 1966, entitled "The Only True Glory," delivered at the annual meeting of the Cincinnati Human Relations Commission. The text is reprinted in the Appendix of the *Congressional Record,* February 10, 1966, pages A682-4. In this address, Dr. Hannah observed that of the twenty-five major recommendations for changes in Federal law or policy made by the Commission, nineteen had been adopted. Moreover, he outlined briefly the case history of one proposal "because it shows how powerful an idea can be when it is based on unassailable fact and appeals to the American sense of justice."

I would like to make it clear at the outset that after serving as Chairman of the United States Commission on Civil Rights continuously since its inception—more than eight years ago—I did not seek this opportunity to speak here this morning.

When President Henry urged me many months ago to do so, I accepted because I continue to feel that the solution of our civil rights problems in this country is most important, and because I feel that our universities and you who determine their policies and procedures can and should play an important role in advancing their solution.

Perhaps we can best begin this discussion by defining "civil rights," because the phrase is currently being interpreted in many different ways. Indeed, we have seen the term even being used to throw a cloak of respectability over, and give moral sanction to, some campus activities which, without such disguise, would be condemned out of hand. Some of these activities tend to be subversive of the very processes and procedures that are the main safeguards of the individual's true rights in a democratic society.

In seeking a working definition of civil rights, many of us refer almost automatically to the Declaration of Independence, recalling Jefferson's words that all men are created free and equal, and Lincoln's later commentary that of course, men are not born equal in color, size, intellect, moral development, or social capacity, but are indeed equal in their God-given, and hence "unalienable," civil rights: Life, liberty, and the pursuit of happiness.

However much some understanding of history is essential to an understanding of the civil rights problems of today, let us pass on quickly to a consideration of a key question: What, specifically, are those rights?

Civil rights are, by definition, the rights of citizens—all citizens—although under our Constitution many of those rights extend to all persons. Furthermore—and more importantly—they are extended to all equally.

For our purpose today, let us accept as a working definition the statement of the Reverend Theodore M. Hesburgh, my valued colleague on the Commission on Civil Rights and president of the University of Notre Dame. Father Hesburgh defines civil rights to be the rights of *all* Americans to:

1. Equal opportunity to be educated to the full extent of their human talents;

2. Equal opportunity to work to the fullness of their potential contribution to our society;

3. Equal opportunity at least to live in decent housing and in wholesome neighborhoods consonant with their basic human dignity as befits their means and social development; and

4. Equal opportunity to participate in the body politic through free and universal exercise of the voting franchise.

I use this definition of civil rights for two reasons: First, because I fervently believe with Father Hesburgh that if all Americans enjoyed equal opportunity in these four particulars, then the problem of civil rights for all Americans would solve itself; and second, I use this definition because it seems to stake out the areas in which our public universities can and must be active if they are to be the fully responsible agencies that the American people intend and expect them to be.

Herein their challenge and opportunity plainly lie, because there is little they can do to defend the citizen's right to life and liberty. But there is a great deal they *can* do to facilitate his pursuit of happiness, as they have demonstrated repeatedly for more than a century.

Indeed, it may be that the universities represent the most effective instrumentality for accomplishing great social good in those areas where legislatures and courts find limits to their effectiveness. As much was suggested in the original charter of the University of Georgia, adopted in 1875, where it was proclaimed: "A free government can only be happy where the public principles and opinions are properly directed and their manners regulated. This is an influence beyond the sketch of laws and punishment, and can be claimed only by religion and education."

Let me ask you this: Is there really any question whether the public universities will participate in working out the solutions to this, the greatest domestic problem of our times?

A realistic appraisal of the situation would seem to argue that the public universities do *not* have a choice, that they must enlist—or be drafted—for this cause of social improvement as so often in the past.

Consider these facts:

Eighteen years ago—in 1947—the President's Commission on Higher Education for Democracy, said this about equality of educational opportunity:

The time has come to make public education at all levels equally accessible to all, without regard to race, creed, sex, or national origin. If education is to make the attainment of a more perfect democracy one of its major goals, it is imperative that it extend its benefits to all on equal terms. . . . Educational leaders and institutions should take positive steps to overcome the conditions which at present obstruct free and equal access to educational opportunities. Educational programs everywhere should be aimed at undermining and eventually eliminating the attitudes that are responsible for discrimination and segregation—at creating instead attitudes that will make education freely available to all.

In 1948, many persons, including educators, dissented. Since then, the Supreme Court has spoken. Since then, the Congress has repeatedly acted in the area of civil rights. Since then, the attitude of the American people has changed tremendously. Who would openly dissent from such a pronouncement today? A year ago, forty-two major public institutions of higher learning in

America were segregated. By latest count, only seven have now failed to assure the Federal Government that they will not discriminate in the admission or treatment of students.

Today, it has been decided that school segregation is against the national interest. More than that, it has been decided that schools and colleges and universities are to be the instruments through which the goal of a better society is to be achieved. Plainly the American people have decided to place their reliance on education to perform a miracle of social evolution as it has performed miracles of scientific development and been responsible for much of our unmatched economic and political progress.

The American people are committed to a war on ignorance, on poverty, on intolerance, on injustice, on inequality of opportunity. The doors of the Federal treasury have been opened in consequence, and we in education are confronted, not by the accustomed shortage of financial support when new burdens are imposed, but with a plethora of Federal programs, each liberally financed. Our current embarrassment may become one of riches, not of penury.

Will our public universities stand aside and refuse to participate in this gigantic national effort to improve the condition of American life? The question, as you recognize, is rhetorical, for public universities would disown their heritage and deny their purpose if now they were to remain aloof.

No, ladies and gentlemen, the choice is not ours to make. The decision has been made for us. We are committed as a people to the elimination of these ugly blemishes in our social system. Education has been cast in a leading role in this social drama, and it is a role that cannot be refused with grace or good conscience.

Perhaps my case is being argued not so much from fact as from faith, because the participation of public universities is plainly indispensable for two major reasons:

First, only the public universities, and their sister universities not under public control, have the resources to do the job that needs to be done. Their faculties represent a tremendous reservoir of knowledge, of experience, of intellectual curiosity, of social commitment. No other combination of agencies—not all of our community relations commissions, not all of our legislatures, not all of our Federal Government—can muster such an array of brilliant and useful talent.

Second, the universities of America possess the confidence of the public in the highest degree, a confidence earned by faithful and effective performance through the past decades and into the present day. The people will trust a university when it speaks where they might be skeptical of a political agency or of an economic interest group.

If we agree, then, that public universities are and must be in this fight to the end, then each must ask itself what the extent of its participation is to be. Will it assume an active role of leadership, or do only enough to keep its skirts clean and its reputation unblemished, exerting an effort that could be described as only a token at best? Some, I regret to say, are doing only that little today.

Let us make no mistake, it would be easy to shirk. A university need only take shelter behind high standards of admission, or use them cynically to screen out those who have mental capacity, but who have been poorly prepared for college through no fault of their own. Or, a university can fall back on the pressures of increasing enrollments, over commitments to research or public service to justify reluctance to assume new responsibilities.

Admittedly, there are the elements of a true dilemma here. We would not advocate the dilution of the quality of education or the lowering of legitimate standards, nor the acceptance of burdens beyond capacity to fulfill them satisfactorily.

I believe that we are intelligent enough to find ways to do what must be done, just as universities have found solutions to complex and delicate problems so often in the past.

One thing we might do is to stop giving encouragement, by spoken word or silent acquiescence, to the popular notion that a four-year college education is essential to a happy and productive life. We need not—should not—dangle before every young American what President Henry P. Tappan once called, in another connotation, "the bauble of an academical degree."

It is sheer sophistry to encourage the belief that only a college diploma can open the door of opportunity. It is worse than sophistry—it is calculated cruelty—to encourage all young Americans to strive for a prize that is plainly beyond the grasp of so many, given the state of society and the differences among individuals.

But it is not sophistry, it is not cruelty, to encourage every young American to do the best he can, to keep persistent pressure upon him until he has gone as far as his background and mental capacity will let him go, be it through high school, or the junior college, or the vocational school, or the technical institute, or through the four-year college, or through the graduate school to the Ph.D. degree.

To this audience, it is a temptation to say that our only immediate concern should be how to create a desire on the part of young Negroes for higher education. It is a temptation, because the total problem is so broad and so complex that the easy way out would be to narrow the discussion—and to restrict our responsibility—to only one aspect of it. It would be so convenient to say that we should concern ourselves only with the duty of finding places in the public universities for the Negroes who manage to fight their way upward into the category of admissible students, or to find places on our faculties for those Negroes, pathetically few in number, who succeed in acquiring their doctorates. But the task is not that easy and our responsibility is not that limited.

My concern is not for the Negro alone. It extends to the white child in the slums as well as to his black brother; it extends to the youngster on the cutover farms of northern Michigan, the child of the unemployed miner in Appalachia, and to the offspring of the tenant farmer in the South as well as to those in the ghettos of our big cities. Your concern is certainly the same.

But at the same time, our concern for the Negro must be more intense and possibly more immediate, for the simple reason that he labors under handicaps more severe, more humiliating, and more destructive of will and motivation, than any of the others.

What we need to do is persuade him that education offers him the best way out of his present economic and social condition.

This opportunity other Americans, be they fourth-generation or newly arrived from foreign lands, have been quick to exploit. Immigrants to these shores have either already known, or quickly learned, that education could open the doors of opportunity. Perhaps it was too late for them, but not for their children. The comedian's phrase "My son, the doctor" is more poignant than humorous.

The Irishman, the Hungarian, the German, the Italian, the Swede, the Armenian, the Greek, bore no physical characteristics that made him different from others in this country and hence a fixed target for discrimination.

All of us in this room, unless there be full-blooded American Indians among us, are the descendants of immigrants. But who can tell about the majority of us, except perhaps from the clue of surnames, from what country our progenitors came? Furthermore, who cares?

But not all of us enjoy this immunity from categorization. The Negro is forever marked by the color of his skin as one apart. He cannot lose himself in the homogeneity in which the rest of us take refuge. He is forever marked as being of another race, fellow-American though he be, and he suffers under a dreadful handicap as a consequence. He begs us to be color-blind, and those of good will try desperately to be, but we can be color-blind only figuratively, no matter how hard we try, because it is impossible for us with normal eyesight to be color-blind literally.

The task of religion and education is to persuade people that color makes no difference, but until we achieve widespread acceptance of that undoubted truth, then the color of his skin will be a handicap with which the Negro will have to live.

There may be some comfort, and perhaps some hope, for him in something a Jewish friend confided to me one day. Discussing the problems of civil rights, in which he takes an active interest, he said: "You may not know it, but for centuries in the ghettos,

Jewish mothers have counseled their sons: 'My boy, to be recognized as silver, you must be gold.'"

To be recognized as silver, the Negro may have to be not only gold, but platinum as well. We must help to persuade him, that for him, education is the surest alchemy.

Doors of opportunity, so long closed arbitrarily to him, are slowly opening in the professions and higher vocations. Business and industry are beginning to accept the principle of equality of opportunity. Unfortunately some labor unions still bar the door. Some have removed all forms of discrimination, and others are struggling to open their membership and apprentice programs to all. To change the metaphor, the skies are brightening, too slowly for most, but they *are* brightening, and the wind is fair.

The Negro in America labors under another handicap, this one so subtle that he may not recognize it, but it is there, all the same. This handicap is that his own cultural heritage is lost in the mists of African antiquity; he has no long tradition of participation in the struggle for individual dignity and collective freedom such as most of us enjoy; he has had, perforce, to adapt to a culture and a tradition to which he was not naturally born.

To illustrate the richness and significance of the American tradition as it derived from the Judeo-Christian traditions of the West, let me quote a comment on the effects of the American Revolution by Professor Frederick Rudolph. It appears in his delightfully readable history, *The American College and University.* Doctor Rudolph has this to say:

The Revolution . . . may have begun as an effort to define the limits of political authority or as an effort to redefine the economic relationships between mother country and colony. It may have become a movement for independence, but before it was over it was also a movement for democracy: A full-blooded statement to the effect that in America, man counted for more, took less account of his superiors—indeed frequently denied their existence—achieved whatever distinction his own ability and the bounty of the land allowed him, looked any man in the eye and knew him as an equal before the law and before God.

But this was for the white American, not the Negro, who if he had looked any white man in the eye and declared himself an equal might not have lived to pass the story on to his descendants.

To our regret and shame, two hundred years of slavery have left their mark on Negroes, who still struggle to escape psychic bonds. They have no great tradition of hardy pioneers, no lasting tradition of success, no tradition of one of their fellows rising from a log cabin to the White House. In saying this, I hope I do not offend any of our Negro friends, for certainly that is not my intent and the situation is not their fault.

To appreciate the significance of tradition one needs to travel extensively in Africa and come into intimate contact with African peoples in areas where there has been no persistent domination by whites. In those areas the Africans are proud; they are self-reliant; they are confident; they are ambitious. They ask our help to bring their countries fully up to twentieth century standards, but they look us in the eye while doing it. There is no attitude of master and servant; one superior, the other inferior. One can only speculate what the position and attitude of Negroes in America would be today if their ancestors had come originally as free men rather than as slaves.

Thus far, we have been concerned with general observations. Not to leave you without any specific suggestions, let me answer the pertinent question: What can the public universities do best to encourage our disadvantaged minority groups to make the best use of their educational opportunities?

One answer is suggested in the data recently supplied by our reliable Mr. Ostar. He informed us that the member universities of this association prepare 25.7 per cent of all of those going into teaching, and 41.5 per cent of those going into the non-teaching educational fields. Surely this is a potent force with which to exert some beneficial influence.

The trouble, as is becoming increasingly clear, is that we prepare these young teachers for jobs in schools in middle-class neighborhoods and the affluent suburbs, where they will enjoy fine facilities and pleasant working conditions. We do not point out to them that the need for their valuable services is greatest in the crowded schools of the central city, where facilities are likely to be less than good, and working conditions less than pleasant.

We prepare them to teach youngsters with backgrounds much like their own, not children who come from broken, fatherless homes, not children whose psychological set may be against education, not children who resent discipline, not children who are difficult to teach, and difficult to manage because outside the classroom they have to fight to survive.

We need to emphasize the preparation of teachers for the slum school, not the suburb. We need to bring to bear the tremendous research resources of our universities to ferret out the still-elusive secret of the learning process and how teaching can best facilitate it. We need to offer our tremendous resources to local boards of education, which may have all of the will in the world to improve the education of minority groups, but simply do not know how to go about it. We need to help persuade the public that to correct this social deficiency will require money, and lots of it, and we need to convince the public that there is true equity in investing more tax dollars if necessary on the slum school than on the one in the advantaged suburb, and that such investments may well pay bigger dividends to society in the long run.

Moreover, we need to do this now, for we are already late. The brave, imaginative programs like Head Start and Upward Bound will have their effect in time, but the effect will be minimal because they represent a piecemeal attack, not the broad assault conditions demand. Much of what I have said about educating teachers applies with equal force to those we educate to be social workers, workers in the fields of human health, the urban planners, and many others.

Let me make one more general observation, and then conclude: We must accept the fact that the real problems of civil rights are not to be found exclusively in the South, but in the East and North and West as well. Events in Rochester, and Chicago, and Los Angeles color the pages of our current history as well as those in Selma, and Little Rock, and Birmingham.

To be fair, we must recognize that problems in the North are different from those in the South, but they are no less menacing because they are different. What Dr. James Conant called "social dynamite" is piling up everywhere, and a single glowing spark may still touch off a chain reaction.

If my years of experience have taught me one thing, it is that problems of civil rights will be solved, not by national programs, but by local programs; not by Federal action, but by community action. Michigan must deal with the problems of the 500,000 Negroes in Detroit; Illinois must deal with the problems of the more than 800,000 Negroes in Chicago; California must deal with the problems of the 400,000 Negroes in Los Angeles; Pennsylvania must deal with the problems of the more than 500,000 Negroes in Philadelphia; Ohio must deal with the problems of the 250,000 Negroes in Cleveland; and New York must deal with the problems of the more than 1,000,000 Negroes in New York City. The civil rights problem must be solved where it exists, North or South, in Mississippi or in Minnesota, or in your state.

This throws the problem directly back to us in the state universities and land-grant colleges, to us who boast that the boundaries of the campus are the boundaries of the state, and that we are the servants of *all* of the people.

For many in the land-grant colleges, the decision to go into the cities may be difficult to make, accustomed as they have been to giving priority to the problems of rural people. But we must face up to the fact that this is no longer a rural, but an urban society. Our major problems are in the cities, and we must, like good military commanders, march towards the sound of the guns.

The call to this new public duty should not sound strange in the ears of the public universities, founded as they were and maintained as they are to advance the public good through education, research, and service.

To single out those universities I know best, the land-grant institutions especially should find this a familiar challenge. They were established more than a century ago, we must remind ourselves, specifically to serve the underprivileged of that day—the sons of farmers, and mechanics, and laborers, and shopkeepers who were being denied equal opportunity for liberal and practical education in the several pursuits and professions of life.

The spectacular successes of that assault on inequality, and the tremendous benefits that have accrued to the nation in consequence, should give us all of the justification we need for undertaking this new assignment, and all of the confidence we need that it, too, can be carried out successfully.

This is not the place to suggest the specific programs in which our universities should engage. Such suggestions have already been made in volume, and still others are being formulated by this Association, by the American Council on Education, by the Educational Policies Commission, and by many others.

The primary task, in summary, is to prepare all of our students, regardless of race, or color, or national origin, to live comfortably, to work productively, and to serve effectively in an integrated society. Meanwhile, our universities can make enormous contributions to the solution of the complicated puzzle of human relations through encouraging the research and service programs we already have to put a high priority on work designed to advance progress in the entire field of civil rights.

But as always, our primary task is to prepare young people to become effective citizens in this democratic society, which has now reaffirmed its belief that all men are indeed created equal, and renewed its pledge to extend the right to equal treatment to all who call themselves Americans.

Ladies and gentlemen, our duty is plain. Let us have the courage to do it.

A CHICAGOAN GOES SOUTH [6]

Charles H. Percy [7]

The 1966 senatorial nominations will bring to national prominence several attractive young aspirants who regard the revitalizing of the Republican party as an important phase of their political mission. Edward W. Brooke will try for the seat occupied by Leverett Saltonstall of Massachusetts. Charles H. Percy, who recently resigned from his position as board chairman of the Bell & Howell Company, will seek the office held by the redoubtable Paul H. Douglas, Democrat of Illinois. At seventy-three, Senator Douglas remains a formidable figure: skilled in speaking, very much at home before political meetings, and not afraid to engage issues in head-on argument. Reportedly, however, he has said that in the forthcoming contest with Mr. Percy there will be "no point in rhetoric. It won't help. I will simply run on the record."

In the campaign, Mr. Percy will be facing his former teacher. While at the University of Chicago, he took instruction under Senator Douglas, then a professor of economics. Before he received his bachelor's degree, however, Mr. Percy had joined Bell & Howell, rising successively and swiftly to the top administrative posts in the company. A director of the firm at twenty-three, he moved on to the presidency when he was twenty-nine. Commenting on his business experience, in a speech at the University of Illinois on January 4, 1966, Mr. Percy disclaimed anything unusual, however, about his early career. He told his audience about a group called the Young Presidents' Organization, composed of more than two thousand businessmen, in which membership is limited to persons who became corporation presidents before the age of forty.

Mr. Percy is a vigorous campaigner. Although his first venture into politics was unsuccessful—he lost his bid for the governorship of Illinois in 1964—he is counted on to make a strong comeback in the senatorial race, if he receives the nomination, which seems likely.

The speech reprinted below is fairly typical of Mr. Percy's method and style. The analysis of subject matter is relatively simple, the manner of expression is down-to-earth, the identification with the audience is direct. The speech was given on February 17, 1966, at Jackson, Mississippi, before the Mississippi Council on Human Relations. It contains a note of political aspiration and an endorsement of Republican philoso-

[6] Text furnished by Charles H. Percy, with permission for this reprint.

[7] For biographical note, see Appendix.

phy; but more importantly, it expresses his credo on civil rights, especially with regard to fair employment opportunities and the right to vote.

I come to the South not, I hope, as an intruder, but as a native son.

For generations, my branch of the Percy family lived in Alabama, and a second branch lived here in Mississippi. My grandfather was a drummer boy at the headquarters of Robert E. Lee, and later he served on the faculty at Washington and Lee University. My father spent most of his life in Mobile, and I was born across the Bay in Pensacola, Florida.

I am not, then, a stranger to the South.

Tonight I would like to discuss equal opportunity, first as a businessman, and then as a Republican politician.

When I talk of equality, I do not do so under a halo of self-righteousness, for I live in a glass house. My city, Chicago, has nearly a million Negro citizens. They do not have equal access to jobs. They do not have equal education. They do not have equal housing. I myself live in a village of 3000 persons where there is only one Negro family; this is not a sociological accident.

Cloaked in hypocrisy, discrimination in the North is just as real as discrimination anywhere. Our racial problems, especially in the cities, are at least as serious as yours. Martin Luther King has made no mistake in coming to Chicago to mount an assault against our wretched slums. We in the North must work just as hard as you in the South to hammer out a society of justice, equality, and dignity.

A good place to begin is in the field of employment. I submit to the businessmen here among you that job discrimination is not only bad democracy—it's bad business. To support my point, let me give you a brief case history.

In 1949, when I became the president of Bell & Howell not one Negro was employed by the company. I had been concerned about this for a long time, but I was not in a position to do anything about it until I assumed the presidency.

Once that responsibility was mine. I carefully examined the reasons the company did not hire Negroes. These reasons, I found, included every myth ever used to discriminate. Essentially, I was told that a reversal of company policy wouldn't work.

I am pleased to report that it did work. I called a meeting of all supervisors and department heads, and made it clear that we would begin hiring Negroes on the same basis as whites. Anyone who disagreed with the new policy was free to resign. No one did.

Now, after seventeen years of experience as an equal opportunity employer, we can say unequivocally that the performance of Negro employees has met our standards in every way.

Despite our record at Bell & Howell and at numerous other companies, we in the North have not yet attained equal job opportunities for all citizens. In Chicago alone, Negroes represent 26 per cent of the population but account for 43 per cent of the city's unemployment. With labor critically short in some areas of our state, one out of four Negroes in East St. Louis is still without work.

In many communities, then, the most serious problem facing the Negro is employment—securing and holding a job that not only enables him to support himself and his family, but makes him feel that he is truly a member of the community. Negroes and whites in Chicago have told me of the overwhelming hopelessness that comes when a man can't find a job. Inevitably, unemployment engenders resentment and despair—a despair I saw in my own father when we were on relief during the depression. Welfare does not change this. Too often the price for public assistance is a sense of lost human dignity.

What we are talking about here is what Martin Luther King has called "a sense of somebodiness." I think the business community here in Mississippi, as in Illinois, has a great opportunity to provide many more of its citizens with that "sense of somebodiness," while at the same time doing itself an important favor.

I have seen your advertisement in the New York *Times* which urges outside companies to come to Mississippi. It was an attractive ad, and perhaps it will help to bring new industry to your state. But as a businessman, I can tell you that much more appealing is the potential of the labor force in Mississippi—a potential which many regions of our nation cannot provide.

It is up to you to realize that potential—to educate that labor force, to give it needed skills, to open up opportunities for it. When you have done that, there will be less need to advertise for outside industry.

Both in the North and in the South, we must see to it that Negroes are not the "last hired and first fired." And we must do better than to make surface concessions to racial decency; the illusion of equality is not enough. It is not enough simply to require the Negro worker to wear a white shirt, a jacket, and a tie, while asking him to continue to perform the same menial chores as before.

The opportunity to advance is as important as the opportunity to work. Let us all look to the example of Marietta, Georgia, where the biggest single airplane factory in the world employs highly-placed Negro engineers, mathematicians and technicians—where Negro foremen supervise both white and Negro workers.

And so I urge the businessmen of the South, as I have urged the businessmen of the North, to give the Negro the equal opportunity, the equal treatment, the equal break that is rightfully his. Do it for your own sake, for your country's sake, and for the sake of the harmonious human relations this council seeks to foster.

As some of you may know, I recently ended a quarter-century career as a businessman to begin what I hope may be an equally long career of public service. However, as I learned in 1964, job opportunities in politics are not always what they seem, and the competition for advancement is very tough indeed.

I am now running for the Senate against Paul Douglas. If the Mississippi press should ever comment on our race, I can only hope it will deal more gently with us than the Jackson *Mississippian* dealt with an earlier Senate race in Illinois. The *Mississippian* stated that the South could have no choice between "a pair of depraved, blustering, mischievous, low-down demagogues." At that time, the paper was speaking of Abraham Lincoln and another Douglas—Stephen Douglas—during their famous 1858 campaign for the Senate.

In talking to you about civil rights as a Republican, I do not speak for myself alone. Many share my views.

As a Republican, I have long been proud of much of our civil rights record. And one need not go back to Lincoln to find cause for pride.

The recommendations of the Eisenhower administration led to bipartisan enactment in 1957 of the first Federal civil rights legislation in over eighty years. Republican governors like Rockefeller in New York, Scranton in Pennsylvania, Romney in Michigan, and Hatfield in Oregon, are providing strong leadership in the field of equal rights.

It was two Republican representatives, Halleck of Indiana and McCulloch of Ohio, who made it possible in 1963 for President Kennedy to get the civil rights bill through the House Judiciary Committee.

And as much as any man, it was Senator Everett Dirksen from my own state of Illinois who was responsible for the passage of the Civil Rights Act of 1964.

In the spring of 1964, the Republican Critical Issues Council, headed by Dr. Milton Eisenhower, recommended Federal legislation to ensure fair employment practices and to guarantee access to public accommodations to all Americans. These recommendations were included in the Civil Rights Act of 1964 which won the support of 80 per cent of the Republicans in the Eighty-eighth Congress. And in the Ninetieth Congress, I look forward to joining Hatfield of Oregon, Brooke of Massachusetts, and Taft of Ohio in reaffirming the Republican commitment to effective civil rights legislation.

Ironically, the Republican 1964 presidential candidate found it impossible to vote for the Civil Rights Act of 1964 because he considered the sections on fair employment practices and public accommodations to be unconstitutional. And it was his negative vote, I believe, more than any other factor, which enabled the

Republican party to carry the Deep South in the 1964 national election.

As much as any Republican, I am anxious to see the South in the Republican column on election day, but not for the reasons that it was there on election day, 1964.

Some people voted for the Republican ticket in protest against the Democratic Administration's stand on civil rights. Some people voted for it in the hope that a Republican administration would take a far weaker stand, or perhaps even squelch the Negro revolution.

I am not proud of those votes.

In 1964, the Republican party won five southern states by setting foot upon what has been called "the shifting racist sands," and that was a triumph neither for Republicans nor conservatives.

Such a victory will not serve the future success of our party, or of any party. For what we succeeded in doing in 1964 was to drive practically the entire Negro vote in the United States into the Democratic camp.

With each passing year, the Negro vote will—and should— grow, as more and more Negroes register with the help of the Federal government and of private groups. In many states, the Negro has the opportunity to become the decisive factor in determining the outcome of elections.

As a Republican, I can only hope that the American Negro will judge my party by its *complete* record, and not by an isolated aberration of that record. I hope, too, that he will keep in mind that segregationist Democrats dominate public offices in southern states, and that 90 per cent of the poor in America have lived under Democratic rule in southern and urban areas for the past several decades.

However they decide to judge us, I ask Negroes not to be indifferent to the opportunities and duties before them. Negroes have the opportunity—and the duty—to fulfill the responsibilities that come with their long-delayed rights. First-class citizenship requires equal rights *and* equal responsibilities.

No right, no responsibility, is quite so formidable as the vote. With it, Negroes have a potential to effect change that they never had before. As one New Orleans minister has said, "The answer to police brutality is the vote." And it is the answer to much, much more, if only it is applied to good advantage. Properly used, the votes of Negroes could provide the final thrust in the struggle for equal opportunity. And wisely used, those votes will not form a one-party bloc. For we have seen in Chicago that when one party takes the Negro vote for granted, that vote loses much of its power.

If the Republican Party ever hopes to attract that vote—if it wishes to remain the progressive party I think it is—then we Republicans must heed the lessons of 1964.

We must make it unmistakably clear that the traditionally progressive position of our party on civil rights will never again be betrayed by subtly appealing to a backlash of white resistance.

Both parties must be on guard lest they become the tools of the racists. There are some Republicans here in Mississippi who are no more interested in true Republicanism than George Wallace is interested in the fundamental principles of the Democratic party. In each case, these men are using respected party labels in an effort to perpetuate segregation and inequality.

We must never forget that the Republican Party was founded as a party of reform; when we abandon reform, our vitality is drained.

And we must above all be the party of justice and freedom in the field of civil rights and civil liberties. We must see in *every* man the work and genius of God. We must respect, support, and actively defend the rights of every American, as an individual and as a citizen. To do less would be to deny our heritage.

All those, both Republican and Democratic, who deplore the breakdown of states' rights, who look with horror upon Federal intrusion into state and local government, should be as concerned about states' responsibilities as states' rights.

If every state had met its responsibilities to assure the rights of all citizens, there would have been no need for a Federal Civil Rights Act of 1964, and there never would have been the strife and the anguish this country has witnessed in recent years. As Ralph McGill has observed, if political and public leadership had supported the processes of law in 1954 when the Supreme Court's school decision was handed down, "the South—and the nation—would have avoided the bitter and disgraceful harvest of hate . . . that has been so much a part of the years since."

Those of us who wish to see state and local government remain effective must remember the past. For it has been truly said that those who cannot remember the past are condemned to live it again. If, for instance, we in Chicago fail to respond to the challenge of our slums, then we may be sure that the Federal Government will increasingly assume the responsibilities in urban housing which should be ours.

And similarly, if you here in the South do not move with greater energy, speed, and sincerity to give the Negro his vote, to abolish injustice to Negroes and to civil rights workers at the hands of all-white juries, to advance the cause of civil rights across the board, then you can be assured that the Federal Government will—and should—pass more and more of the legislation which so many southerners abhor.

In the social revolution of the sixties, it is incumbent on each of us, northerner and southerner, Republican and Democrat, black and white, to look ahead and to plan ahead—not to temporize, not to drag our feet in the sands of the past. With open minds and hearts, we must decide what is needed, and then we must do it.

President Johnson thinks a Great Society is possible, and that is a worthy goal he shares with all Americans. But I believe that before a society can be great, it must be just.

A just society will provide equal opportunity to every citizen, whether he lives in Philadelphia, Pennsylvania, or Philadelphia, Mississippi.

A just society will ensure the dignity of every citizen, from the South Side of Chicago to South Carolina.

A just society will guarantee the rights of every citizen, whatever his color, his creed, his cause.

A truly just society will not be easily attained. We have learned that the hard way. The shaping of such a society is a complex and delicate task which requires and deserves patience, as long as patience is not cynically invoked as a screen for inaction.

But a just society *can* be achieved. In a short time, we have already moved a long way toward it. We can move still further, still faster, if, individual by individual, institution by institution, in Watts and in Harlem, in Chicago and in Jackson, we voluntarily set the just society as our goal. All of us working together can hasten that day when democracy will truly work for every American.

We in this room, we in the Republican party, and we in the United States, could do no better than to follow Abraham Lincoln's personal creed. "I shall try to correct errors when shown to be errors," he said, "and I shall adopt new views so fast as they shall appear to be true views . . . and I intend no modification of my oft-expressed personal wish that all men everywhere might be free."

A NEW LOOK AT AN OLD PROBLEM

THE TWO AMERICAS [1]

J. W. FULBRIGHT [2]

During an interview in September 1965, Chalmers Roberts of the Washington *Post* asked Senator J. W. Fulbright to comment on the reasons for the Administration's displeasure with some of his speeches. In his reply, the Arkansas Democrat reflected on the complaint "that the Congress hasn't developed any debate, that there has been no discussion, that we are a rubber-stamp Congress. Then when I make a speech . . . it is a terrible thing. You are criticized for starting a debate. I don't think you can have it both ways." Mr. Fulbright speaks out boldly on the crucial issues of our time. Scholarly, articulate, poised, he is sometimes referred to as America's Great Dissenter on foreign policy.

Both in his capacity as chairman of the prestigious Senate Foreign Relations Committee and as private citizen, he has been fearless in striking out against those Administration policies which he considers ill-advised and dangerous. Moreover, he has consistently urged the adoption of measures calculated to improve the educational system in America. But probably he is at his best in the role of the exposer of myths. With seeming intellectual detachment, he scores importantly in his analyses of United States actions abroad.

Within the past two years, he has authored at least three major statements. On March 25, 1964, he delivered the widely heralded and sharply criticized address "Foreign Policy—Old Myths and New Realities." In it he challenged the public officials to give some thought to "unthinkable things." Criticizing the "excessive moralism" in our diplomatic policy, he urged that Americans "learn to welcome rather than fear the voices of dissent and not . . . recoil whenever some heretic suggests "that Castro may survive or that Khrushchev is not as bad a fellow as Stalin was." (The complete text of this speech was reprinted in REPRESENTATIVE AMERICAN SPEECHES: 1963-1964, pages 91-114.) In another speech before the Senate on September 15, 1965, Mr. Fulbright entered an abrasive protest over our intervention in April in the Dominican Republic. Distressed by our questionable judgment and lack of candor, he ventured to believe that "we misread prevailing tendencies

[1] Text furnished by J. W. Fulbright, with permission for this reprint.
[2] For biographical note, see Appendix.

in Latin America by overlooking the fact that any reform movement is likely to attract Communist support.

> We thus failed to perceive that if we are automatically to oppose any reform movement that Communists adhere to, we are likely to end up opposing every reform movement, making ourselves the prisoners of reactionaries who wish to preserve the status quo.

The speech was not joyously received by Administration officials.

The third major pronouncement by Mr. Fulbright dealt as did the others with the broad outlines of American foreign policy, but particularly with our attitude toward Communist China. The Brien McMahon Lecture, reprinted below, was delivered at the University of Connecticut at Storrs on March 22, 1966. Given during the course of the four-week hearings on China before the Senate Foreign Relations Committee, the address is a part of the detailed dialogue on critical phases of American foreign policy. In the Committee hearings, three points of view seemed evident: (1) Put an end to the doctrine of containment of China. She is not a formidable threat to American security. Her rhetoric, though strong, is, according to Professor Hans J. Morgenthau of the University of Chicago, "unrealistic and in good measure absurd—the result of China's traditional ethnocentrism and lack of understanding of the outside world." In short, it is a mistake "to take their rhetoric as an indication of policy." (2) Continue the policy of containment—and this involves a certain posture of military power—but try to end the isolation imposed by our reluctance to recognize Red China as a world power. And (3), maintain generally the status quo. In his testimony before the Senate Foreign Relations Committee on March 28, 1966, Dr. Walter H. Judd, former Republican Congressman from Minnesota remarked:

> Until someone can suggest policies that offer better prospects of success, based on something more substantial than speculation, wishful thinking or just hope, I can see no sound, sensible, or logical reason to change present policies and every reason to continue them, always being flexible in our tactics as required by developments as they come along.

On March 7, 1966—the day prior to the opening of public hearings on China before the Senate Foreign Relations Committee—Mr. Fulbright advised the Senate of the ultimate objective of the testimony: "the prevention of war between China and America." And he stressed the necessity, if the "fatal expectancy of war" was to be altered, of America's learning more about the Chinese people and government. "Americans and Chinese [must] come to know each other in human terms." This makes it imperative for

Americans to be open-minded and inquisitive, to set aside ideological preconceptions and try to learn all that we can about the Chinese and their behavior and attitudes, and especially to try to find out why exactly the Chinese are so hostile to the West and what, if anything, can be done to eliminate that hostility.

In the lecture at the University of Connecticut, Senator Fulbright returned to the role he performs exceedingly well—that of discerning critic and dissenter. He asserted that "it is never pleasant to criticize one's own country but, seen in perspective, criticism is an expression of confidence; it bespeaks a faith in the capacity of our country to realize its own best possibilities." His examination of the rationale of our Latin American and Asian policies prompted him to observe that

Whatever wisdom or lack of it our emphasis on communism has had in the past, the realities of the present require a reversal of priorities as between opposing communism and supporting nationalism. The basis of my criticisms of American policy in both Southeast Asia and Latin America is a belief that American interests are better served by supporting nationalism than by opposing communism, and that when the two are encountered in the same country it is in our interest to accept a Communist government rather than to undertake the cruel and all but impossible task of suppressing a genuinely national movement.

Going back to the theme of his address of March 25, 1964, he called for the dispelling of old myths about China and the recognition of new realities:

It is, of course, a gamble to allow China to continue building its strength, including a nuclear arsenal, in the hope that by the time Chinese power is truly menacing it will be wielded by less dangerous men than those who now rule Peking. But when one considers that the alternative is a preemptive war—a war which would inflict temporary physical damage on China but irreparable moral damage on the aggressor—it seems clear that we have no real choice except to take a chance that China, like Russia, will evolve toward moderation.

Historian Arnold Toynbee once remarked that it is "a paradox and a tragedy that today America should be China's No. 1 enemy." Perhaps the speeches and debates of the Fulbrights and other citizens will in good time help give witness to the injunction in Matthew 5:24-25:

First be reconciled to thy brother. . . . Agree with thine adversary quickly, whiles thou art in the way with him; lest at any time the adversary deliver thee to the judge, and the judge deliver thee to the officer, and thou be cast in prison.

There are two Americas. One is the America of Lincoln and Adlai Stevenson; the other is the America of Teddy Roosevelt and General MacArthur. One is generous and humane, the other narrowly egotistical; one is modest and self-critical, the other arrogant and self-righteous; one is sensible, the other romantic; one is good-humored, the other solemn; one is inquiring, the other pontificating; one is moderate and restrained, the other filled with passionate intensity.

We have tended in the years of our great power to puzzle the world by presenting to it now the one face of America, now the other, and sometimes the two at once. Many people all over the world have come to regard America as being capable of generosity and far-sighted behavior but no less capable of pettiness and spite. The result is an inability to anticipate American actions which in turn makes for apprehension and a lack of confidence in American aims.

The inconstancy of American foreign policy is not an accident but an expression of two distinct sides of the American character. Both are characterized by a kind of moralism, but one is the morality of decent instincts tempered by the knowledge of human imperfection and the other is the morality of absolute self-assurance fired by the crusading spirit. The one is exemplified by Lincoln, who found it strange, in the words of his second inaugural, "that any man should dare to ask for a just God's assistance in wringing their bread from the sweat of other men's faces," but then added: "let us judge not, that we be not judged." The other is exemplified by Theodore Roosevelt, who, without question or doubt as to his own and his country's capacity to judge right and wrong proclaimed the duty of the United States to exercise an "internal police power" in the hemisphere on the ground that "chronic wrongdoing, or an impotence which results in a general loosening of the ties of civilized society, may in America . . . ultimately require intervention by some civilized nation. . . ." Roosevelt of course never questioned that the "wrongdoing" would be done by our Latin neighbors and we of course were the "civilized nation" with the duty to set things right.

After twenty years of world power, the United States must decide which of the two sides of its national character is to predominate—the humanism of Lincoln or the aggressive moralism of Theodore Roosevelt. One or the other will help shape the spirit of the age—unless of course we refuse to choose, in which case America may come to play a less important role in the world, leaving the great decisions to others.

The tendency of recent months has been toward a more strident and aggressive American foreign policy, which is to say, toward a policy closer to the spirit of Theodore Roosevelt than of Lincoln. We are still trying to build bridges to the Communist countries and we are still—in a small way—helping the poorer nations to make a better life for their people; but we are also involved in a growing war against Asian communism, a war which began and might have ended as a civil war if American intervention had not turned it into a contest of ideologies, and in Latin America we remain trapped by the consequences of an ideologically motivated and politically unsuccessful intervention in the Dominican Republic.

Our national vocabulary has changed with our policies. A few years ago—even some months ago—we were talking of détente and building bridges, of five-year plans in India and Pakistan, of agricultural cooperatives in the Dominican Republic and land and tax reform all over Latin America. Today these subjects have an antique ring. Instead of emphasizing plans for social change, the policy planners and political scientists are conjuring up "scenarios" of escalation and nuclear confrontation and "models" of insurgency and counterinsurgency; in Latin America they seem more interested in testing the "images" of armies than in the progress of social reform.

Commenting last October on the reaction to those who have opposed the war in Vietnam, a European observer wrote:

The airy contempt with which many of the unofficial defenders of official policy nowadays treat such "sentimental" considerations as international law, neutral opinion, or even the wishes of the unfortunate people of Vietnam, is indeed something new in responsible American circles; to one European who has just spent a year in the United States, it sounded ominously similar to the notorious *Realpolitik* of Imperial Germany, while the protesters seemed to embody the American democratic tradition.

The change in words and values is no less important than the change in policy, because words *are* deeds and style *is* substance insofar as they influence men's minds and behavior. What seems to be happening, as Archibald MacLeish recently put it, is that "the feel of America in the world's mind" has begun to change and faith in "the idea of America" has been shaken, for our own people as well as for the world. MacLeish is suggesting—and I think he is right—that much of the idealism and inspiration is disappearing from American policy, but he also points out that they are not yet gone and by no means are they irretrievable. ". . . If you look closely," he said, "and listen well, there is a human warmth, a human meaning which nothing has killed in almost twenty years and which nothing is likely to kill. . . . What has always held this country together is an idea—a dream if you will—a large and abstract thought of the sort the realistic and the sophisticated may reject but mankind can hold to."

The foremost need of American foreign policy is a renewal of dedication to an "idea that mankind can hold to"—not a missionary idea full of pomposities about saving the sinful and civilizing the heathen but a Lincolnian idea expressing what Aldous Huxley has called "the simple human preference for life and peace."

A year ago, in domestic affairs, we vigorously reasserted our "preference for life and peace;" it seemed that the United States might be about to undergo something of a social revolution. With a degree of partisan harmony that would have seemed inconceivable a few years ago the Congress in 1965 adopted sweeping legislation to expand education, to provide health care to the aged, to combat urban and rural poverty on a large scale, to renew our cities and purify our streams, and to meet many other long-neglected problems. These accomplishments reflect brilliant legislative leadership, for which President Johnson is justly famed, and they also are an expression of the humane and idealistic side of the American character.

Vigorously executed and adequately funded, the legislation adopted in 1965 can open the way to an era of abundance and opportunity for all Americans, but, for the present at least, the inspiration and commitment of a year ago have disappeared. They have disappeared in the face of deepening involvement in an Asian war, and although it may be contended that the United States has the material resources to rebuild its society at home while waging war abroad, it is already being demonstrated that we do not have the mental and spiritual resources for such a double effort. In concrete terms, the President simply cannot think about implementing the Great Society at home while he is supervising bombing missions over North Vietnam; nor is the Congress much inclined to debate—much less finance—expanded education programs when it is involved in debating—and paying for—an expanding war; nor can the American people be expected to think very hard or do very much about improving their schools and communities when they are worried about casualty lists and the danger of a wider war. My own view is that there is a kind of madness in the facile assumption that we can raise the many billions of dollars necessary to rebuild our schools and cities and public transport and eliminate the pollution of air and water while also spending tens of billions to finance an "open-ended" war in Asia, but even if the material resources can somehow be drawn from an expanding economy I do not think that the spiritual resources will long be forthcoming from an angry and disappointed people.

Wars breed war fever; when a nation is involved in a bitter foreign conflict, hopes give way to fears and creative and generous attitudes give way to a false and strident patriotism. That, I believe, is what is happening in America today, and there can be no cure for it except an end to the war in Asia. As long as the war continues, whatever our material resources, the harsh and egotistical America will prevail over the generous and humane America. It will prevail not only in Vietnam but, to one degree or another, depending upon the length and size of the war, in relations with the Communist world, with the neutrals, with our allies and in relations with each other here at home.

How have we come to this state of things? How has it come about that the greatest and richest of nations, a nation with a tradition of decency and humanity in its conduct both at home and abroad, a nation with the will and resources to contribute powerfully to peace and development in the world, is now caught up in a spiral of violence in a poor and backward Asian country, with results that are damaging our foreign relations all over the world and poisoning our political life at home? Is it entirely, as the Secretary of State seems to believe, because of the evil and malice of the "other side"? Or is there something wrong on our side as well, some failure of judgment, some weakness of character, some blind spot in our view of the world?

Before suggesting an affirmative answer to the last question, I emphasize that I do not think our country is the author of the world's misfortunes, or any significant part of them, but only that we are no more immune than the rest of humanity from failures of insight and judgment. It is never pleasant to criticize one's own country but, seen in perspective, criticism is an expression of confidence; it bespeaks a faith in the capacity of our country to realize its own best possibilities.

A society can never be any better than its citizens require it to be. In one of his *Letters to a German Friend,* Albert Camus wrote in 1943: "This is what separated us from you; we made demands. You were satisfied to serve the power of your nation and we dreamed of giving ours her truth. . . ."

In this spirit, I say that I do think there is something wrong with our foreign policy; I do think there is a discrepancy between two Americas, one magnanimous and humane, the other arrogant and self-righteous, a discrepancy, which has nothing to do with the faults and failures of the "other side."

The resulting ambivalence of our policy, as currently manifested in Vietnam and Santo Domingo, arises specifically from the fact that in the years since World War II the United States has been simultaneously committed to policies of opposing communism and supporting nationalism. Insofar as the two have been separate, United States policy has been largely successful. In such instances as the Soviet threat to Western Europe in the late forties and the Cuban missile crisis of 1962 the danger was clearly one of Soviet power and the United States had little difficulty in deciding on effective counteraction. In the case of the colonial revolution in most of Asia and Africa the United States took a strong lead in supporting national independence movements. Only in such instances as the Cuban and Dominican revolutions and the war in Vietnam, in each of which communism and nationalism became closely associated with each other, has the United States encountered cruel dilemmas in the shaping of policy and signal failures in its execution.

For complex reasons, deriving in large part from our early postwar experience with Soviet Communist imperialism, we have tended to give our opposition to communism priority over our support for nationalism. The result has been that, with certain exceptions, we have strongly, and for the most part unsuccessfully, opposed those genuinely nationalist movements which have been controlled or influenced by Communists. The most notable—and rewarding—exception has been Yugoslavia, whose national independence we have supported since 1948 with the result that it has posed a powerful barrier to Soviet aspirations in Southeastern Europe—a more powerful barrier, it should be noted, than many non-Communist governments have been able to erect.

Whatever wisdom or lack of it our emphasis on communism has had in the past, the realities of the present require a reversal of priorities as between opposing communism and supporting nationalism. The basis of my criticisms of American policy in both Southeast Asia and Latin America is a belief that American interests are better served by supporting nationalism than by opposing communism, and that when the two are encountered in the same country it is in our interest to accept a Communist government rather than to undertake the cruel and all but impossible task of suppressing a genuinely national movement.

Far from being unified in a design for world conquest, the Communist countries are deeply divided among themselves with widely varying foreign policies and widely varying concepts of their own national interests. Unless, therefore, we accept the view that Communist ideology in itself constitutes a threat to the free nations, we are bound to regard Communist countries as menacing or not depending on whether their foreign policies are aggressive or benign. If we accept the premise that it is aggression rather than communism which endangers us, then it follows that the existence of a strong Communist state which poses a barrier to expansion by an aggressive Communist power may be more desirable from the viewpoint of American interests than a weak non-Communist state whose very weakness forms a vacuum which invites conquest or subversion.

Such a nonideological approach may commend itself to the practical and humane strand in our national character but it is anathema to that other, puritanical strand, which predisposes us to ideological conflict and, indeed, suggests, that there is something immoral about any other kind of conflict. The ambivalence in our foreign relations seems to arise, therefore, from the discrepancy between the two Americas, the one making us the friend of social revolution all over the world, the other making us an enemy to communism in all its forms, and the two together making for a troublesome inconstancy and self-defeating policies.

It is with this dilemma in mind, and with a view to encouraging a renewal of the spirit of humanitarian idealism in American policy, that I turn now to comment on some of the issues that agitate the American people and their leaders.

The tragedy of Vietnam is that a revolution against social injustice and foreign rule has become a contest between Asian communism and the United States. In the years after World War II an unenlightened colonialism bred a militant form of communism in Indo-China. A nationalist movement that might have developed peacefully and democratically as in India and the Philippines was driven to Communist control by France's insistence on reasserting her prewar colonial authority. The West represented by France thus came to be regarded as the enemy of Vietnamese nationalism and communism was able to play the role of its friend.

The United States has found itself in the difficult and undesirable position of sustaining a series of governments in Saigon which have signally failed to reflect or advance Vietnamese nationalist aspirations. The United States, it must be remembered, did not create this situation but inherited it. In the case of the Philippines, by contrast, for which we had initial responsibility, the commitment to national independence was made even before the Second World War. Our difficulties in Vietnam are the direct result of the ambivalence in our policy in a situation not of our own making involving both communism and nationalism. The United States has opposed more nationalist movements than it should have but this has happened not because of a conscious decision to support counterrevolutionary forces in the world, nor for lack of sympathy with the national aspirations of emerging peoples, but primarily because of errors in judgment in the face of genuine and apparent threats of expansion by Communist powers.

The fact that the United States did not cause or precipitate the Vietnamese tragedy does not make it less of a tragedy. However worthy the motives for our involvement, however contrary it is to our wishes—and our interests—we are committed once again to the support of an unstable and unrepresentative regime. One very striking indication of the weakness of that regime is the low morale of the South Vietnamese army, from whose ranks no fewer than ninety-six thousand soldiers are reported to have deserted in 1965. The tragedy of Vietnam is summarized in one extraordinary sentence written from Saigon by James Reston on August 31, 1965: "Even Premier Ky," wrote Reston, "told this reporter today that the Communists were closer to the people's yearnings for social justice and an independent national life than his own government."

So-called "wars of national liberation" are political wars, whose outcomes depend on a combination of political and military factors. The Communist guerillas in Malaya could not have been beaten without hard fighting, but neither, in all probability, could they have been beaten if Malaya had not been given its independence. The Hukbalahaps were defeated in the Philippines primarily because of the political isolation imposed on them by the reforms of President Magsaysay. The major reason for the success of the Vietcong in South Vietnam has not been aid from the North but the absence of a cohesive alternative nationalist movement in the South. Both the success of the Communists in South Vietnam and their failure in India, Burma, Malaya, Indonesia and the Philippines strongly suggest that "wars of national liberation" depend for their success more on the weakness of the regime under attack than on the strength of support from outside.

Nationalism, rather than Western democracy or Soviet or Chinese communism, is the dominant force in Southeast Asia, as it is in much of the rest of the world. Because of the heritage of colonialism, national self-assertion often and naturally takes the form of hostility to the West. It would seem to follow that friendship with the West will be possible for many colonial peoples only when the West no longer plays a dominant role in their national lives. It would also seem to follow that as long as American military forces are fighting Asians on the Asian mainland—*regardless of their motives and purposes and regardless of the character of the enemy*—Asian nationalism is likely to retain its anti-Western character and communism will continue to be able to offer itself as the true friend of national aspirations. The American military presence in Southeast Asia thus has a kind of "counter-domino" effect, strengthening the very forces it is meant to contain.

I have suggested a number of times what seems to me a promising approach toward peace in Vietnam and I will not elaborate again on these suggestions here. Very briefly, I believe that the United States should recognize the Vietcong as a belligerent with whom it is prepared to negotiate peace along with the government of North Vietnam and that we should use our considerable influence to persuade the South Vietnamese government to do the same. I have also recommended that we state forthrightly and explicitly in advance of negotiations, that we are prepared to conclude a peace agreement providing for an internationally supervised election to determine the future of South Vietnam and, further, that we are prepared to accept the outcome of such an election, *whatever that outcome might be.* Beyond that I have proposed that we use all available channels to persuade the North Vietnamese and the Vietcong that, whatever the future political complexion of Vietnam, Communist or non-Communist, united or divided, it can enjoy a secure and independent national existence and normal relations with the United States as long as it respects the independence of its neighbors and as long as it upholds its own independence of China.

It is contended that if the United States makes major concessions in Vietnam the credibility of our other guarantees and commitments will be undermined and countries which depend on American support, from Thailand to Germany, will lose faith in the United States. As H. L. Mencken once said, there is something in this but not much. In fact, many of America's allies are more inclined to worry about an undue American preoccupation with Vietnam than to fear the consequences of an American withdrawal, provided that withdrawal is orderly and based on a negotiated agreement. One hears German commentators, for example, expressing the fear that in its preoccupation with Asia the United States may be losing interest in Germany and Berlin. In his press conference of last February 21, General de Gaulle cited as one reason for his decision to withdraw French forces from NATO in 1969 the danger that the United States might drag its European partners into non-European wars. As to the small Asian nations bordering on Vietnam, it is possible that the violence and inconclusiveness of the war have raised doubts in their minds as to whether it is not more painful to be saved than to be abandoned by the United States.

Our major allies are not supporting us in Vietnam. There are three possible explanations for their refusal to participate in the war, each of which, if valid, suggests that there is something wrong with American policy: First, they may believe that it simply does not matter, from the viewpoint of their own security, who wins the Vietnamese war. Or, secondly, they may believe that their security is affected but there is no point in becoming involved because the United States, under what has been called the "Rusk doctrine," is unilaterally committed to resist any and all threats to the free world and will take all the risks and accept all the costs regardless of what anyone else does. And finally, our allies may have judged that it is neither necessary nor possible to engage China successfully on the Asian mainland and that their security, and ours, can be defended from the islands and waters off the coast of Asia where our sea and air power are dominant.

If there is merit in any of these arguments, there is something wrong with American policy. My own view is that there is some truth in all of them but it is the last which suggests the basis of a constructive new policy in Asia. The issue on which everything else depends is the shaping of a new relationship between the United States and China in the rimlands of Asia.

History and logic and common sense suggest that a viable settlement in Vietnam must be part of a general settlement in Southeast Asia. The central issue is the contest between Chinese and American power and the prospect for a lasting peace depends far more upon the resolution of that issue than it does on the matter of who is to participate in a South Vietnamese government and by what means it shall be formed. If the issue between Chinese and American power in Southeast Asia can be resolved, the future of Vietnam should not be too difficult to arrange; but if the issue of Chinese and American power is left unresolved, even a total victory in South Vietnam is unlikely to solve very much. As long as China and America are competitors for predominance in Southeast Asia, there can be no lasting peace or stability in that part of the world.

It seems to me possible that the crisis in Southeast Asia can be resolved on a lasting basis by the withdrawal of American military power to the islands and waters around the coast of Asia coupled with a political arrangement for the neutralization of the small countries of the Southeast Asian mainland, notably the Indochinese states, Thailand, Malaysia and Burma. China is profoundly fearful of American bases on her periphery, as she demonstrated by intervening in the Korean War in 1950 only when American troops approached her Manchurian frontier. Fearful as she is of American military power in Southeast Asia, China might well be willing to purchase its removal by a commitment on her own part to abstain from military intervention. It would seem to me highly advisable that, by one means or another, we indicate to the Chinese that we are prepared to remove American military power not only from Vietnam but from all of Southeast

Asia in return for a commitment on the part of China to abstain from military intervention and respect the political independence of the Southeast Asian states. Such a neutralization agreement could and should be placed under the guarantee of the major powers with interests in Southeast Asia, notably the United States, China, the Soviet Union, Great Britain, France, India and Japan.

There is even some reason to believe—and I say this in full awareness that it contradicts the strongly held view of most Americans—that China may not wish to subject the small countries around her borders to her military and political domination. China undoubtedly wants "friendly" countries around her periphery in the same way that Russia insists on friendly governments in Eastern Europe and the United States wants friendly governments in Latin America. This requirement, which is characteristic of great powers, can be applied with varying degrees of stringency: it can mean total subordination as Stalin required of the Eastern European states; it can mean a high degree of domestic autonomy and a small degree of independence in foreign policy, such as the Eastern European countries have enjoyed under Khrushchev and Kosygin; or, as in the case of the United States and Latin America—except of course for Cuba—it can mean full independence as long as a country does not align with the enemies of the United States or adopt a Communist government.

The ferocity of Peking's language has obscured the fact that in practice China has tolerated a high degree of independence on the part of her neighbors. Burma, for example, despite the fact that it is weak and nonaligned, remains independent and, so far as one can tell, untroubled by her Chinese neighbor. North Vietnam, despite its dependency on China for economic and logistical support for the prosecution of the war, remains substantially in command of its own affairs; and it seems logical to suppose that if there were no war, if there were normal relations with the United States, North Vietnam would be even more independent of China. One does not know, of course, but the thought that the Chinese, despite their colorful language, may actually not wish to subjugate their neighbors is less "unthinkable" on examination than it might at first glance appear.

The most interesting example is North Korea. During and after the Korean War North Korea was occupied by hundreds of thousands of Chinese troops. Then in 1958, despite the fact that there was no outside pressure to compel them to do so, the Chinese withdrew from North Korea. In the wake of that withdrawal the North Koreans purged many pro-Chinese officials from their own government and acquired substantial freedom of action in their relations with both China and the Soviet Union.

A highly respected expert on Far Eastern affairs told me in a conversation some weeks ago that it is possible that the North Vietnamese, noting the North Korean experience and recalling their own dependence on China in the war against the French, may be less fearful of Chinese military intervention than is generally supposed by United States policy makers. This same expert suggested that the differences between the North Vietnamese and the Chinese regarding the war may be no deeper than, say, the squabbles between Generals Montgomery and Eisenhower during World War II and that the attitude of the North Vietnamese toward Chinese military intervention might even be comparable to the British attitude toward the American forces in England during the Second World War: they didn't much like having them there but neither were they afraid that the Americans would not go home when the war was over.

If this is the case, if, as the expert to whom I refer contends, it is superficial to stress too much the North Vietnamese fear of Chinese intervention, then our policy makers may be underestimating the danger of Chinese participation in the Vietnamese war. If, as seems possible, the North Vietnamese are not fearful of permanent Chinese domination, then it would be dangerous indeed for American policy makers to suppose that North Vietnam would sue for peace in the face of escalating force rather than call for Chinese assistance.

American policy makers seem convinced that China is determined to subjugate her neighbors, but they also contend that there is little likelihood of Chinese intervention in the Vietnamese war. I have already suggested some reasons for questioning China's aggressive intentions. I am at the same time less sanguine than some Administration officials about Chinese abstention from the war.

The danger of war between the United States and China cannot be discounted, for one reason, because China is ruled by men who are intensely hostile to the United States, men whose long isolation and narrowly ideological outlook have left them dangerously ignorant of the outside world, particularly of the United States. The extent of their misinformation about America was apparent in an article published on March 3 in the Chinese Communist party newspaper (*Jenmin Jih Pao*), which described both "hawks" and "doves" in the United States as a "bunch of fools" and asserted that "there is no fundamental difference of opinion between them with regard to aggression against Vietnam." (I can only say that this is interesting news to all us "hawks" and "doves"; maybe the "consensus" is more solid than we thought.)

We do well, in the face of such patently misinformed assertions on the part of the Chinese Communists, not to become angry and denounce them as hopeless fanatics but to remember the wise words of United Nations Secretary General U Thant, that in a "difficult stage of development" such as China is going through "countries will show certain emotions, certain strong reactions, certain rigidities, and even certain arrogance." "Countries, like individuals," said the Secretary General, "have nervous breakdowns," and it is the duty of the community to try to understand and find some solution.

Another reason why the danger of war between China and the United States cannot be discounted is the continuing danger of miscalculations on our part resulting from our own lack of knowledge of the mind and character of modern China. To most of us China is a strange, distant and dangerous nation, not a society of 700 million individual human beings but a menacing abstraction.

I believe that the most immediate need in our policy toward China—and possibly the only useful thing that can be accomplished for some time to come—is a concerted effort to dispel myths with realities, to get to know something about Chinese behavior and attitudes, about the Chinese past and its effects on the present, about why the Chinese are so hostile and inflexible and what if anything can be done about it. It was in the hope of helping to increase congressional and public knowledge of China that the Senate Committee on Foreign Relations undertook the public hearings which are now in progress. I myself have found these hearings highly instructive and I hope that they are having some effect around the country—including the District of Columbia.

There are two ways of looking at China, one of which commends itself to the puritanical strand in the American character, the other of which commends itself to the pragmatic and humane strand in our national character. One can harbor a nightmare view of China as an insane and predatory creature, as the fulcrum of "Asian hordes" which at any time may spill over the world like lava from a volcano. Or, on the other hand, we can treat China according to the standard suggested by U Thant, which is to say, as a respected member of the world community now going through a period of dangerous chauvinism and warranting our best efforts to rehabilitate her to the world community.

At present our Government seems wedded to the nightmare view of China. On February 23, 1966, Secretary of Defense McNamara declared before a joint session of the Senate Armed Services Committee and the Senate Subcommittee on Defense Appropriations that "the long range objective of the Chinese Communists is to become dominant in the Asian, African and Latin American countries, and to frustrate the process of peaceful development and free choice in the developing nations."

The basis currently cited in support of the nightmare view of China's intentions is the doctrine enunciated in September 1965 by the Chinese Minister of Defense Lin Piao. The Lin Piao doctrine divides the world into two parts, the "cities," so-called, consisting of the United States, Western Europe and the Soviet Union, and the "rural areas," of Asia, Africa and Latin America, which will gradually surround and conquer the cities in the same way that the Chinese Communists started from the countryside and gradually took over all of continental China.

All this, in Churchill's eloquent phrase, is "jaw jaw jaw." It is a terrifying doctrine no doubt, but it is only a doctrine not an existing fact. The Chinese have a ferocious vocabulary but surely some distinction must be made between what they say and what they do, and between what they might like to do and what they are able or likely to be able to do. As I have already pointed out, this is no clear evidence that China wishes to conquer and subjugate her neighbors. In Vietnam itself, one must remember, the United States has over 200,000 troops and the Chinese have only work teams supporting the North Vietnamese.

China's ability to implement the Lin Piao doctrine is even less clear than her desire to conquer Southeast Asia. In fact China is doing very badly in foreign policy: within the last six months, for example, Chinese influence has been destroyed in Indonesia, Ghana and Cuba. As we look ahead, it is difficult indeed to see how a country still in an early stage of industrialization and burdened by the enormous task of feeding its population of 700 million is going to be able at any time in the foreseeable future to overturn the governments of Asia, Africa and Latin America, much less those of Europe and America.

Chinese doctrine is bloodthirsty indeed but Chinese policy is cautious and, at the moment, strikingly unsuccessful. The question for the United States is whether it is to base its policy on Chinese words or on Chinese deeds. It is a fateful choice, going to the very heart of the ambivalence of the two Americas.

If we are to base our policy on Lin Piao's doctrine rather than on what China is actually doing or able to do, then I suppose it would be logical for us to take the first good excuse that comes along to strike a devastating military blow against China while she is still relatively weak, especially against her incipient nuclear capacity. The trouble with this option is that it would disable China temporarily but not permanently while converting her present enmity into an enduring fury. It would also outrage the conscience of peoples all over the world, including, I would expect, the American people. Some might call such a course "realism." I myself think that it is unrealistic, because one simply cannot engage in barbarous action without becoming a barbarian, because one cannot defend human values by calculated and unprovoked violence without doing mortal damage to the values one is trying to defend.

The other possibility in our relations with China is to continue doing what we must to contain her power while doing what we can to encourage more responsible Chinese behavior. The second option, in short, is to take a chance that China will change and that a new generation of leaders will not try to do what the aging men who now rule in Peking insist they will do, that is, engage in relentless conflict with the non-Communist nations until they have been destroyed. One hopes that the Chinese people, with their high civilization and great traditions, increasingly will bring a peaceful and constructive influence to bear on their rulers.

Do we dare take the second choice and gamble that China will change as Russia has changed, toward a better understanding of the world and more moderate policies? I think that we can and we must take that chance, first, because we cannot take the first option of preemptive war without destroying the democratic values we wish to preserve, and second, because it is completely reasonable to anticipate change in China—and in every other society for that matter—because change is the law of life, if indeed there is a law of life.

It is sometimes said that communism is unaltered and unalterable in its goals and strategy. The more I think about this hypothesis, the less I am able to accept it. Since communism as an ideology exists only in the minds of living Communists, and since Communists, however, reluctant we may be to admit it, are human beings, contentions as to the unalterability of communism rest on the premise that a whole branch of humanity is immune from one of the basic facts of human nature, the fact of change and changeability.

Far from being unchangeable, communism has never ceased to change since the Bolsheviks seized power in Petrograd almost fifty years ago. The first generation of Soviet leaders has now mostly passed from the scene and been succeeded by more practical men whose actions seem to have much more to do with Soviet national interests than with ideological zealotry. It is not a certainty, to be sure, but there seems at least a reasonable possibility that when Mao Tse-tung and the first generation of Chinese Communist revolutionaries pass from the scene they will be succeeded, if not immediately then eventually, by less fanatical and more flexible men. China indeed has changed tremendously in the last twenty years and it seems reasonable to suppose that it will continue to change, hopefully in the direction of moderation already taken by the Russians.

It is, of course, a gamble to allow China to continue building its strength, including a nuclear arsenal, in the hope that by the time Chinese power is truly menacing it will be wielded by less dangerous men than those who now rule Peking. But when one considers that the alternative is a preemptive war—a war which would inflict temporary physical damage on China but irreparable moral damage on the aggressor—it seems clear that we have no real choice except to take a chance that China, like Russia, will evolve toward moderation.

Communist China, sooner or later, is likely to become a member of the United Nations. Some will regard this as a calamity; others will proclaim the dawn of a peaceful world community. I do not think Chinese Communist membership in the United Nations will mean either of these things. It seems more probable that it will have little if any immediate effect on Chinese foreign policy or on China's relations with the West. It may, however, help to draw China out of her political and ideological parochialism and start her down the long road toward a realistic assessment of the world and of her own role in world affairs. The journey is likely to be slow and arduous but it represents the only real hope for drawing China into a peaceful community of nations.

There is not a great deal Western nations can do to hasten China's evolution. France is engaged in a long term, and I think constructive, effort to open lines of communication with Peking, albeit at the cost of what seems at times unnecessary rudeness to the United States. About all that we can do for the time being is to learn what we can about China and try to understand her behavior, avoid recrimination and invective—even in the face of high verbal provocation—and continue in a quiet and patient manner to express sympathy for the Chinese people and our desire for friendly relations.

I hope that the generous and humane side of the American character will govern our relations with China in the years ahead. I hope that in its attitude toward China America will act with the magnanimity that befits a great nation by following the advice of Pope Paul, who said in his speech to the United Nations General Assembly:

> Your vocation is to make brothers not only of some, but of all peoples, a difficult undertaking indeed; but this it is, your most noble undertaking. . . . We will go further and say: strive to bring back among you any who have separated themselves, and study the right method of uniting to your pact of brotherhood, in honor and loyalty, those who do not yet share in it.

Nowhere has the ambivalence of the two Americas been more apparent and more troublesome than in the relations of the United States with Latin America. In Latin America as in Asia, the United States, a profoundly unrevolutionary nation, is required to make choices between accepting revolution and trying to suppress it.

Thus far we have been unwilling, or unable, to choose. On the one hand, we have made ourselves the friend of certain progressive democratic governments and have joined with Latin America in the Alliance for Progress, the purpose of which is social revolution by peaceful means. On the other hand, we have allowed our fear of communism to drive us into supporting a number of governments whose policies are incompatible with the aims of the Alliance, and on three occasions—Guatemala in 1954, Cuba in 1961, and the Dominican Republic in 1965—we resorted to force, illegally, unwisely and—inasmuch as each of these interventions almost certainly strengthened the appeal of communism in Latin America—unsuccessfully as well.

The United States thus pursues two largely incompatible policies in Latin America—discriminating support for social reform and an undiscriminating anticommunism that often makes us the friend of corrupt and reactionary oligarchies. These incompatible policies are an expression of the two Americas—the one humane and tolerant, the other strident and puritanical, the one disposed to help its neighbors to be happy, the other disposed to force them to be virtuous.

Over the years since President Monroe proclaimed his doctrine, Latin Americans have had their fill of the second disposition in the North American character. They have had the advantages of United States tutelage in fiscal responsibility, in collective security, and in the techniques of democracy. If they have fallen short in any of these fields, the thought presents itself that the fault may lie with the teacher as well as with the pupils.

When President Theodore Roosevelt announced his "corollary" to the Monroe Doctrine in 1905, he solemnly declared that he regarded the future interventions thus sanctified as a "burden" and a "responsibility" and an obligation to "international equity." Not once, so far as I know, has the United States regarded itself as intervening in a Latin American country for selfish or unworthy motives. Whatever reassurance the purity of our motives may give must be shaken a little by the thought that probably no country in all human history has ever intervened in another except for what it regarded as excellent motives. "The wicked are wicked, no doubt," wrote Thackeray, "and they go astray and they fall, and they come by their deserts; but who can tell the mischief which the very virtuous do?"

For all our noble intentions, the countries which have had most of the tutelage in democracy by United States Marines are not particularly democratic. These include Haiti, which is under a brutal and superstitious dictatorship; the Dominican Republic, which is in turmoil; and Cuba, which, as no one needs to be reminded, has replaced its traditional right wing dictatorships with a Communist dictatorship.

Maybe, in the light of this extraordinary record of accomplishment, it is time for us to reconsider our teaching methods. Maybe we are not really cut out for the job of spreading the gospel of democracy. Maybe it would profit us to concentrate on our own democracy instead of trying to inflict our particular version of it on all those ungrateful Latin Americans who stubbornly oppose their North American benefactors instead of the "real" enemies whom we have so graciously chosen for them. And maybe—just maybe—if we left our neighbors to make their own judgments and their own mistakes and confined our assistance to matters of economics and technology instead of philosophy, maybe then they would begin to find the democracy and the dignity that have largely eluded them and we in turn might begin to find the love and gratitude that we seem to crave.

The Latin American policies of the United States have been distorted by a tendency to identify reform with revolution and revolution with communism. It is assumed, because they have something to do with each other, as indeed they do, that they are one and the same thing, which indeed they are not. The pervading suspicion of social revolutionary movements on the part of United States policy makers is most unfortunate because there is the strong possibility of more explosions in Latin America and, insofar as the United States makes itself the enemy of revolutionary movements, communism is enabled to make itself their friend. The antirevolutionary bias in United States policy, which is rooted in the fear of communism, can only have the effect of strengthening communism.

The Alliance for Progress encouraged the hope in Latin America that the United States would not only tolerate but actively support domestic social revolution. The Dominican intervention has at least temporarily destroyed that hope and it is reported by some observers that for the first time progressive Catholic leaders in Latin America are talking seriously about joining forces with the Communists as the only feasible way of bringing about social revolution and, indeed, as the only possible way of keeping the Communists from dominating social revolutions.

It is not too late for the United States to play an important and effective role in helping Latin Americans to achieve their aspirations to democracy and social justice. These aims after all are the same as those which we seek for ourselves in our own society. Although we are an unrevolutionary society, we have traditionally been sympathetic to the aspirations of people all over the world to democracy and social justice. Despite the strand of harsh puritanism in our national character, I continue to believe that there is a stronger strand of democratic humanism, an elemental decency which has motivated us, despite grievous lapses, to seek social justice in our own society and to encourage it in others, not only because this was the prudent and politic thing to do but also, and perhaps primarily, because it was the decent thing to do.

It is thus in keeping with that which is best in our own character, and it is unquestionably in our interests, that we make ourselves the friend of social revolution in Latin America. It will require a renewed commitment and increased contributions to the Alliance for Progress—contributions which I regret to say do not seem likely to be forthcoming from the Congress in the immediate future. It will also require a drawing away from military and economic oligarchies, whatever the short-term advantages of supporting them. It may require the acceptance of gradual expropriation of United States-owned enterprises. It will certainly require the acceptance of great and rapid change, not all of it necessarily by peaceful means.

It will also require acceptance of the fact that Latin America is coming into its own in the world and can no longer be regarded as the special ward of the United States. We must be prepared to see the Latin American countries, whose channels to the outside world have traditionally run through Washington, enter into new relationships with Europe and with Asia and Africa, some of which may not be much to our liking. We must recognize that paternalism is no longer a workable basis for our relations with Latin America, that, as President Frei of Chile said in France last summer, the people of Latin America "desire true political and economic independence; they want a system without hegemony."

This review of our country's involvements in Asia and Latin America suggests that our people and our policy are troubled by three major questions: First, are we to be the friend or the enemy of the social revolutions of Asia and Latin America? Second, are we to regard the Communist countries as more or less normal states with whom we can have more or less normal relations, or are we to regard them indiscriminately as purveyors of an evil ideology with whom we can never reconcile? Finally, are we to regard ourselves as a friend and counselor and possibly as an example for those around the world who seek freedom and who also want our help, or are we to play the role of God's avenging angel, the appointed missionary of freedom in a wicked and benighted world?

The answer to each of these three questions depends on which of the two Americas is speaking. There is no inevitable or predetermined answer because our past has prepared us to be either tolerant or puritanical, generous or selfish, sensible or romantic, humanly concerned or morally obsessed, in our relations with the outside world.

For my own part, I prefer the America of Lincoln and Adlai Stevenson. I prefer to have my country the friend rather than the enemy of demands for social justice; I prefer to have the Communists treated as human beings, with all the human capacity for good and bad, for wisdom and folly, rather than as embodiments of an evil abstraction; and I prefer to see my country in the role of sympathetic friend to humanity rather than its stern and prideful schoolmaster.

The "Blessings-of-Civilization Trust," as Mark Twain called it, may have been a "Daisy" in its day, uplifting for the soul and good for business besides, but its day is past. It is past because the great majority of the human race are demanding dignity and independence, not the honor of a supine role in an American empire. It is past because whatever claim America may make for the universal domain of its ideas and values is countered by the Communist counter-claim, armed like our own with nuclear weapons. And, most of all, it is past because it never should have begun, because we are *not*, in the phrase attributed to McGeorge Bundy, the "engine of mankind," but only one of its more successful and fortunate branches, endowed by our Creator with about the same capacity for good and evil, no more or less, than the rest of humanity.

We must choose between the two Americas—the one imperious in its wealth and power, the other a civilized example for the world. We would do well in making our choice to consider the words of Pope Paul before the United Nations General Assembly.

"It is pride," he said, "no matter how legitimate it may seem to be, which provokes tension and struggles for prestige, for predominance, colonialism, egoism. . . ." America and all nations would do well to ponder Pope Paul's message, that "pride disrupts brotherhood."

THE ISSUE OF PEACE; THE VOICE OF RELIGION [3]

JOHN C. BENNETT [4]

One of the durable controversies in the religious world concerns the role of the church in temporal affairs. Should the churchman take a stand and express his view on the social and political issues of the time? Should the clergy's duties extend beyond the sanctuary? Among the many distinguished and widely known clergymen who believe that the church must be an actively creative force in secular society are Bishop James Albert Pike, the Reverend Dr. Eugene Carson Blake, the Reverend Dr. Robert J. McCracken, and the Reverend Dr. John C. Bennett.

During mid-March 1966, the National Inter-Religious Conference on Peace held a three-day meeting in Washington, D.C. Some five hundred delegates from religious bodies throughout the country were in attendance. The keynote address was delivered on March 15 by the Reverend Dr. John C. Bennett, president of Union Theological Seminary in New York City. His speech, reprinted below, illustrated clearly how active churchmen conceive of their obligation to society; how the organized churches and synagogues can and should speak out on international crises, just as they mobilized domestic support in the civil rights cause.

In his orderly analysis, Dr. Bennett recognized that "nations at the present time are the only units of power that can do many things that need to be done." Moreover, he acknowledged the criticism of some who believe that the church and its leaders are outsiders, not competent to speak on matters that the experts and policy makers alone can understand. But he singled out six areas "in which persons who combine religious perspectives and moral sensitivity with a careful attempt to understand the relevant facts, even though they are not specialists or insiders in the Government, have a duty and right to speak."

The issues on which Dr. Bennett focused the sharpest light concerned the view we hold of communism and the attitude the United States continues to take toward China. "China today," said Dr. Bennett, "is relatively weak." But

> If we take advantage of her weakness to keep her down and deny her even her natural role as the greatest power in Asia, a role that we assume for ourselves in this hemisphere, if we isolate her and continue to express our own hostility against her, punctuated by

[3] Text furnished by Dr. John C. Bennett, with permission for this reprint.
[4] For biographical note, see Appendix.

moral lectures about what is the result of a tragic history to which the great powers of the West have contributed so much, we may find ourselves face to face fifteen years from now with a powerful China that has every reason to seek revenge upon us.

Admittedly, the China question has olympian dimensions. And it is complicated by our pledges to defend the integrity of Taiwan. It is reasonable to believe, however, that the candid hearings before the Senate Foreign Relations Committee, the continuing debates in the Senate and elsewhere, the statements outside congressional halls by knowledgeable men such as J. W. Fulbright and Walter Judd, and the testimony of religious leaders such as John C. Bennett will help to clarify the issue and, it is hoped, draw the peoples of the world into a closer harmony.

A statement on religion and peace should begin with some affirmations about the bases that our churches and synagogues have for speaking and acting in the sphere of international relations.

Underlying all else that we may say or do here is the biblical faith that God is Lord of our nation and of all nations. As the prophet said, "All the nations are as nothing before him, they are accounted by him as less than nothing and emptiness" (Isaiah 40:17). As Amos said earlier: "Did I not bring up Israel from the land of Egypt, and the Philistines from Caphtor and the Syrians from Kir?" (Amos 9:7). The faith that all nations are under the judgment and providence and mercy of God is central to biblical religion. Since it is the nation that so easily becomes the ultimate object of loyalty for its citizens, this faith in God transcending the nation is always a warning against national idolatry. And in our time it is political idolatry, the worship of any social group or system, that is the greatest obstacle to the tolerance and humaneness which are essential conditions for decent relations among nations, essential conditions for peace. The form that idolatry takes with people of some sophistication is not so much the explicit worship of the nation as it is the assumption that God is always on the side of one's own nation, an easy assumption when our adversaries are atheists!

A second basis for all that we say or do may be ultimately derived from biblical faith, but even without being aware of its religious background many people are, fortunately, able to see the truth of it and to be claimed by it for their own lives. I refer to the moral imperatives that, when translated into a social ethic that is relevant to public life, call us to care for the welfare and dignity of all neighbors including enemies, to seek for them justice and freedom. When I speak of justice, I mean a transforming justice that continually raises the level of life of those who have been at a disadvantage. Most of our neighbors in the world are victims of poverty and hunger. Only a revolutionary justice can help them. I am not suggesting that there are some religious shortcuts to the proper balance in our world of justice and freedom, both of which depend upon some kind of political order. But our religious imperatives do press upon us to seek these values. Our churches and synagogues should continually disturb us and press us to do what is in our power to deliver God's people everywhere from poverty and hunger, from humiliation and oppression, from anarchy and war.

Our problems begin when at a given time we find the quest of one value such as freedom interfering with another such as order or justice. There will be some differences of opinion about this, but I believe that a conference on peace should begin by recognizing that peace is not the only good, that at times it may have to be sacrificed for the sake of other goods. And yet we may still say that total war would probably destroy all the goods for which we strive and that the burden of proof upon those who defend even limited wars must be a heavy one, for limited wars may escalate into total war and nations, including our own, have a habit of assuming too uncritically the moral and political efficacy of military solutions.

I shall add to these bases for what we may do here one more: a realistic understanding of the temptations to which nations are especially vulnerable. Reinhold Niebuhr has a chapter in his *Moral Man and Immoral Society* on the "morality of nations." This is a classic statement of the situation. Let me mention two of his chief emphases: The first is that "patriotism transmutes individual selfishness into national egoism." This enables good men to become the instruments of the pride and ambition and greed of nations. He also emphasized the tendency of nations, including the United States, to clothe the national will with idealistic pretensions. He says that "perhaps the most significant moral characteristic of a nation is hypocrisy." This is a hard saying, but I recommend this chapter as devotional reading to all the speech writers in Washington.

Professor Herbert Butterfield emphasizes the way in which democracies especially become victims of their own frenzied national self-righteousness. He makes much of the idea that the most furious and cruel conflicts are between what he calls "giant organized systems of self-righteousness" with each system only too delighted to find that the other is wicked, each only too glad that the sins give it the pretext for still deeper hatred and animosity (*Christianity, Diplomacy and War*). This is a fairly accurate description of the relations between the United States and China.

George Kennan reminds us of our own national frenzy in the First World War when our enemy was the Germany of Kaiser Wilhelm II, a moderate compared with subsequent adversaries. Kennan says:

There is, let me assure you, nothing more egocentrical than the embattled democracy. It soon becomes the victim of its own propaganda. It then tends to add to its own cause an absolute value which distorts its own vision of everything else. *Its* enemy becomes the embodiment of all evil, *its* own side, on the other hand, is the center of all virtue (*Russia and the West*).

National self-examination and national repentance are difficult though not impossible. But citizens, each with his own background of faith and commitment, can and do repent on behalf of their nations. A national repentance usually depends upon events, often catastrophic events, which convince men of ordinary prudence that the nation has been following a wrong road. One of the responsibilities of churches and synagogues is to interpret such events.

Let me at once put in a corrective for what I have said: from such a statement about the temptations of nations it would be a great error to deduce that we should therefore say "a plague on all houses" and hold ourselves aloof in personal self-righteousness from all of the strivings of our Government. We may be tempted to become personally self-righteous because of our criticism of national self-righteousness. Nations at the present time are the only units of power that can do many things that need to be done. Nations have responsibilities that are commensurate with their power. National ideals are not necessarily mere rationalizations of crude national interests. Also, what is in the real national interest of the citizens of a nation has its proper claim so long as it is not dressed up with idealism and ideology and made into an absolute.

Whatever the errors and self-deceptions of the United States, our country was not wrong about the threat of Hitlerism to humanity and it was not wrong about the need to develop power in the defense of Western Europe against Stalinism. The United States is right today in trying to keep as much of the world as possible open so that nations may choose their own social systems; but it does exaggerate the role of military force in this effort, it is guided by a persistent notion of American omnipotence, and it does clothe its policies with far too simple ideas of freedom and with too absolutistic an anticommunism.

I come now to a question that is asked on all sides whenever churches and synagogues or their leaders speak about these problems of foreign policy and international relations. Always we hear it said that these high matters belong to the experts or to policy makers on the spot who live with the changing details of the problems and who may have access to classified information. We are often believed to be outsiders who are said to have no competence to speak.

It is very difficult to disentangle the moral factors from the technical and in the broadest sense strategic factors in any complicated situation. I shall speak of six areas in which persons who combine religious perspectives and moral sensitivity with a careful attempt to understand the relevant facts, though not specialists or insiders in the Government, have a duty and right to speak.

First, they have a duty and a right to call attention to the immediate human consequences of any policy. This in itself may not be decisive because there is always the question of the probable human consequences of changing the policy. Yet, this question should not silence the critic. The human consequences of an alternative policy in many cases may be quite speculative and, however one judges that, what our nation may now be doing to people needs to be kept to the fore.

Second, the determination of the goals of policy is a matter of moral choice. Dean Acheson, in his provocative speech at Amherst College in 1964 about morality and foreign policy was right in dismissing many moral slogans as inadequate guides to policy, but when he came to his own statement of the goal of American policy he said that our goal was "to preserve and foster an environment in which free societies may exist and flourish." Is not his own phrase "free societies" another one-sided moral slogan? How is this freedom to be related to a transforming justice and to order and viability in a nation in a period of tumultuous and revolutionary change?

Without taking time for analysis, I shall dogmatically state four goals that should guide our policy. They are all moral goals but they are all consistent with a wise estimate of the conditions for our own national welfare and security in the long run. They are as follows: (1) the prevention of war and especially the prevention of the escalation of any conflict into general nuclear war; (2) the preservation of as wide an area as possible of openness in the world in which nations have freedom to choose their own social systems, in which there is diversity and mutual respect among those who choose diverse paths; (3) the helping of nations that are struggling against hunger and poverty to achieve justice and access to plenty and to do so in their way and not necessarily in our way; (4) support for the United Nations and development of its functions to enable nations to find security and multilateral substitutes for the present arms race, to extend the rule of law among nations and encourage the growth of mutual confidence and human relations between them. At any given moment there may be a fierce debate among moralists concerning the priority that is to be assigned to each of these goals. This is where morality necessarily becomes contextual. But let no context in which we may be called to act obscure any one of them. The assignment of priorities is not a matter for the expert alone. It does not depend on classified information. It should not be the monopoly of the policy maker. It should be a subject of continuous national discussion to which churches and synagogues can make an essential contribution.

The *third* area of moral concern has to do with the means used to achieve any or all of these ends. Here there will be much debate among us between those who represent a religious pacifism and those who believe that we must allow for the use of military force to check force or to overcome oppression. I belong to the latter group but the issues are so difficult that I often wish that I did not. For one thing, I am much impressed today by the probability that even uses of force that have some justification easily escalate and even when this process remains limited, do more harm than good. Can we not agree on two forms of limitation of force? One is that we should not use bombs, nuclear or conventional, against centers of population as was done in the Second World War and as our own Government now threatens as a last resort. I know that we are at a stage in which it is plausible to allow some license to what may be called "deterrent talk" even though it is murderous. I am not clear about this myself except that I believe that this cannot go on for long without being very much a source of moral corruption to a nation that engages in it. The other form of limitation of force is to resolve never to use nuclear weapons first. There are difficult technical problems here mixed with moral problems; for example, problems involving the differences between types of nuclear weapons and their relation to conventional weapons.

While we discuss these matters in general terms, we should give strong support to those in our Government who resolutely refuse to bomb Hanoi or to extend our bombing to China. If it is true that the President feels stronger pressure from those who would expand the war than he does from those who would restrict it or end it now, whatever else we may think about our policy in Vietnam, we should be able to agree on our responsibility to counteract that pressure.

A *fourth* area in which religious groups can make a contribution is in helping the American people to see the world as it appears to other countries and especially as it appears to people in Asia and Africa and Latin America—for they get less of a hearing among us than the European nations. Our churches have close relations with the churches in these other continents. What we hear from our fellow churchmen there reflects much more than an inside church point of view; it reflects widely held views in their nations.

Let me give one illustration of this kind of contribution: The General Board of the National Council of Churches in a message to the American churches last December put great emphasis on the self-defeating character of our action in Vietnam because of its effects on the sensibilities of Asians. Here is one very forthright statement:

> We believe that if the United States follows a unilateral policy in Vietnam, no conceivable victory there can compensate for the distrust and hatred of the United States that is being generated each day throughout the world because we are seen as a predominantly white nation using our overwhelming military strength to kill more and more Asians.

The Central Committee of the World Council of Churches made a similar statement in February:

> The primary objective must be to stop the fighting as the most effective step to starting discussions and negotiations. This is not an easy task and we are not unaware of the deep-rooted obstacles which have thus far prevented progress from the battlefield to the conference table. This is all the more urgent because by continuing the conflict both sides face acute problems. On the one hand the United States of America and its allies face increase of bitter racial and other resentments against the West, and on the other hand the Vietnamese face the vast destruction of their people and resources. The prospect of victory at the end of conflict does not justify this inevitable cost.

I do not suggest that churches have a monopoly of wisdom concerning the more intangible effects of our policies on other peoples, but they do have an inside track to this kind of understanding and it is easy for the policy makers and experts in any one country to be so absorbed with a problem from the dominant point of view in their country that they fail to see how self-defeating their policies may be. Also they often gain a vested interest in policies and so rather than admit an error, they extend the range of their commitment in the hope of proving that they were right. This need not be a conscious process.

The *fifth* area in which those who are not specialists and those who are not policy makers on the spot may make a contribution has to do with the presuppositions of policy, expressed or unexpressed. Is it not probable that on important matters of foreign policy that go beyond limited tactical decisions, our makers and defenders of policy are governed less by facts of which they may have a monopoly, than they are by various assumptions about our period of history? Assumptions on many matters are determinative, e.g., about the dynamics of communism in its various stages, about the role of military power in the containment of communism in a revolutionary situation, about the meaning of social revolution on other continents, about the place of freedom in relation to other values, about the relevance of our experience in dealing with Hitler and Stalin in Europe to the way in which we deal with problems in Asia, about the degree of the risks of nuclear war involved in our policy and about our moral right to take such risks. Military expertise is no guarantee of wisdom about any one of them. And on some of them decisions may be made on the highest level on the basis of an unexamined line of thought that has become dominant.

Churches and synagogues have no monopoly of wisdom about these matters either, but they do have their contribution to make. These issues belong to the sphere of public debate. They need the widest possible ventilation from all sides with many voices heard from other countries. I believe that at the present time, especially in relation to Asia and Latin America, our policy makers are in a rut about many of these issues.

A *final* contribution the churches and synagogues can make to the national discussion of these issues, is to criticize the false uses of religion and morality that are so common. This means criticism of the psychology of the "holy war" that is one factor in the American attitude toward the cold war. This means alertness concerning all forms of national self-righteousness. It also calls for a continuous examination of the use of such words as "honor," "obligation," and "commitment," when our policy in Vietnam is defended by spokesmen in Government. Honor is an especially ambiguous word and it is difficult to distinguish between its use to refer to national face-saving and its use to refer to a genuine moral obligation.

I shall limit myself to a discussion of one of these issues that seems to be most pervasive, and that is the view that we hold of communism. At the present time in many situations one major source of error in the determination of policy is an absolutistic anticommunism. I do not believe that this is always so, for in relation to European communism this outlook has been in large measure abandoned. The breaking of the Communist monolith by the Sino-Soviet split, the gradual humanization of society in the Soviet Union and most of the Eastern Communist countries, the diverse paths taken by these Eastern European nations—these developments fortunately have influenced American policy. We now know intellectually, even if this knowledge is not fully absorbed, that for a nation to become Communist does not mean that it is lost for all time to Stalinist slavery. The American rhetoric of a decade ago that kept contrasting the free world with the slave world has fortunately disappeared in the highest circles of government, though to a considerable extent it continues to influence the public.

No influence has been more helpful in counteracting the American anti-Communist obsession than that of Pope John XXIII and the Vatican Council. Pope John did much to expel the holy war psychology in relation to communism from his Church and from other churches. It is most significant that the Vatican Council refused to take action condemning communism and that it initiated steps leading to dialogue with atheists, including Marxist atheists.

Yet the American obsession with anticommunism keeps appearing, especially when we seem ready to declare that we must oppose all wars of liberation in Asia and Latin America if they are inspired by one of the branches of international communism.

I believe that we should help nations that can be helped to find alternatives to communism because, however much a Communist society may improve after some decades, it does bring terror and tyranny in the early stages to any country that embraces it. I do think that we should put over against this fact the recognition that Communists have no monopoly on terror. The recent slaughter of Communists in Indonesia by the hundreds of thousands should remind us of this. Political cruelty on all sides in tumultuous situations is so common that it should perhaps gain our attention more than it does.

The axiom that communism is the worst fate that can ever come to any country is false. It may not be worse than years and years of civil war; it may not be worse than some rightist tyrannies; it may not be worse than some decades or even generations of neglected social and economic problems. Communism is cruel in its early stages and it has not been successful in dealing with all problems, the problem of agriculture for example. But after the revolutionary period it does become in many ways constructive; it does overcome anarchy, it does deal radically with famine and poverty and disease and illiteracy. If it can be gradually humanized, as it is in European Communist countries, our nation should not take all measures to prevent a nation in Asia from becoming Communist. It may be that people will vote themselves into communism, but how far self-determination in this sense can be a reality in situations of civil war and revolution is debatable. One fine day there might be a free election, but what is to prevent its results from being overturned six months later? The pressure and counter-pressure of political movements in such situations seem to determine the fate of nations whether there are elections or not. We in America do not like to have it so, but there are some things that are beyond our control and when we try to control them we may do far more harm than good, despite fine motives.

I cannot speak of communism without dealing with China. As we face the reality of China as a vast human power—whether it is moved primarily by communism or by nationalism—churches and synagogues have no expert knowledge of what is happening in that country; nor can they read the minds of the Chinese leaders, those who will pass from the scene or those soon to assume power. The doctrines and slogans of the Chinese which seem to scare our Defense Department are paranoiac, even though Chinese behavior has so far been prudent and cautious. Who is to decide how significant the doctrines and the slogans are? James Reston raises the question as to whether this is for the Defense Department to decide. Without attempting to decide we can ask ourselves some questions.

Communism has been the instrument by which China has been unified, by which it has become able to assert itself among the nations, by which it has been able to purge itself of the effects of generations of humiliation at the hands of the white West. Why must we take all that China does now against us with such seriousness and forget for how long she has been the victim of the Western powers of which this nation is now the chief representative? Why must we have a double standard and do near the borders of China what we would never allow China to do near our borders? Why are we still involved in the Chinese civil war as the major ally of Nationalist China? Is there no possibility of our changing our attitudes toward China even though we know that a tragic history and the fanaticism of early communism make it unlikely that China will soon change her attitude toward us? How long are we to be engaged in diplomatic efforts to keep Communist China isolated? Should our policy not be designed with all the imagination we can muster to undercut the paranoia of China, not exacerbate it?

In our religious communities there should be continued efforts to counteract national attitudes in regard to China. The General Board of the National Council of Churches called recently for a reversal of American policies that are designed to isolate China and for preparation for the widest variety of relations between the United States and China.

China today is relatively weak. If we take advantage of her weakness to keep her down, to deny her even her natural role as the greatest power in Asia, a role that we assume for ourselves in this hemisphere, if we isolate her and continue to express our own hostility against her, punctuated by moral lectures, we may find ourselves face to face fifteen years from now with a powerful China that has every reason to seek revenge upon us. I do not say that this prospect should be the main motive for a change of attitude and a change of policy but it does indicate the kind of judgment that will come upon us if we do not do so.

Churches and synagogues should provide an environment in our country within which these questions are continually raised and in which new attitudes can begin to form. I hope and pray that new relationships will become possible between our religious communities and the people of mainland China. We often hear that our Government would like to change its policy in many respects but that it is afraid of the people. If so, let us do what we can to support its desire for change among the people and let us ask the representatives of Government to give some leadership if they do seek such change.

One final word. I have said very little about the United Nations and the institutions of world order, but I believe that churches and synagogues should not only give strong support to the United Nations and to efforts to improve its working but should now put great stress on the need for multilateral judgments upon American actions. The United States gets some support for its Asian policies from European allies and from nations on the eastern fringe of Asia, and doubtless it is always easy to find people around the world who are somewhat ambivalent because they see in the power of the United States the only countervailing power east of Suez. But let us not expect very much of this support and let us not allow it to lead to self-justification. Whatever anyone here may think of American policy to date in Vietnam, there is a terribly dangerous momentum in our power. We may easily become its prisoner. Also, the mounting of national self-justification may gradually cause the self-criticism that now exists to erode. There is danger that more complete moral isolation is not far away. Unless we find ways to submit our policies—policies that affect all mankind—to a far broader judgment than is now the case we may become a nation possessed by a destructive determination to have our own way in Asia. Our religious communities are called to be an inner check on this development. This first interfaith conference dealing with these issues should begin to prepare to meet this call.

SUMMONS TO FRESH INQUIRY

IS GOD REALLY DEAD? [1]

HAROLD A. BOSLEY [2]

With nearly 125 million Americans holding some tie of affiliated membership in religious bodies in the United States, it may seem paradoxical that such a theological furor should have arisen over the inquiry "Is God Dead?" But the controversy is not precisely over atheism versus belief. The principal figures in the movement are Christian thinkers, although some of their critics may prefer to call them Christian atheists. At any rate, the "God Is Dead" dialogue, upsetting as it may be to orthodox conceptions, does not necessarily imply a surrender of faith in Christ. Rather, it asks whether the notion of God has not become outmoded, whether it is relevant to the problems of our time. In neither thought nor experience, say the "radical" theologians, can modern man any longer experience or know God.

Doubt in religious matters is indeed no new phenomenon. And America's great preachers do not react to the present ferment frivolously. They engage the issue directly; in fact, some of them may even rejoice in its presence, feeling, perhaps, that perceptive doubters help rebuke the apathy so commonly associated with the acceptance of conventional beliefs.

Among the distinguished preachers who have entered the debate and have served as thoughtful critics of the "God Is Dead" theologians is Dr. Harold A. Bosley, senior minister of Christ Church, Methodist, in New York City. In a sermon at his church on November 21, 1965, he expressed a measure of sympathy with much that "our current crop of atheists are saying," but he found himself disagreeing "with the mistaken way in which they are trying to say it." He then discussed "certain facts—yes, facts is the word—that have become an essential part of any thoughtful person's understanding of God." Readers of Dr. Bosley's carefully organized and developed sermon, reprinted below, may find profit in examining an article entitled "The Convergence of Science and Religion" by the Nobel prize-winning physicist Dr. Charles H. Townes in the March-April 1966 issue of *Think*. Dr. Townes believes that the eventual confluence of science and religion is inevitable.

---

[1] Text furnished by Dr. Harold A. Bosley, with permission for this reprint.
[2] For biographical note, see Appendix.

Dr. Bosley brings to his preaching duties an extensive experience in speechmaking, including debate activities during his undergraduate years at Nebraska Wesleyan University. In 1963 he received the Distinguished Alumni Award of Pi Kappa Delta, national forensic honorary society.

A recent article in *Time* magazine startled and shocked many with the headline: "The Death of God." The lengthy news item that followed dealt with a number of contemporary theologians who are insisting that, for them, God is meaningless, that God is, in effect, dead.

What a time we have been having over that phrase ever since—"The Death of God"! Beginning with last week's issue [November 13, 1965], the *New Yorker* magazine is running a series of three long, excellent articles on it. A great university in Atlanta is convulsed by a public quarrel over whether to keep or to fire a young professor who says that God is dead. Some incensed alumni of that university have taken a full page in one of the Atlanta papers to proclaim that the university ought to fire him and, until it does, no loyal alumnus should give a dime to the institution!

Like every other preacher, I have been confronted with the article many times of late. While participating in the World Order Study Conference of the National Council of Churches held in St. Louis three weeks ago, I was asked to participate in a radio interview. Thinking the questioner would surely concentrate on the many serious problems before our conference—Vietnam, China, Cuba, the Dominican Republic—I was surprised to have him lead out with "The Death of God." He asked if I had read the *Time* article, and when I confessed that I had, he wanted to know, "But is God really dead?" I was tempted then and, though I did not, I now wish I had asked him what difference it would make to him, personally, that very minute, if I should answer, "Yes, God is dead, really dead." I wonder: What difference would it have made in terms of his life and his work, his problems and hopes, his values and dreams? I wish I had put the question to him, but I think I know why I did not: I had no right to foist my troubles on him. I have problems of my own with questions like that. I ask you as I ask myself, then, What difference would it make to us if we believed, really believed that God is dead?

Any way we look at it, that is a hard ball to handle—it certainly has taken a bad bounce. We had better play it carefully and honestly or we will come up with a glaring error.

I suggest that we ought to look carefully at what is being said when thoughtful men make this claim. We ought to be quite clear on what we mean when we say that we believe in God—if we say it. And, above all else, let us try to be honest as to whether it really makes any difference to us one way or another.

It is just possible that this claim and the questions it raises point up one of the great contradictions in the life of modern man. On the one hand we have the Harris poll of last summer which assures us that 97 per cent of the adult citizens of this country believe in God. On the other hand, we have still another survey of several hundred thousand young adults, 65 per cent of whom said they were neither atheists nor theists—they just did not care one way or another and were not interested enough to try to reach a decision.

I am not sure we can reach a decision here that will convince everyone of its validity, but it is possible to take a steady look at the matter that is now "top news" even though it is deeply rooted in theology. Personally, I think we owe these young theologians a real vote of thanks. Grappling with the challenge they have thrown out may make honest Christians out of us yet! They say that God is dead. And while we may not say it, is it not true that some of us act on this assumption much of the time? We act as though he were dead even though we may not bring ourselves to state it just that way. There are ethical atheists as well as theological ones!

The assertion that God is dead is not new; what is new is that it is being said by some persons in departments of religion and theological seminaries. To say that 99 per cent of their colleagues disagree with them openly if not violently only describes the problem; it does not settle it. Time was when Copernicus, Galileo, Newton, Darwin, and Harvey stood almost alone among their peers in the positions they were taking in the various sciences. What we are witnessing today may well prove to be a repeat performance of the old play that "one man with truth is a majority." We do not settle matters like this by counting noses, by measuring the volume of ayes and nays, much less by organizing ourselves into a mob of vigilantes for lynching offending faculty members who take the position.

The only point of issue is the problem they raise when they say that God is dead. What do they mean by it? Does it make sense in the light of reason and fact? Does it make as much or more sense than any modifying or contradictory claim? Is it possible to appreciate and appropriate the truth in what they are saying without being misled by the falsity that also may be there?

Christian thinkers have had to grapple with atheism in one form or another from the very beginning of the Christian enterprise. Indeed, atheism was old when Christianity came into existence. Several hundred years before Jesus was born, Aristophanes was writing the credo of many Greek intellectuals when he cried: "Zeus is dead; Whirl is King."

Stoicism was the reigning philosophy throughout the entire area in which Paul lived, preached and launched the Christian mission. And Stoicism was basically atheistic, paying little or no attention to God or the gods except as incidental symbols of excellence and ultimacy.

Over the last thirty years we have witnessed the growth of an authentic atheistic philosophy in Europe as well as our own country. A number of our significant artists, Ingmar Bergman for example, have been developing in terms of the contemporary situation the theme Thomas Hardy put in his poem "The Funeral of God," written a hundred years ago.

Yet there is something in the very claim "God is dead" that brings us up sharply. We may feel with a crusty old French philosopher, Comte, when he heard of deism as a religion without God. He exclaimed, "A religion without God? My God! What a religion!" Or we may feel with Gamaliel Bradford, "The whole world crumbles without God!" But that is just the question each of us must ask himself with all seriousness, "Does our world crumble in whole or in part without God?"

I wish it were not so easy to stand up and affirm in unison "I believe in God the Father Almighty, maker of heaven and earth. . . ." The almost casual way in which we do this ought to be jolted seriously by the way in which the editors of *Great Books* begin the article on God, "The arguments for the existence of God constitute one of the greatest attempts of the human mind." As Job discovered in his day, and Paul in his, and we in ours, a clear conception of God, a great faith in God, a vital companionship with God lie on the far side of a hard fight with every stubborn fact, every jeering demon of doubt, and every sirenlike invitation to early and easy repose in something less or other than a sincere, intelligent belief in God.

I repeat, the simple statement "I believe in God" is easily the greatest formulation of the human mind. No man acquainted with the centuries of experience and thought which have gone into its making will treat it lightly. I wish it were possible to sum up quickly the centuries of human experience that have gone into it. But it is not. Yet it lays a heavy requirement upon us if we are to appreciate it. Emerson warned off all who want quick and easy answers with his question, "What is so odious as polite bows to God?" We are not interested in that sort of thing as we grapple with the challenge in the claim that "God is dead." Alfred North Whitehead, the greatest of modern philosophers, writing twenty-five years ago, put it neatly, "The only really important question before us today is this: What do you mean by God?"

When he wrote this and when our young colleagues today are challenging us with their atheism, they are calling attention to the fact that religious ideas and institutions, like machines and industrial plants, grow old and must be remolded or discarded. *Obsolescence,* you call it in business, and obsolescence it is in the field of religion too.

That, as I understand it, is the really creative and critical charge in the claim that "God is dead." Our traditional ideas of God no longer persuade or inspire. The conceptions of God that have been cherished by men for generations no longer fit our understanding or ourselves, or history, or the world in which we live. They are meaningless; they are irrelevant; they belong on the museum shelves of history, not in the marketplace and in the dwellings of men.

I must confess that as I read what our current crop of atheists are saying I find myself in sympathy with much that they are trying to say, yet in complete disagreement with the mistaken way in which they are trying to say it. My mind goes back to seminary days, now over twenty-five years ago. I recall, as though it were this morning, the clarity with which it was hammered home to me that the idea of God with which I had grown up, under the guidance of which I had gone into the Christian ministry, was no longer tenable in the form in which I had known it. The choice before me was clear: either I could admit that, for me, God was dead and give up my calling in the ministry, or I could search for a reformulation of the idea until it made sense in terms of fact. Actually, I could not give it up because there were so many facts and values in life that demanded some kind of ultimate statement, and when I started on that I discovered that I was talking of God in new terms. So, for me the long search through the entire field of man's understanding of God began and has continued to this day. I discovered at the outset that the Christian faith in its best moments has never asked anyone to accept belief in God as an item of blind faith.

There are certain facts—yes, *facts* is the word—that have become an essential part of any thoughtful person's understanding of God. I do not, for a single moment, think it either wise or possible to try to drag an unwilling person into a profession of faith in God by a simple recitation of historic reasons for believing in him, but the cold fact remains that unless we are willing to face up to certain facts and deal with them justly, we cannot believe in God or anything else that lies beyond the end of our nose. We ought always to have before us this understanding: when we ask someone to believe in God, we must be able to tell him what it is we have in mind. Above all, we must make it clear that we are not asking him to embrace as true a fiction or a fantasy or an invention, or a simple projection of human frustration. Rather, we are asking him to accept as true a fact known in part in experience, and available to all who are willing to participate in that sort of experience. The reality of God is not so much proved by argument as it is felt in life. In answer to the query, then, what do you mean by God, the Christian faith has formulated answers that continue to make sense even though our inherited formulations of them must be radically reformulated, even discarded because of obsolescence.

This, then, is the first fact that goes into the great fact of God: *There is a principle of orderliness in the world we know.* Thanks to the investigations of the sciences, we are kept humble by the complexity of this order. We are keenly aware that there is undoubtedly more that we do not know, and may never know, than we do know about this universe in which we live. But, even within these broad limits, we are confident that reliable orderliness stretches from atom to galaxy, from amoeba to man. We have an obligation to keep faith with our knowledge as well as our ignorance in this matter!

The scientist, then, better than anyone else knows that we live in a cosmos, not a chaos. Were this not true, he would be unable to conduct the experiments or make the explorations that are meat and drink to modern science. Standing firmly on what he knows and believing that it is truly related to what he does not know, he moves with confidence into the unknown. But without complete confidence that an orderliness pervades the universe, and that this order stretches from what he knows to what he does not know, even the most astute scientist would be as helpless as a baby.

Our spiritual forefathers unhesitatingly insisted that the principle of order is an essential part of the idea of God. And a long line of eminent scientists testify to the fitness of this term.

It was my good fortune to be seated beside Dr. Kirtley Mather, now emeritus professor of Harvard, on a recent journey. I asked this great scientist if he had any reason to reconsider or repudiate a statement he made long ago, "We live in a universe, not of chance or caprice, but of law and order." Quick as a flash he said, "I not only will not repudiate it, but I would underscore it as even truer than it was when first I wrote it."

Nor can I forget what Albert Einstein wrote shortly before he died, "Certain it is that a conviction, akin to religious feeling, of the rationality or intelligibility of the world lies behind all scientific work of a higher order." I am impressed by the way these eminent scientists see a deeper and more ultimate meaning in the facts they discover and put together in their separate disciplines.

When the astronomer pictures innumerable galaxies majestically wheeling through the silences of eternity, the religious spirit, listening with the ears of faith, not fear, cries out in adoration, "The heavens declare the glory of God and the firmament sheweth His handiwork." When the biologist speaks about the billion-year-old development which stretches between the earliest life forms and the emergence of man; a development which begins with an amoeba-like unity of preconscious life capable of only a few simple acts of self-preservation and slowly sweeps upwards culminating in the glorious possibility of self-dedication to the great ideals of truth, beauty, goodness and love—when the biologist invites us to stand before this canvas, the religious spirit humbled by the ancient and costly foundation on which it stands, whispers, "And the Lord God formed man of the dust of the ground, and breathed into his nostrils the breath of life; and man became a living soul."

I have read with care the writing of our current crop of atheists and I do not discover a repudiation of the reality of this principle of order. Neither do I find a single one of them doing justice to it in any statement he makes about the essential character of reality.

Still another fact demands expression as an essential part of the idea of God: *the every-day experience of value.* The most distinctive thing about our life is the network of values by which we live. Work, play, love, friendship, remembrance of things past, things hoped for, things of the future—what would life be like without these values? We not only cannot imagine what it would be like—we take them so for granted—but it certainly would not be worth living if they were not real. Though they are intimately personal and our life cannot be separated from them, they are not our own creations. They are a *discovered part of daily life.* We do not make up the laws of health or enduring relationships. They are already made up and we either discover them and obey them or we miss them and are destroyed without them. The truth of the matter is this: these values make us; they mold the personalities we are; they give substance and meaning to the lives we live. Values are God's laws for life, His way of creating and recreating us. They are God's hand on man's shoulder guiding him through the gradations of growth and the shifting patterns of life, giving it meaning, content, and form.

It is the faith of profound religion that where values are, God is. He is as dependable as truth, as eloquent as beauty, as strong as goodness, as vital as love. So far from being afar off, He is the heartbreak of our sorrow, the joy of our laughter, our strength for tragedy. To feel His hand on our shoulder in these everyday experiences of value is to know beyond all doubt that He will not desert us in our hours of need. "Yea though I walk through the valley of the shadow of death, I will fear no evil, for Thou art with me."

Do our contemporary atheists deny the reality of value in life? Quite to the contrary, they exalt the value of life and work! They actually want to place their whole life within the area of this search for meaning, ever deepening meaning, until they are involved with the whole life of mankind. They pray, as did one of the agents in Bergman's *Winter Light,* as she, torn by her unbelief yet need, knelt at the altar and cried, "Give my life meaning." And the anguish of her cry reminds me of the man in the New Testament days who said to our Lord, "Lord, I believe! Help Thou my unbelief!"

The Christian understanding of God is inseparately related to Jesus Christ. However much Christian theologians may have disagreed over many things they have been in complete agreement for over nineteen hundred years in the judgment that *to know Jesus Christ is to know God.* Certainly there is no accounting for Jesus Christ—His life, His faith, His teachings, or His influence on men then and through history—apart from His understanding of God as the one who was working in and through Him. His life began and ended in God—this He believed. His faith began and ended in the claim of God upon Him and His response to that claim. We may want to back away from the theological assertion that He is God, but we cannot ignore the historic fact that in and through Him God was and is working a mighty work of transformation and renewal in human life and history.

As we look at Him with care in the fragmentary records we have, we discover certain things about Him. He knew man. He knows us. He stood where men stood; yes, He stands where we stand! No alien intruder in the human sphere, He saw more deeply into life than any other teacher or prophet we have any record of. In and through Him the meanings of life—the ultimate meanings of life—as they come to expression in human relationships become incandescent with eternal significance.

Yet His discoveries about God and man came where ours must come—in the hard and high way of daily experience. The incredible thing about Him is this: living among people like us, He still believed in man and in God as the creator of man. He went among men throwing open the door to an ultimate meaning that completely transformed their lives. "You are the children of God," He said to a way-lost generation. And then He put it in terms of the symbols that made sense to them, "God is seeking you in love as a shepherd seeks a lost sheep. If you will respond to His approach, if you will put first things first, you will discover the ultimate significance of your own life and God will help you every step of the way. Through difficulties, failures, dangers, even death, He will not leave you comfortless."

Now, I ask you as I ask myself, is it an accident—an historical accident—that He who opened the door to a new life for so many persons should Himself become the symbol of a new life to all who through the ages have come to know Him? That is precisely what happened. "Thou hast the words of eternal life," cried a disciple. "Behold, old things have passed away; all things have become new," exclaimed Paul. Two hundred years after Jesus' death, Irenaeus, exultant with renewed life, could only say,

"He brought everything new by bringing Himself." From our own day comes the testimony of a great English thinker, John Caird: "He is the light of all our seeing. . . ." Explain it how we will, theologically, the plain historical fact must be faced that, in Him, God was working a mighty work of redemption in human life and history.

He opened the door to a new life. He became the symbol of new life. And the gospel, the good news, to our generation is this: That door is still open! Enter it and we will find God, and in finding Him we too will find new life; life with strength, courage, joy, peace and purpose.

This, I am confident, is what Paul Tillich had in mind when, at the very heart of his theological system, he writes, "Christianity was born, not with the birth of the man called Jesus but in the moment when one of his followers was driven to say of Him, "Thou art the Christ." And Christianity will live as long as there are people who repeat this assertion: "Christianity is what it is through the affirmation that Jesus of Nazareth, who has been called 'the Christ' is actually the Christ, namely, he who brings the new state of things, the new being . . . this is the central story of the Gospel. Reduced to its simplest form, it is the statement that the man Jesus of Nazareth is the Christ." And, Tillich continues, "The distinctive thing about the confrontation of man with Christ is this, "He calls for a decision, namely, *the decision for God.*"

Do our contemporary atheists who proclaim that God is dead brush Jesus Christ aside? Not at all—and this is the hardest thing to understand about them. Without exception, they see in Him one at whose side they want to stand; they find in Him one whose life is the life of deepest meaning because it is of ultimate involvement in the human enterprise.

Why, then, you ask, do they say that God is dead? They affirm the reality of order and meaning and the ultimate significance of Jesus Christ. Yet they are repelled by the traditional conceptions of God which have included many things in addition to these. I would say of them, their work has just begun. If they will take with complete seriousness the reality of order, meaning, and Jesus Christ, they will be led into an awareness of what men have meant by God as the one in whom we live and move and have our being. They may never feel at home with traditional Christian conceptions of God—I have no way of knowing about that. Nor would I want to say of them that because they are not at home in my conception of God they are without any conception of God. The word *God* has been cheapened by so much casual use and misuse that they no longer find it capable of interpreting the ultimate meanings of life which they find and are trying to describe. I honor them for their humility even as I question the necessity or the finality of the position they take.

For me, the question, "What do you mean by God?" is the most creative question we can face. It points to the never-ending search for ultimate meaning which has engaged the best efforts of poet, philosopher and ordinary man alike. The full record of this search would be a catalog of the visions of the mystics, the intimations of the poets, the hypotheses of the philosophers, combined with the moments of insight of ordinary people. And throughout the entire catalog, we will find certain points made over and over again:

(1) We live in a world of meaning: Our life has a "dimension of depth" which many of us explore very little or not at all.

(2) There is need for deepening our awareness of this world of meaning through insight and experience.

(3) It is the part of responsible living to enlarge the area of meaningful experience in which we live.

It is the contention of religious thinkers like Tillich, Whitehead, Wieman, and many others, that the more we investigate and attempt to think about our experiences of meaning, the more certainly we are led to the conviction that there is an essential unity in the separate meanings of life, *and this unity they call God.*

Is God really dead? Of course not! But how shall we affirm our faith—in terms of words alone? Or shall we let it be known by what we say, think, plan and do that to believe in God makes a difference—a discernible difference in the way we live. Actually there is only one way to say that we believe in God and that is by what we are!

CRISIS IN THE TWO-PARTY SYSTEM [3]

Edward W. Brooke [4]

In January 1967, when Senator Leverett Saltonstall, Republican from Massachusetts, retires, the urbane Attorney General of the State hopes to take over the post. Edward W. Brooke, the forty-six-year-old aspirant, announced his candidacy for the seat in late December. Hopefully, he expects to receive his party's endorsement in June; failing in that bid, however, he has intimated that he will enter the primary in September. Although he suffered defeat in 1950 and 1952 for state representative, he has been a strong vote-getter in his bids for the attorney generalship. In 1964 he won with a plurality of nearly 800,000 votes.

Mr. Brooke shares a view held by many Americans, namely, that the two-party system in our Government is in danger. The speech below attests to his deep concern over the plight of the Republican party. Delivered as part of the Distinguished Lecture Series at Boston University on January 5, 1966, it represented a sort of clinical analysis of the party's present condition, its continuing problems, and its unanswered challenges. And underlying all was the persistent call for a revitalization of minority opposition, for a return to serious competition of ideas through meaningful debates between the two major political parties.

In a sort of testament of faith entitled "Where I Stand" (based upon his recently published book *The Challenge of Change*), in the *Atlantic* of March 1966, Mr. Brooke commented on the enormous waste of physical and human resources in the United States. Emphasizing particularly the blight that poverty imposed upon our society, he urged consideration of a reverse income tax. According to such a plan, poor families that incur no tax obligation because their potential exemptions are larger than what they earn would receive from the Federal Government a sum equal to the difference between exemptions and total income. Defending the scheme against the charge of "outlandish charity," he remarked that special tax exemptions are currently given as incentives to certain individuals and businesses and added, "Why not use our tax laws to combat poverty—as a form of assistance to the oppressed to help themselves."

[3] Text furnished by Edward W. Brooke, with permission for this reprint.
[4] For biographical note, see Appendix.

Mr. Brooke believes that the Republican party is traditionally committed and prepared to encourage people to help themselves. But the hour for action is late. These "are times when cursing the darkness has become unacceptable to the vast majority of American people." The majority is now "waiting for us to strike the match."

"If we could first know where we are and whither we are tending, we could better judge what to do and how to do it." Those words were spoken many years ago by Abraham Lincoln who, together with Theodore Roosevelt, recognized the responsibility of American Government, the primary obligation of the Republican party, and the duty of both to accommodate to social and economic change.

A politician talking about his party often begins by explaining how eagerly he joined it, how deeply he respects it, and how conscientiously he is working for its improvement. Let me dispense with these themes under the assumption that they are always more interesting to the teller than to the listener. Nothing is quite so tedious, self-righteous, or usually irrelevant to the fate of his party than a politician reminiscing about himself. I shall try, therefore, to confine my discussion to more significant subjects.

However, I do want to mention two personal matters before I begin. The first concerns my relationship to the Republican party. As the saying goes, it has been good to me. It has given me extraordinary personal opportunities and I have enjoyed all the advantages of party support in my campaigns. It is commonplace to talk of one's debt to his party; in my case, the debt is immense.

My political career began some sixteen years ago with an unsuccessful campaign for election as representative to the lower house of the Massachusetts legislature. That defeat was repeated in 1952. Then followed in 1960 another defeat in a campaign for Massachusetts secretary of state before I was elected the Commonwealth's attorney general in 1962 and reelected in 1964. I mention this because some may be less than eager to listen to an appraisal of a national political party by a state attorney general.

I had hoped that more Republicans of national stature would publicly discuss the grave problems facing our party. But too few of our leaders have addressed themselves to our critical, underlying difficulties, and I fear we may approach the next national election as we approached the last one—woefully unprepared. Almost all Republican leaders whose approach to major issues I share have avoided the painful task of speaking out about our dilemmas. If we are alarmed with the course of events in recent party history and with the party's prospects, much of the blame must be placed on the reluctance to address ourselves directly to our troubles. The "good people" of the party have kept silent too long.

As long as the Republican party remains highly unsuccessful, criticism becomes not a matter of personal feeling, but the first order of party business. What might, in the flush of victory, be dismissed as individual whims or personal dissent must, in the sober quiet of repeated defeat, be considered seriously as possible sources of our troubles. Somehow we Republicans must come to grips with the attitudes of academicians, journalists, and the majority of Americans who speak and vote against us. It is in this spirit that I make my personal feelings public, and I urge others to do the same, no matter how severe their criticism.

No great powers of prophecy are required to predict that many of you will disagree with my opinions. But if my talk helps provoke discussion about the future of the Republican party, it will have done its work. If it prompts Republicans and non-Republicans—politicians and laymen, liberals and conservatives, those of you who are mildly or passionately concerned with politics—to debate my ideas, or even reject them publicly and loudly, I shall assume it has performed a service. For the Republican party needs nothing so much as it needs debate, criticism, reappraisal and above all *ideas*.

But there are far more compelling reasons for Republican self-appraisal than the promotion of partisan self-interests. So marked is the present weakness of the Republican party that the very foundation of our two-party system has become structurally undermined. When one of our major parties is dangerously weakened, its strengthening becomes a matter of national, rather than purely partisan concern. Were it the Democratic party that was drastically weakened, I would, I believe, feel as strongly about the need for restoring its ability to compete as I do now about reviving our own party.

At first glance one might conclude that "as the Democratic party goes, so goes the nation." After all, it enjoys huge majorities, large enough to determine the nation's future with a freedom of action rarely available to an American party. But in a larger sense, the opposite is true: unless the imbalance of political parties is corrected, much more fundamental changes in the nation's political life will result. The country will suffer all the damage inherent in a permanent impairment of the two-party system. Therefore, I think it fair to say, "as the *Republican* party goes in the next decade, so goes America." More than anything else, this consideration prompts me to speak out about my party and its problems.

My criticism should be preceded by a qualification. It will be directed principally to abstractions such as "the party," "the leaders of the party," "Republicanism," or "most Republicans." Everyone knows, however, that there is no such thing as "the party"; it is composed of a great number of nearly autonomous groups and individuals. And although there are, of course, "leaders of the party," they are rarely of one mind about given issues. On the contrary, there has always been considerable diversity among party leaders. Abstractions such as "the party," therefore, while convenient shorthand for "the mainstream of Republican thought and action," are bound to oversimplify specific cases.

Moreover, generalizations about the party frequently do injustice to my own segment of it. In my state of Massachusetts, for example, the Republican party has often been the party of social reform, of pioneering legislation, of intelligent application to the problems of the present and future. It has often been the party of action and innovation, while the Democratic party has often been mired in temporizing talk, as you have witnessed in the unforgivable indecision and inaction of the overwhelmingly

Democratic majority in the Massachusetts legislature in the past year. Much of what I say about Republicans in general, therefore, will not necessarily apply to state and local Republican organizations.

Ambiguity of this sort is inherent in the nature of American parties which are essentially local rather than national. Nevertheless, some generalizations about the Republican party as a whole have to be made, based on how *most* Republicans have reacted most often to most issues. This is the sense in which I use the terms "the party" and "the party leaders," and I hope those who think of the many exceptions to the rule will not be too disturbed by my generalizations. Describing even the major exceptions would be an endless task. Thus, I shall try to analyze the Republican "consensus," such as it is in the nation as a whole.

In criticizing this consensus, I do not have in mind the millions of registered Republicans who comprise the party in its largest sense. For the Republican consensus is molded by a relative handful of party leaders and officeholders—just as the Democratic consensus is molded by Democratic leaders and officeholders. Those who make pronouncements, hold press conferences, and manage affairs in our legislative bodies are the makers of what becomes known as party opinion. The makers of Republican policy have been largely Republican members of the Congress—opposition leaders for the most part, who have acquired great seniority by virtue of continued reelection from long-standing Republican districts. My criticism is directed primarily to them. For better or worse, their statements and votes determine what is known both to historians and the public at large as the Republican position—even if they do not faithfully reflect a genuine consensus.

Statistics testifying to the present crisis of the Republican party have been reproduced often enough in the last several years, but I wonder whether their significance has fully penetrated our collective consciousness. Republicans ought to ponder these statistics for the most obvious reasons. Yet like all politicians we are inclined to make light of our electoral failures in order not to give the fatal appearance of discouragement. And in so doing, we are apt to mislead ourselves. Let me therefore repeat some of the salient statistics here. They require no dramatization.

In the last national election, the popular vote for the Republican presidential candidate was 38 per cent, a dismally small percentage in terms of traditional American voting habits. That figure of 38 per cent is commonly cited as a symbol of Republican distress. Actually, other figures testify even more dramatically to our weakness at the national level. In Congress, for example, there are now more than two Democratic senators to every Republican (68 Democrats to 32 Republicans), and the ratio in the House is even worse than two to one (295 Democrats to 140 Republicans). Every aspect of our national politics, from the composition of legislative subcommittees to the quality of debate in Congress and the press, is affected by these statistics. Republicans occupy fewer than a third of our national elective offices. And as so often happens in politics when opposition strength deteriorates so drastically, our influence is in many ways less significant than our numbers might suggest.

There is a level at which effective opposition in a two-party system becomes impossible. I fear we have sunk to that level. The Democrats, surfeited with votes and legislative power, are now free to manage the affairs of state more or less as they see fit. We Republicans are more like spectators than participants.

But the national statistics, sorry as they are, fail to convey the profundity of our crisis. At state and local levels our position is even more precarious. Scores of statistics document our plight. Of 50 state governors, a mere 17 are Republican. On the national average, Republican representation in the state legislatures has been reduced to one lawmaker in three. Republicans now control both legislative houses in a mere six states, and in areas throughout the country where, as the political commentator Richard Rovere recently put it, "Providence was believed to have ordained Republican dominance," Democrats are enjoying comfortable majorities.

Our representation in city, county and town councils, on judges' benches and in sheriffs' and district attorneys' offices is roughly at the level to which it fell during the worst years of the Depression. Only a thorough state-by-state, county-by-county review can convey the extent of our weakness at the local level. I urge Republicans to make such a review for themselves. Here, it is enough to recognize that we are weak nationally and weaker locally.

Nor is there anything encouraging about our strength among voting "blocs" throughout the country. Among every religious, ethnic, and professional group, from executives of the nation's largest corporations to unskilled and unemployed laborers, from "native" white Protestants of New England towns to ethnic minorities in major urban centers, Republican influence and appeal has waned sharply. The single exception is to be found in the rural South—an exception which is more cause for alarm than for satisfaction. Among union members and management officials, college graduates and high school dropouts, city residents and farmers, Negroes and whites, Jews, Catholics and Protestants—in all of the categories of sex, education, income, religion into which voting statistics are divided—support for the Republican party has declined sharply.

Voters who had once considered themselves Republican by instinct and who remained faithful to the party from their earliest voting years are now voting Democratic. Once allegiance of this kind is shattered, it is virtually impossible to restore a sense of permanent personal identification with the party. And most disheartening of all is the Republican showing among the youngest generation of voters. In 1964 the greatest Republican weakness was in the twenty-one to thirty-nine age category: a mere 30 per cent of this group voted Republican. Moreover, there was a drastic decline in Republican affiliation among voters registering for the first time. Voting habits of a lifetime are often established in these early years—and the habits now being established bode ill for the future of the Republican party. To an entire new generation of voters, Republicanism means something obscure but negative. There has been enthusiastic talk of a Republican re-

vival among young people, but the facts are contrary: we are
gaining some support loudly, but losing more of it quietly. Even
among college-educated Americans who have traditionally supported Republicans, we sacrificed our majority in 1964.

One can search recent election tallies for encouraging trends,
for pockets of hope, for categories of voters on which to concentrate future campaigns and appeals. Isolated victories can be
discovered here and there across the country, but nothing that
might honestly be called a solid structural foundation upon
which to base consistent Republican majorities.

My own state of Massachusetts is occasionally cited as an example of encouraging Republican victories. Despite the Democratic landslide of 1964, as national Republican leaders like to
point out, Republicans captured the three most important constitutional offices by electing a Republican governor, lieutenant
governor, and attorney general. But the whole story is by no
means encouraging. For the Democrats carried Massachusetts for
President Lyndon B. Johnson by over a million votes, and elected
a United States senator and three state constitutional officers.
And as national Republican leaders fail to point out, Republicans
elected but 12 of 40 state senators and 69 of 240 state representatives. And most tragic of all, registered Democratic voters now
outnumber registered Republican voters by almost two to one in
Massachusetts.

I could go on. Statistic after statistic might be quoted, one
more appalling than the next, but all testifying to an ominous
weakness of the party at almost every level of political activity
and in almost every section of the country. The most shattering
of all statistics pertains to the percentage of voters across the nation who feel a sense of personal identification with the party. In
1964 only one American voter in four considered himself a Republican.

But statistics alone never tell a complete story. They tell
nothing about discouragement and demoralization of party workers and damage to party organizations. They say nothing about
the distrust harbored by independents and Democrats, without
whom very few elections can be won. Statistics only hint at the

loss of confidence, among Republicans and others, in the party's ability to govern the nation.

For a political party is not merely a compilation of statistics —not merely a percentage of supporters among the voters. People can be counted; numerical strength can be measured. But the intangible assets of a party—its ideas, plans, programs; its sense of purpose and direction; its aura of confidence and demonstrated ability to direct the affairs of the nation cannot be measured arithmetically. These intangible assets are at least as important to a party as its electoral percentage. The real test of a party measures its pulse, its cohesion, its confidence, its responses to daily political give-and-take as well as to crisis—its inner resources rather than merely its performance at the polls. And it is here that the Republican party is weakest—weaker, I am afraid, than our numbers indicate. There is a growing sentiment in the country, strengthened by a new generation of voters who have known but a single Republican national administration, that the natural role of the Republican party is the role of opposition. And there is a growing disenchantment about even that secondary role. Generalizations of this sort are dangerous, but I think it safe to say that millions of Americans simply do not take us seriously as a party that can be trusted to govern. "We ought to have some Republicans around," I often hear, "but not running things."

So weakened is our stature that many voters do not consider themselves faced with a genuine choice. In the voting booth the decision makes itself: Democrats appear to be the traditional governing party, the traditional winners—and we the traditional losers. As often happens in politics, defeat breeds defeat in a cumulative process, from election to election and from generation to generation.

I do not believe, as several political commentators appear to, that the party is in danger of withering away. American political parties have an extraordinary resilience that is woven into the very fabric of our political life. As Professor Clinton Rossiter, one of the most respected political scientists in the country, has observed, each major party is "a citadel that can withstand the impact of even the most disastrous national landslide." The Republican party, like others in American history, has made strong recoveries in the past. Our return to at least respectable minority status after the humiliating defeat of 1936 is the most outstanding example. So great are the resources, the commitments, the forces of tradition and the means of access to the public, the strains of obstinacy and stability in the two-party system, that there is an almost built-in guarantee against total collapse. In the business and political worlds, major corporations and parties may stumble, but the odds against total bankruptcy are very great. There are plausible reasons to expect that the Republican party may survive and to hope that someday it will again become the moving force in American politics.

It would be senseless, however, to underestimate our present weakness and difficulties. We may survive, to be sure, but we do not now possess the political resources, either in terms of ideas or organizational strength to compete successfully in a two-party system. For those Republicans who do not accept my estimate of the seriousness of our plight, I ask them to do their own research. And if there are many who do not believe our situation is grave, then in fact the situation is more grave than I had imagined. Not to be alarmed about the status of the Republican party is, I fear, a sympton of impending *rigor mortis*. Or, to change the metaphor, it is a symptom of intoxication with the heady and dangerous illusion that all is well—or if not quite well, that the passage of a little more time will cure all.

The decline of the Republican party was manifest well before the 1964 presidential election. Only a party weakened, tired and confused could have succumbed to the infection we suffered in that year. Our troubles have been increasingly grave and our appeal increasingly feeble for more than a generation. One might even argue that the 1964 disaster was a blessing in disguise, for it forces us—it should force us—to face some unpleasant facts about ourselves that had not been quite unpleasant enough before to demand general attention. For decades we have been coasting downhill in a state of relative calm; 1964 was a plunge that should shock us to our senses. After this shock, we should welcome the challenge to reexamine the attitudes and policies that have failed us for a generation.

It would be comforting to assume that accident or fate, bad luck or a bad image have reduced the Republican party to chronic minority status. But these vagaries rarely produce a consistent, prolonged political phenomenon such as the thirty-five-year decline of Republican popularity. I think more fundamental causes are responsible. Our principal weakness has not been poor salesmanship, but poor programs; not a poor image so much as poor leadership. We are losing elections because Republican leaders, with too few exceptions, have been reluctant to embrace, and to mold, America's social transformations during the past three decades. They appear unprepared to guide the momentous changes now taking place. Too many Republican leaders are failing to cope with too many issues that concern too many people.

And it is all too easy to assume that we can rehabilitate the party simply by improving our tactics, image, and organization. But tactics, image, and organization are only the outward reflections of a party's outlook and philosophy—of its substance. It is to that substance that the Republican party must turn its attention.

The Republican party cannot reverse its decline by thinking of its own needs. It must think primarily of the needs of the country. For political parties are not ends in themselves. They are meant to be agencies for promoting the national welfare, for expressing and shaping the general will.

Yet in a real sense, the fate of the Republican party itself has become a national issue of major proportions. Ordinarily the interests of the nation far outweigh the interests of any of its political parties. But under present circumstances, the nation has no greater interest than the rebirth of a dynamic Republican party.

This proposition is illustrated by one of my favorite political stories. It took place in 1933 when Republican fortunes and prospects seemed even more gloomy than they do now. After President Franklin Roosevelt's extraordinary congressional successes during the period known as The Hundred Days—a period in which Republicans all but ceased to function as a party—the President asked the late Felix Frankfurter, on the eve of Mr. Frankfurter's trip abroad, for some parting advice. "Get yourself an opposition," Mr. Frankfurter replied.

Get yourself an opposition—it was sage advice, for the country more than for President Roosevelt. No doubt President Lyndon Johnson would not agree that he or the country now need a stronger Republican party. But in this respect at least, President Johnson is outside the American consensus. For the very foundation of American politics, the two-party system, has been undermined by present Republican weakness. And even the most partisan Democrat agrees that America suffers in every respect when it lacks a strong two-party system.

The two-party system was not established by the Constitution or even by law, but it has become so integral to the workings of American government that any serious damage to it is by the nature of things damage to our entire political structure. We do not now enjoy the benefits of genuine two-party competition. And unless Republican strength is restored, there is no guarantee that we will enjoy those benefits in the foreseeable future.

Do I exaggerate? I fear not. It is not so much one-party rule in the totalitarian sense that we must fear, as the breakdown of the checks and balances—the principal advantages—of competition. Our government, like our trials at common law, is grounded in the adversary system. Just as a fair trial in the common law presupposes conflict between two sides roughly equal in skill and resources, good government presupposes conflict between two political parties roughly equal in numbers and influence. When one side is palpably weaker than the other, the system loses its balance, its logic, and soon thereafter, its integrity and effectiveness.

More than fifteen years ago, when Republican fortunes were considerably brighter than they are now, an ardent Democrat, Arthur Schlesinger, Jr. warned that "while Democrats may gain short-run benefits from the present absence of competition, thoughtful members of that party understand the long-run dangers from absence of competition. An essential function of a party in our system is to secure the concurrence of that part of the community which it represents, and if a party becomes so feeble and confused that it turns into an object of public pity or contempt, it can no longer assist in securing that concurrence. As a result, our whole political fabric suffers. . . ."

It suffers in a dozen ways. At the local level, the absence of competition encourages wrongdoing by public officials. I have had to spend too much of my time as attorney general of Massachusetts fighting corruption by elective and appointive officials at state, county, and local levels. While I cannot say that one-party government is the sole cause of corruption, my experience has consistently confirmed what is commonly assumed about corruption in government: one-party government provides a climate in which all forms of dishonesty and unethical behavior flourish in the conduct of the public business. I am often chided by people who say I enjoy prosecuting wrongdoers because I am "only getting rid of the Democrats." My answer has been, "There is no one here but Democrats." Actually, I have had to prosecute Republicans and Democrats—but more Democrats, logically enough, because Massachusetts is fast becoming a one-party, Democratic state.

Neither political party has a monopoly on corruption or a monopoly on virtue. But voters *are* creating a Democratic monopoly of public office in Massachusetts and in the nation. A climate therefore exists in which the tendency toward virtue struggles unevenly against the tendency toward corruption.

But the effects of corruption under one-party government cannot be measured simply in terms of stolen dollars, of bought jobs, of conflict of interest. In a larger sense, our very political atmosphere is corrupted by the absence of serious competition. In state capitals and in Washington as well, the conflict of political principles is reduced to a sham battle. Meaningful debate becomes rhetoric for the record. Controversial proposals and decisions lose their sense of controversy. Legislative and administrative policies are no longer hammered out and put to the test of a strong, self-confident opposition, but are handed out, untested, by an over-confident majority party. Effective investigations, careful review in committees, minority reports on legislative proposals, the sharpening and dramatizing of issues in floor debates—these crucial functions are feebly discharged by a feeble minority. The opposition itself, recognizing its impotence, loses its sense of responsibility. And inevitably, the members of a party enjoying a lopsided majority become arrogant and lazy. A system theoretically based on competition between near-equal partners becomes a caricature of that system.

If I were starting in politics today, without question I would join the Republican party. For here is where the great challenges and opportunities lie. If one wants to participate in the political process and is serious about improving America, here is the opportunity to channel political energy where it will do the most good. Equal work will produce far more results in the Republican party than in the Democratic party.

For the restoration of two-party government in America, I make a plea for active support to intellectuals, to members of minorities, to young voters and to those who have, through family ties and background, through labor union affiliation, through habit and empathy, always considered themselves "Democrats."

The Republican party must attract intellectual talent and youthful energy. The Republican party must broaden its over-all base. The Republican party must not accept the outmoded proposition that the Democratic party is the logical and natural political home of first-, second-, and third-generation Americans. The Republican party must, by person-to-person contact, work with people who live in America's cities and demonstrate to them a genuine and sincere concern for their problems and aspirations. This is the only road to Republican recovery. It will be long and the obstacles formidable, but that is all the more reason for intellectuals, minorities, and young people to join the march.

I am well aware that the present leadership of many Republican organizations may not encourage intellectuals, minorities, and eager young people to join the Republican party. But that should not dissuade them, for American intellectuals have always loved challenge and here is an opportunity for them to respond with meaningful political activity to a clear-cut challenge vital to the nation's stability. Here is a chance for them to channel their zeal for improving the country into direct action. It has been all too easy for the nation's intellectuals to stand aside and criticize the Republican party without committing themselves to its improvement. But those intellectuals who have refused to make the commitment, who have reserved their skills and energy for deriding our condition, are not less responsible for that condition than the Republican party they criticize. To allow the Republican party to "stew in its own juice" is as irresponsible as some of the positions Republican leaders have taken in the last thirty-five years for which intellectuals have most criticized our party.

The same reasons that have disaffected the intellectuals have caused young people to avoid the Republican party. Since the advent of Franklin D. Roosevelt, members of minority groups have, rightly or wrongly, believed that the Democratic party would best serve their interests. And immigrants, their children, and grandchildren have, by and large, shared that belief. Because of this, the composition of the Republican party has lacked that pluralistic quality which has benefited the Democratic party so much. The voices of these groups have not been heard in Republican party councils. We learn about their problems second hand. We have not had the advantages of their thinking or their suggestions for solutions to their problems. Worse, their absence has left an intraparty political void—they have not been present as participants to influence the direction in which the Republican party should move.

They have maximized their philosophical differences with the Republican party and minimized their philosophical differences with the Democratic party. They have put practically all of their political eggs in the Democratic party basket to the detriment of the two-party system and to their own detriment, for they have been taken for granted by the Democratic party. The leverage they could assert by a better distribution of their strength between the two great political parties in America has never been fully utilized.

I have tried not to minimize the difficulties facing the Republican party. I realize the enormous efforts which will be required to overcome our inertia and to infuse Republicanism with the qualities necessary for leadership. I know that the very people who avoid us are precisely the people we need most in order to help us overcome our grave handicaps in popularity and dynamism. But I am fully aware that a welcome may not be extended by party leadership for some time. And because of this, I urge them to force their way into the Republican party. I urge them to join Republican city, town, ward, and precinct committees. I urge them to *participate*. I ask them to intensify their efforts. And I say to them that even though it may not be apparent, the great majority of Republicans in this country welcome them with open arms.

It is no secret that an intense ideological struggle within the Republican party can probably not be avoided—a struggle which, I trust, will be waged without rancor and bitterness. But the Republican party is not going to wither away; it is an established American institution with enormous resources for survival. The question is, which direction will it take? Its future, and the future of the country and perhaps the future of the world, hangs in the balance. No political activity can have more immediate and direct effect on American and world politics as a whole than participation in the struggle within the Republican party. For those who yearn to do something constructive for America, to commit themselves to a worth-while cause and to engage in meaningful political activity, the challenge is clear. I urge the skeptical, the critical, the fearful, and the disillusioned to put aside the crutch of noninvolvement and join *this* good fight.

It perhaps is no news to most of you that last week I announced my candidacy for the Republican nomination for the United States Senate and in practicing what I preach, I seek the ideas, counsel, and support of the intellectual community. It is also my intention to have an active, and I trust enthusiastic, "Brooke for United States Senator Committee" in every university, college, and institution of higher education in the Commonwealth of Massachusetts.

I cannot quarrel with Shakespeare that the "past is prologue." But—for the Republican party—I hope that the recent past—the past of 1964 particularly—will not be prologue—rather that we will look to the past of Teddy Roosevelt—and further to the past of Abraham Lincoln as the prologue to Republican attitudes, planning, and policies of today and tomorrow.

I end with high optimism and with a prediction that the Republican party will soon become the majority party. I believe that there is a great future in store for us. I have faith in our determination to govern. I have faith in our ability to govern. I have faith in the intelligence of the American people to give us the opportunity to govern. And, above all, I have faith in the wisdom and willingness of the Republican party to respond to the challenge of change so essential if we are to govern.

REFLECTIONS ON THE AMERICAN EXPERIENCE

THE CONSENSUS COMPLEX VS. THE FREE MARKET [1]

George Champion [2]

Readers will have observed long before they reach this page that many of the speeches included in the present volume are symbolic indicators of a preciously guarded democratic privilege, namely, the right to dissent. That is equally true of the address by George Champion, chairman of the board of the Chase Manhattan Bank.

In this address, delivered before the Colorado Association of Commerce and Industry at Denver on November 18, 1965, Mr. Champion asserted that the Federal Government was not above criticism. Rather, its actions should at all times be subject to responsible appraisal:

> We should be completely free to question the Government's actions and, if necessary, to alter them in a democratic way.
>
> We should be free to debate important issues such as the so-called voluntary guidelines, instead of having them thrust upon us without discussion in Congress or appeal through the courts.
>
> We should be free to criticize the Government's implementation of its policies without being chided like children about the desirability of consensus.

Whether big government is good or bad is a perennial topic of controversy. In a speech before the San Diego Open Forum on January 9, 1966, Roger A. Freeman, senior staff member of Stanford University's Hoover Institution on War, Revolution and Peace, remarked that in 1965 the American people had a $675 billion economy and a $210 billion Government. This inevitably posed the question of "what Government should be doing—or leave alone." After an extensive analysis, Mr. Freeman concluded, among other things, that "it is high time for us to quit devising new programs which government may adopt or enlarge as substitutes for personal effort and to start thinking of means to strengthen the challenge to the individual to deal with his own problems."

The object of Mr. Champion's criticism was the bureaucratic insistence that the free market system was outmoded and that the central

---

[1] Text furnished by George Champion, with permission for this reprint.
[2] For biographical note, see Appendix.

government must assume a firmer control over the economy. In support of his critique, Mr. Champion dealt specifically with three lessons provided by the Soviet economy, which he believed pointed up the failure of authoritarian economic control and which offered hints to America on what not to do. Noting the proliferation of Government influence, he warned the audience that

> Unless we educate public opinion to the meaning and need for a strong free-opportunity system, we shall continue to see that system chipped away until it has been destroyed. But if enough people understand how our system works, I am confident that public opinion as the final arbiter of all great issues in this country will see to it that the present dangerous trends are corrected.

Though the songwriters show a perverse preference for "Springtime in the Rockies," I personally have always been partial to autumn. So I'm delighted that your invitation gave me an excuse for a visit during my favorite time of year.

It's easy to understand why the sage, Elbert Hubbard, remarked that "many wise men have come here from the East—and the wiser they are, the sooner they come."

Frankly, I wish I had come sooner myself so I could have found out how you managed to bring about the very constructive merger of your two business organizations into your fine new Colorado Association of Commerce and Industry. We tried to effect a similar merger in New York last year when I was president of the Chamber of Commerce, and that explains why I address you tonight as an ex-president!

Our merger proposal failed by a scant eight votes to get the required two-thirds approval of the membership, so I suspect that if I had applied some of your Colorado wisdom I might have influenced the results. When we first began considering a merger in New York, I assumed that the issue would stir about as much emotion as a plan for moving a cemetery. But I found out differently, as I suppose some of you people did.

When it was all over, I could truthfully say with Sir Winston Churchill that I had "benefited enormously from criticism and at no point did I suffer from any perceptible lack thereof!"

At any rate, I applaud your merger move because I'm convinced that businessmen must get together and speak out more forcefully if they are to make themselves heard in the halls of government. Never, in my judgment, has this been more essential than it is today. We businessmen have the greatest story in the world to tell about our free-opportunity system, but we have been reluctant to tell it with the vigor and enthusiasm that the Communists muster in depicting their so-called heaven on earth.

To my mind, nothing points up the validity of our story more dramatically than recent economic developments in the Soviet Union. The Communists have openly admitted that their system of central planning has failed to solve the economic problem.

The billions of rubles plowed into the national economy for industrial expansion have not brought satisfactory returns. Something is clearly wrong. So after almost half a century of rigid planning, Soviet production is increasingly being geared to what the people want rather than what central planners prescribe. The government is trying desperately to decentralize the process of economic decision-making. Managers are being given greater freedom in deciding how to run their factories. Not for a moment have the Soviet leaders lost sight of their long-term goal: the spreading of communism around the world. But out of self-interest, they are borrowing some capitalistic methods to improve their economy.

What a strange turnabout! It was only a few years ago that Nikita Khrushchev boasted about burying capitalism, that Soviet planners boldly predicted the U.S.S.R. would soon overtake the United States, and that many in our own country pointed to the success of the Sputniks as indisputable "proof" of the Communist system's superiority.

Now we see Communists—not only in Russia but in Poland, Czechoslovakia, and other satellite countries—flirting with that old bugaboo of Marxism, the profit motive. More and more consumer goods are being turned out under a kind of profit system, with price flexibility and greater attention to consumer demand. The "cult of the plan" is being raked with scornful broadsides in the press and other public forums. Some Kremlinologists look upon this as the beginning of a gradual transformation of the face of Soviet society.

Whether this assessment turns out to be correct or not, I think all of us can learn valuable lessons from this latest failure of authoritarian economic control. Tonight, I'd like to discuss three of these lessons with you.

The first is that the individual is the key element in the successful operation of any economic system.

For a long time, the Communists ignored this central fact and got away with it. Eventually, though, the Soviet consumer refused to buy what failed to please him and began to want more of everything from hand creams to hairdos. As the Soviet government newspaper *Izvestia* admitted: "The urge to have one's own car is as compelling as technical progress itself." Or as it was summed up in a recent U.S. cartoon that had one Communist official saying to another: "Know something? The entire dialectic of Marxist revisionism can be reduced to one simple formula— 'money talks.' "

Soviet consumers are now being given a greater voice in determining the kinds of goods to be produced and are enjoying a larger share of life's amenities. Somewhat belatedly, the Politburo is coming around to the viewpoint of the Russian novelist Dostoevski that even "tragic freedom" may be preferable to "compulsory happiness."

In our own country from the very beginning, we have emphasized the importance of the individual, both as a person and as a consumer. This emphasis on unleashing the individual's energy, ability, and initiative and providing him with the freedom to make the most of his opportunities has been largely responsible for the great economic strides we have made.

From pioneer days, self-reliance has been an ingrained characteristic. It was as vital to the frontiersman's survival as his musket or his horse. To meet his daily needs, he had to develop a wide range of basic skills. He built his own home, shaped his own furniture, grew his own food, and defended his family against lawlessness. When emergencies struck, the frontier family dug down into deeper reserves of patience, faith, and determination. Their prideful boast was that they were beholden to no man. Well did they know the exhilaration that comes from proving one's competence and steadfastness under hardship.

Our insistent emphasis on the individual accounts for the preeminent position we have always accorded education and training. The huge expenditures for public and private schools and colleges are, of course, familiar to all of us. Not so well known, perhaps, are the wide-ranging educational efforts on the part of business. By some estimates, the bill for corporate educational efforts will hit $4.5 billion this year—fully half of what it costs to run the nation's colleges and universities. U.S. companies are far ahead of those anywhere else in the world in the training of staff and line people at all levels. This is one reason they have been so successful in decentralizing the decision-making process.

Our concern for the individual has also been reflected in the various work-and-study programs by which needy students with a willingness to apply themselves have been assisted in getting a college education. Dr. Fred Patterson, former president of Alabama's famed Tuskegee Institute, told me just recently that many of his alumni of truly outstanding accomplishments were graduates of Tuskegee's five-year program, in which they attended evening classes while working during the day for the first two years of their college course. The business community has long recognized that the person who worked his way through college had qualities that were deserving of special consideration.

Today, I'm dismayed to say, our traditional emphasis on the individual is becoming diluted. Security is being exalted above personal freedom. Day by day, Government is being called upon to make choices that once belonged exclusively to the individual.

It used to be that when you wanted something, you worked to earn it. Now, it seems, you stage a demonstration to get it at Government expense.

It used to be that if you lost your job, you took whatever work you could find or you went where there was work to be done. Now many of those drawing unemployment compensation turn down a job unless it suits their fancy.

It used to be that a family would work and save for a lifetime to earn a taste of security. Now more and more people are de-

manding that the Government guarantee them an annual income
without any effort on their part.

We seem to have lost sight of the fact that, throughout our
history, the great advances have come, not from paternalistic
Government but from the venturesome and creative individual.
Henry Ford did not adapt the assembly-line technique to auto
production in response to a Government directive. Nor did
Thomas Edison develop the incandescent lamp with the help of
a Government subsidy. These achievements were the product of
individual initiative, of strongly-held minority views, of a social
climate not of conformity, but of variety and diversity. In my
view, we would do well to work toward a revival of such a
climate in our country.

A second lesson we can learn from recent developments in the
Soviet Union is that the individual must be given adequate incentives if he is to perform up to his full capabilities.

The Russians learned this to their sorrow, first in their agricultural program and later in their industrial buildup. Under
the strict socialistic system, there was no incentive for a factory
manager to increase production. If he did, the planners would
simply raise his quota the following year. So the temptation was
to insure that targets were set as low as possible. Since shoddy
goods counted as much as any others under the quota system,
there was little motivation for a manager to improve the quality
of his product.

The current search for incentives to get the Russian economy
moving again is eloquent testimony to the failure of one of communism's chief tenets: that the profit motive is unnecessary in
running a society.

In our own country, we learned long ago that profits serve a
vital role as both stimulant and regulator. Our system has been
fashioned on the basis that one must produce more than his needs
if he is to contribute to the general well-being. It has a built-in
drive for improvement and a built-in fear of falling behind.
When incentives are substantial enough, individuals and corporations work harder, invest more, assume the risk of new ventures.

The result is economic growth, more jobs, a better competitive stance in the world marketplace—all of which add up to a higher standard of living and a more rewarding way of life.

Lately, though, I detect disturbing signs that some Government bureaucrats would like to de-emphasize incentives.

Discussions about future tax cuts center on the need for increasing purchasing power rather than bolstering incentives, despite the fact that the tax system still levies heavy penalties on successful performance.

Constant pressures for higher social security and unemployment benefits, and for relaxed standards in welfare payments, tend to reduce the incentives to take and keep jobs.

Mounting controversy over work rules in labor-management discussions, and over the idea of granting wage increases solely on seniority, reflects a resistance to change that can blunt incentives.

These are not healthy symptoms, and we must do something about them promptly if we are to restore incentives to the position of primacy they have traditionally occupied in our country.

It's a curious fact that overseas more and more nations are coming to recognize what many in the United States fail to grasp: namely, the enormous power generated when the individual is not restricted and is appropriately rewarded for his efforts. It is becoming increasingly evident that an economy based on individual incentives and private initiative produces far more real wealth and improved living standards than one that is stifled by government regulations. No better evidence can be cited than the case of the two Germanies where we see growth and prosperity under freedom in the West, misery and stagnation under collectivism in the East.

As I travel around the United States, I hear profits criticized as exorbitant, unfair, monopolistic, inflationary, even antisocial. I sense a deep-seated suspicion that they are something subtracted from the well-being of the general public and added to that of the wealthy. I detect a growing feeling that profits are contrary to price stability and a sound dollar. I conclude from these observations that our incentive system is being widely misjudged, misunderstood, and indeed misrepresented, and it's high time we in the business and financial community did something about it.

A third lesson to be learned from the Soviet experience is that the free-market system, with its respect for the individual and its stress on incentives, provides by all odds the best allocation of economic resources.

What we are seeing in Russia now is a deliberate effort by the planners to unplan part of their economy. The Communist system has simply not been working according to its elaborate plans. Instead of the promised "miracles of production" that were supposed to put free enterprise to shame, the reverse is happening. Waste, inefficiency, and confusion are rampant.

Pravda told recently about a seemingly unbeatable plan for production of sewing machines. The only trouble was that somebody forgot to coordinate production and distribution. The result, said *Pravda,* was that "Himalayas of sewing machines" were piling up in warehouses. Government planners had decided how many sewing machines should be produced, and produced they were, long after the quantity had surpassed the demand.

It's as if our own Government had been turning out automobiles and had built the Edsel. Chances are we'd all be driving Edsels today. But because U.S. consumers decided in the marketplace that they did not want Edsels, we now have the new and improved Mustangs and Thunderbirds, even though the miscalculation cost the company a quarter of a billion dollars.

This illustrates the fundamental difference between a free-market economy and a controlled economy. It is profoundly disturbing these days to hear some bureaucrats insist that the free market is, in many ways, a chaotic method of doing business and that we ought to find a better one. Whatever may have been the market system's achievements in the past, they say, it has now been rendered obsolete by the forces of history. Competitive markets are simply not to be trusted, so the Government must take a firmer hand in the matter.

Do we want to abolish poverty? Then, say the bureaucrats, let the Government impose uniform standards of housing, nutrition, education.

Do we want to sustain prosperity? Then, say the bureaucrats, let the Government prescribe terms for labor-management settlements and decide how much General Motors, Ford, and Chrysler should charge for their new models.

Do we want to assure our senior citizens a carefree retirement? Then, say the bureaucrats, let the Government take a few dollars more here and a few dollars more there and set up a new welfare program.

The refrain is a familiar one . . . "Let the Government do it." The Germans heard it from Adolf Hitler. The Italians heard it from Benito Mussolini. In fact, we could trace the pattern clear back to the Pharaohs who built some impressive pyramids through central planning.

There is no doubt that authoritarian government can concentrate the resources of a country and produce spectacular results in a narrow area. But no government by itself has ever solved the economic problem of production and distribution for use and enjoyment by consumers. Why? Because government can never duplicate the variety and diversity of the free market. By imposing uniform standards, it may possibly raise the level of performance for a while. In the process, though, it usually substitutes uniform mediocrity for the wide-ranging experimentation that can transform today's laggards into tomorrow's leaders.

As former President Eisenhower has said: "Too much Government planes off peaks of excellence, hones down differences, dries up competition, and leaves a drab and unhappy community where once dwelt thrift, zeal to excel, and ambition for human betterment."

The free market works to correct mistakes; Government often tends to perpetuate them. Replace the free market with the Government directive and you get a system riddled with inconsistencies, inequities and absurdities. Consider a few examples:

> While one Government unit pays out $4 billion annually to farmers to limit their production of food, another spends millions to irrigate new lands for food production, and a third supplies low-cost fertilizers to increase the output of crops already in surplus.

While the Government spends billions to prop up farm prices, we are selling commodities like wheat, tobacco, and poultry more cheaply abroad than we sell them to our own citizens.

While the Government exerts pressure on unions and management to hold down wage increases, Government workers' pay has been going up one-third faster than that in private industry.

While the newly created Office of Economic Opportunity bears responsibility for our antipoverty program, a substantial proportion of the decisions are still made by the Departments of Interior, Labor, Agriculture, and Health, Education and Welfare.

While one Government department forbids the use of certain pesticides in national forests as unsafe, another urges the public to spray them on lawns, trees, and rose bushes.

While one Government agency subsidizes tobacco production, another is conducting a massive campaign to frighten people away from smoking.

The list of examples could be expanded endlessly, as one of the senators from my home state of Connecticut pointed out recently. Senator Abraham Ribicoff was talking about how easy it is these days to get lost in Washington. If you wanted to find out what the Federal Government is doing—or not doing—about highway and traffic safety, he said, you'd have to call on the Departments of Commerce, Defense, Post Office, Labor, and Health, Education and Welfare. When you finished with them, you'd have to try the Interstate Commerce Commission, the General Services Administration, the Federal Trade Commission, the Interdepartmental Highway Safety Board, and the Federal Safety Council. Then for a refresher course, you'd have to spend some time with the President's Committee for Traffic Safety.

While this proliferation of Government influence has its ludicrous aspects, it is becoming a matter of mounting concern to citizens across the land. A special Gallup Poll disclosed recently that the proportion of Americans who look upon Big Govern-

ment as a major threat to this country has more than doubled in
the past five years. Apprehension has risen sharply at almost
every social and economic level. Widely varied occupational
groups feel it almost identically. Forty-two per cent of people in
professional and business households consider Big Government a
threat; so do 38 per cent of those in workers' households. "Big
Business" and "Big Labor" scare people much less than monster
Government.

This concern, as I see it, is a good sign. It shows that we have
not grown too weak or too complacent to care about the future.
I, myself, have become increasingly concerned about the en-
croachments that are being made on our freedom in the name of
"consensus." This is a perfectly respectable word with noble
antecedents in our country going back to the Founding Fathers.
The root of the word is the same as the root of *sense,* and it
means a "feeling together." It denotes widespread voluntary
agreement. It carries no suggestion of compulsion, no hint of
forcing people to go along against their will.

Yet today in Washington, we have what might be called the
"consensus complex" stifling constructive critical comment on
Government policies to an extent that is dangerous to our national life.

In the name of consensus, we find Government telling labor
and management what wages are acceptable, telling aluminum
producers what prices are justified, telling banks what rates are
permissible. In the name of consensus, we find Congress pres-
sured into passing grandiose laws in haste and without adequate
debate, and with little thought as to the ultimate costs or effects.
In the name of consensus, we find press criticism of the Government frowned upon, and critical suggestions from the business
community brushed aside.

Thus, consensus in modern dress has become alarmingly syn-
onymous with conformity which Dr. Norman Vincent Peale has
called "one of the most fundamental dishonesties of all [because]
when we reject our specialness, water down our God-given in-
dividuality, we begin to lose our freedom."

It is a serious mistake, in my judgment, to suppose that the Federal Government is either honored or helped by being placed above criticism. On the contrary, its policies should be the object of constant vigilance by every citizen, and its decisions subjected at all times to responsible criticism.

We should be completely free to question the Government's actions and, if necessary, to alter them in a democratic way.

We should be free to debate important issues such as the so-called voluntary guidelines, instead of having them thrust upon us without discussion in Congress or appeal through the courts.

We should be free to criticize the Government's implementation of its policies without being chided like children about the desirability of consensus.

One of the strongest tenets of our political philosophy has been to insure that viewpoints at odds with prevailing doctrine will not be rejected out of hand. Through the years, we have devised elaborate legal and constitutional safeguards to protect the dissenter. Indeed, tolerance of dissent is one of the chief characteristics of our cherished open society, and I find it hard to square this tolerance with the "consensus complex."

At a time when the voices of restraint are so few and so muted, it is up to us in the business and financial community particularly to speak out for the principles we believe in.

It is up to us to impress upon our friends and associates the profound lessons of recent events in the Soviet Union.

It is up to us to remind our fellow citizens continually of the importance of individual freedom, the need for adequate incentives in our competitive society, and the advantages of the market system over state control.

In a democracy such as ours, sound economic policies are dependent largely on the public's understanding of the issues at stake. Unless we educate public opinion to the meaning of and need for a strong free-opportunity system, we shall continue to see that system chipped away until it has been destroyed. But if enough people understand how our system works, I am confident that public opinion as the final arbiter of all great issues in this country will see to it that the present dangerous trends are corrected.

THE AMERICAN THEATRE AND THE
SPEECH PROFESSION [3]

ESTHER M. JACKSON [4]

Dr. Esther M. Jackson believes that the theatre "has been among the last professions to respond to the challenge of the sixties." This circumstance contains a painful irony. Traditionally, she asserts, the theatre has been in the "vanguard of change"; but today it has "arrived at nothing resembling a clear purpose in regard to the function which it should assume in this period of political and social transition." Accordingly, "the agonizing issues—family disintegration, racial conflict, and the threat of nuclear war—have been left to the interpretation of the communications media, while theatre has increasingly removed to the world of purely private dreams and longings." To help solve the theatre's artistic and professional problems, and insure its exercising a more decisive role in orderly social change, she calls upon the speech profession to help strengthen the arts, and particularly the theatre in American society.

A former director of education of the New York Shakespeare Festival, and author of the widely acclaimed *The Broken World of Tennessee Williams,* Dr. Jackson is currently a professor of speech and theatre at Adelphi University, Garden City, New York. The speech reprinted below was delivered in New York City on December 29, 1965, at the annual convention of the Speech Association of America.

The American theatre of the sixties appears to have entered a period of transition which may have a decisive effect on its subsequent history. This marked alteration in the course of American theatre arts may be traced to the kinds of social and political changes which are taking place in the nation at large. For America of the sixties is a society characterized by the rapid extension of human possibilities; particularly, by the expansion of opportunities for hitherto unrecognized social, economic, and professional classes.

One result of this extension of opportunity has been the assignment of a greater level of societal responsibility to the theatre,

[3] Text furnished by Esther M. Jackson. Reprinted by permission of the author and the Speech Association of America.

[4] For biographical note, see Appendix.

as to the arts community in general. As in earlier periods of history, the assumption of increased societal responsibility on the part of the arts has had both fortunate and unfortunate results. Certainly, the theatre stands to reap the benefits of that increased financial support offered by Federal legislation in support of the arts. But such responsibility must inevitably create new problems for the theatre, not only in regard to its fundamental relationship to the society, but in regard to the kind of artistic context in which it exists. It is not surprising, therefore, that at this point of confrontation, the American theatre seems momentarily to be without a clear sense of professional purpose.

Oddly enough, the arts in general have seemed least prepared to cope with the major social, political, and cultural changes of the sixties. The sciences, reinforced by massive funding and by decades of organized activity, have responded brilliantly to the often painful realities of this era. Indeed, it may be claimed that the sciences—with their image of man against the unknown of space—have usurped the ancient function of epic, creating new myths which capture the spirit of twentieth-century man perhaps more effectively than the contemporary theatre. But even more conservative professions such as religion, medicine, and public education have begun the revision of many of their traditional practices and have evolved new methodologies, techniques, and goals consistent with the new shape of our society. Certainly, the response of the religious community to the pattern of political and social action initiated in the past decade, marks a change in our understanding of the principle of separation of Church and State. Even more significant may be the evolution of a new theology which attempts to provide new insights relevant to the context of crisis in which most Americans live today. One of the most impressive adjustments to change has been that of a relatively new complex of disciplines: the social sciences, which have, in a relatively brief period, moved to build conceptual, methodological, and practical support for the programs of the Great Society. In reward for this decisive use of professional resources, the social sciences have earned virtual control over a vast professional empire, including programs in education, technology, and the arts.

It is, therefore, disappointing to note that the theatre—traditionally in the vanguard of change—has been among the last professions to respond to the challenge of the sixties. Though the complex theatre community has acknowledged the effect of change upon its own national role, it has, as yet, arrived at nothing resembling a clear purpose in regard to the function which it should assume in this period of political and social transition. The failure of the theatre community to clarify its new responsibilities is all the more distressing, since many of the acute problems which characterize this period can be alleviated only through the appropriate and effective use of the theatre arts. It is, for example, no exaggeration to claim that one of the primary roots of permanent cultural disadvantage is insufficiency of those complex imaginative faculties which fine theatre develops most fully. Psychologists of learning tell us that the ability to perceive relationships between image, symbol, concept, and reality is fundamental to the total pattern of the individual's intellectual, social, psychological, and cultural growth. The theatre is not primarily a recreational device; it is a powerful and sensitive instrument in the total process of human growth, the source of basic understandings, available in no other form of knowledge.

In this context, it is a matter of concern that the record of the American theatre in responding to the crises of the sixties is less than admirable. Although substantial funds are today available for the support of theatre through the National Foundation for the Arts, the Office of Education, and the Office of Economic Opportunity, the theatre community has yet to propose any program comparable to that in operation in behalf of the sciences, social sciences, or education. Unlike the sciences, the social sciences, medicine, religion, or—for that matter—professional sports, the theatre community has simply allowed its facilities, personnel, and basic contents to be requisitioned to social and political uses without assurances for the validity or integrity of that use..

We might be persuaded to offer excuses for this reluctance in assuming responsibility for the use of the drama in the pursuit of social, political, and intellectual objectives, except that the central failure of the American theatre in the sixties is, in fact, artistic.

An examination of the history of the past decade indicates that its reputation rests on the achievement of the twenties, thirties, forties, and early fifties. Although our theatre productions demonstrate a technical excellence which is virtually unmatched in Western theatre—except perhaps for those of Germany and Poland—we have as yet developed no acting company which can compete successfully with the great ensembles of England, France, Russia, Germany, or, for that matter, Canada. We have been unable to apply our celebrated ingenuity to the creation and development of an indigenous American style of acting appropriate to the interpretation of classical works. The creative achievement of our great playwrights of the thirties, forties, and fifties—of O'Neill, Wilder, Miller, Williams, and others—remains unchallenged by the leading playwrights of the sixties, Albee, Baldwin, or LeRoi Jones. Our hope for the resuscitation of the theatre—the repertory company—has not proven to be an immediate answer to the problem. In a melancholy note on the current season, the New York *Times* reporter Lewis Funke commented on the difficulties affecting three valiant experiments in repertory theatre: at Seattle, Pittsburgh, and Lincoln Center.

The problems of these three companies are not singular. Rather, they are symptomatic of our failure as a profession to deal with basic problems in a systematic way. For many difficulties in acting which plague these theatres have developed as the repertoire demanded by audiences has become more difficult. Basic problems in acting cannot be solved by a single company, any more than the problems incident to producing space scientists can be solved by a single institution.

Lillian Smith, writing in a recent issue of the *Saturday Review* (October 2, 1965), traces the present difficulties of the American theatre to its failure to engage the great social and political issues of our time. Miss Smith writes that the American theatre has avoided the very themes out of which great and vital drama might emerge: the struggle for human rights, the growing conflict between youth and age, the clash between radical and conservative movements in the political arena. Instead, Miss Smith charges, the new playwrights have become more and more immersed in the expression of narrow personal desires. Our theatre today is concerned primarily with themes relating to interpersonal conflict, ego fulfillment, and the search for pleasure. Although these motives represent an aspect of the drama in all ages, they cannot be interpreted as the foci of our primary concerns in the sixties. The agonizing issues—family disintegration, racial conflict, and the threat of nuclear war—have been left to the interpretation of the communications media, while theatre has, increasingly, removed to the world of purely private dreams and longings.

It is clear both artistic problems and professional failure are related to the way in which the theatre has chosen to confront the realities of our time. How does it happen that the American theatre—a pioneer in the intellectual revolution of the twenties, thirties, and forties—should have failed to respond to such profound social changes? Undoubtedly, the theatre community was badly frightened by the attacks it suffered during the so-called McCarthy Era. Some of its new conservatism may be traced to the hostility which has in the past characterized the attitude of segments of the society to the performing arts community. But more of the problem of the sixties may be traced to misapprehensions within the theatre community itself. Perhaps the most apparent barrier to the formulation of a relevant national policy is the kind of fragmentation which exists within the theatre world. The deep antagonisms and suspicions which characterize the relationship between educational theatre and the professional community have thus far precluded cooperation in regard to professional and preprofessional training. Similarly, many of the difficulties in style which beset both New York and regional companies might have been alleviated through a national program of apprenticeship.

A more serious kind of fragmentation appears in the emergence of a protest theatre, whose aim is the exacerbation of racial and class conflict. It is curious that this "theatre of hatred" should be encouraged and sponsored by elements of the larger theatre community as an alternative to full opportunity in the arts for all people. The folly of continued splintering, the danger to theatre and to the society in general, can be measured by the speed at which a new cult of violence is developing in connection with the new minority theatre movement.

How does it happen that the American theatre today reflects such limited understanding of its new responsibilities? Perhaps the problem may be traced to a lack of true professionalism. By this, I do not mean a lack of technical excellence and occasional bursts of brilliance; but rather a failure to impose upon the theatre activity, in any consistent fashion, that discipline which has characterized all periods of great artistic achievement. The fact is that the larger theatre community does not recognize theatre as a discipline: neither as a serious academic discipline, nor as a disciplined artistic form. Rather, the American theatre community itself is responsible for the impression that theatre is a platform for unfettered personal expression. The American theatre community, unlike its counterparts in other Western nations, protests that the presence of standards is a limiting and restricting influence upon its creativity. The effect of this doctrine of subjectivity may be seen, not only in the increasingly private concerns of our playwrights, but also in the erratic performances which this approach elicits from many of our acting companies.

The source of such misapprehensions about the nature of the theatre arts is not difficult to trace. They have origin in the intellectual history of our country. They are holdovers from those Romantic theories current at the time of our beginning as a nation; but they also reflect a kind of anti-intellectualism which has characterized much of our artistic endeavor. It is interesting, however, to note that no such claims mark the work of our major creative talents in other fields. The work of Martha Graham for example is characterized by exceptional regard for training, discipline, and the unflinching application of stringent standards.

I wish today to suggest that the key to the solution of these problems may rest in the possibility of leadership from the academic community; particularly, in the possibility of national leadership on the part of the speech profession. In the same way as the university has functioned to accelerate the advancement of the sciences and social sciences, so the speech profession may transform the sixties into a new period of growth for the American theatre arts.

A look at our past history of the American theatre would suggest that we should be recovering a function which the academic community has formerly assumed. American forms of drama, dance, and theatrical design were forged in the workshops and scene-shops of Harvard, Yale, Wisconsin, and North Carolina, as in the dance studios of Bennington and Mills. The rudiments of a new grammar of playwriting were evolved and disseminated in seminars at Yale, Iowa, and Michigan. The decisive steps toward the development of public policy in theatre were precipitated by Hallie Flanagan, who evolved much of the theory and practice which she was to put into national operation at Vassar College. In recent years, our most successful repertory theatre began as a kind of experiment, designed by a former professor of dramatic literature at the University of Michigan.

What are some of these problems for which the speech profession should help to find solutions? Perhaps the most immediate task is that of helping to reestablish unity within the theatre community; to arrange for the creation of task forces which shall engage the resources of the entire theatre community. The speech profession should, in this connection, seek to bring to bear upon these problems the considerable resources of other theatre arts, particularly, of dance, cinema, radio, and television. Clearly, many of the theoretical and practical problems which face the drama also involve these related professions. Moreover, these professions hold answers to many problems of theatre. Perhaps the greatest stylist in the American theatre today is Martha Graham who has, in her dance forms, worked out both theoretical and practical solutions to many of the problems which yet elude directors in the spoken drama.

Further, the speech profession might accelerate the solution of problems in professional training by launching a series of pilot programs to test new concepts of training. History has shown that the gifted playwright, actor, or director is likely to be found where the societal conflict is at its height. The theatre requires first-rate acting schools, playwriting workshops, and apprentice programs, not only on eastern university campuses, but at every class level. While some of these workshops should be placed in the colleges of the South, and Middle West, others should be located outside of the university setting, in centers of social and political activity. Such a program would differ from the kinds of activity presently sponsored by the Office of Economic Opportunity, in that it should undertake to establish conditions which could lead to serious professional careers.

Fortunately, Actors' Equity is now engaged in attempting to establish a pilot program for the training of actors. Again, the speech profession has an important role to play if this venture is to succeed. For the establishment of a national academy requires an extensive program of testing, experimentation, and evaluation before we can arrive at the codification of those principles which will support the development of an American classic style.

A third problem to which the speech profession will need to give systematic attention in the next decade is that of developing new curricula in teacher education and new programs in audience education, which will take advantage of the resources of the theatre and, which will at the same time, provide a kind of laboratory for the training of young professionals. Again, we should hope that the speech profession will seek to develop concepts affecting curricula, teacher preparation, and the development of theatre facilities which will revolutionize the teaching of theatre at elementary, secondary, and undergraduate levels. We should hope that through such programs theatre will come to occupy a place in the curriculum as a basic form of knowledge rather than as a kind of recreation; a form of knowledge on par with science, mathematics, languages, and the humanities. In this connection, new methodologies are required for the use of the theatre as an instrument for the eradication of intellectual, cultural, and psychological disadvantage.

A final problem area in which the speech profession can offer the theatre critical assistance is the development of public policy in the arts, at national, state, and local levels. The speech profession has a clear obligation to assist in the training of administrators, teachers, and specialists who can implement those governmental programs in operation, as well as those which are planned. This would suggest that some retraining of personnel is in order. The speech profession might follow the example of the scientific and business communities in the use of short-term seminars, fellowships, and grants, for professionals whose abilities to administer arts programs might be enhanced by an opportunity to explore ideas in a systematic way. It is of equal importance that the speech profession help to supply that kind of research required for the development of a sound national policy for the arts. New methodologies and new research areas should result not only in the accumulation of substantial data, but also in the development of those historians, critics, and methodologists which theatre in the seventies will require.

Undoubtedly, the implementation of these objectives will require a major reappraisal of graduate studies in theatre and indeed of the entire relationship of the speech profession to the theatre. It is my impression that such a reexamination will not result in the narrowing of the scope of theatre studies. On the contrary, I should predict a new alignment. It seems clear, for example, that many of the functions presently maintained by theatre departments should no longer be handled by academicians. Increasingly, the conduct of practical courses must be ceded to the professional actor, director, or designer. It seems likely that we shall increasingly have a university-based theatre, rather than a university theatre. What then will be the new role of theatre in the university? It will be to provide basic education together with those kinds of training which are critical to the advancement of theatre in America. Certainly, the university, particularly, the speech profession, will remain concerned with the general education of the artist. But beyond this, the educational theatre will, it seems to me, be forced to concern itself more and more with research, education, and planning; specifically, with the systematic gathering of data, with the training of scholars and specialists, and with the development of policy and standards.

It would appear to me appropriate, therefore, that the speech profession, in conjunction with other interested organizations, might now elect to establish a national study group for the purpose of reexamining the relationship of university programing to the theatre. One effort is already under way which will undertake to study needs in theatre research. But a second task force is needed to examine the goals, methods, and standards of curricular offerings in speech and theatre departments throughout the country.

Today, it seems clear that the arts, particularly the art of the theatre, may have a critical role to play in establishing those conditions which insure orderly social change. It is reassuring to know that such have been the conditions under which the art of the theatre has always flourished. I believe that the speech profession can offer major impetus to the growth of American theatre by helping to solve its basic problems in a systematic, efficient, and thoroughly reliable way.

Nothing could be more central to the academic function. For we in America believe that the chief use of knowledge is to accelerate human achievement and to improve the fundamental conditions of human existence, so that every man may aspire to grasp the total riches of human existence within his own lifetime.

CONSUMER PROTECTION:
WHAT JOHANNA WON'T READ [5]

JOHN CRICHTON [6]

Business speaking in America is a flourishing business. Apart from a few notable exceptions such as Bruce Barton's "Which Knew Not Joseph," relatively few business speeches, however, make their way into the conventional anthologies and compilations. A variety of reasons may account for it. Frequently the topics are of such transitory nature as to render them swiftly obsolete. Perhaps they do not deal with the "grand themes." Or they may treat of matters which lack a universality of appeal, which fail to touch upon broad principles of belief and action. Or the content may be so specialized as to make it appear unrelated to the average reader's experience and concern.

As an instrument of classroom instruction, however, the good business speech is often very helpful. At its best, it features immediate identification of subject matter with listener interest, laudable brevity and conciseness, rememberable analyses, and a certain instant intelligibility. Moreover, it is likely to make extensive use of devices for the intensification of ideas.

A special interest often attaches to the study of addresses delivered by professionals in mass communications, advertising, and public relations. These men put to work many of the "rules" and theoretical dicta mentioned in the textbooks and discussed in the classroom. Moreover, the advertising men are engaged in what William D. Patterson has called "the most ubiquitous form of public persuasion in this country."

The academic man is occasionally prone to condemn specialists in advertising technique—and sometimes with good reason—for the use to which they put rhetorical and psychological devices. In all candor, however, the critic must acknowledge that what Madison Avenue is practicing, in its distinctive way, is not distantly removed from what teachers of speaking, in their distinctive way, sometimes theorize about when they give instruction in audience analysis.

The speech reprinted below was delivered by John Crichton, president of the American Association of Advertising Agencies, on March 16, 1966, at Houston, Texas, before the Southwest Council Annual Meeting of the American Association of Advertising Agencies.

[5] Text furnished by John Crichton, with permission for this reprint.
[6] For biographical note, see Appendix.

I want to talk today about consumer protection. Sometimes it seems that everyone is talking about consumer protection this year. And the consumer, alas, must sometimes feel as a sheep might feel, surrounded by a dozen shepherds. As we shall see, some of the shepherds are unnecessary, some are unnoticed, and some are uninformed.

I should like to talk about the problem of consumer protection in three respects. First about what consumer protection now consists of, and the substantial amounts of private and public effort going into it. Second about the nature of the consumer, and why some idealized conceptions of her are untenable in the light of what is now known. Third about two responsibilities, the responsibility of the businessman and the responsibility of the consumer.

Let's first take quick stock of our situation. Our economists are talking about a trillion-dollar economy, and we are approaching the three-quarter trillion.

A trillion dollars may seem a little closer here in Texas. It's a one followed by 12 zeros. A stack of one trillion one-dollar bills would reach 67,866 miles—one third of the way to the moon—because of NASA this may have unusual relevance in Houston.

Sylvia Porter once said with a trillion dollars one could buy every American family a $20,000 home, or every adult American a $9,000 limousine. Or, the trillion dollars would pay for a four-year education in college for 100 million students, roughly every American under thirty-five years of age.

It's a lot of money. We're an affluent country. No people anywhere ever were better fed or better housed, and no nation ever put so much money into education, or educated such a high proportion of its people, or gave so generously to charities to improve our society and to care for its casualties.

The last twenty-five years have been years of growth, spectacular in industrial capacity but equally remarkable in every social respect.

Sometimes how widely shared our gains are is not appreciated. Many people do not know that the percentage of family income spent on food by the metropolitan housewife has declined 5.1

percentage points in the last fifteen years. It is, in part, from this reduction in the proportion of income going to food that we have been able to buy travel and education and books.

With this preliminary, let's look at consumer protection. The last time it was carefully surveyed was in 1961. At that point, in the Federal Government, 33 departments and agencies out of 35 considered that they performed consumer protection activities. These 33 units were involved in 118 different activities either protecting the consumer or advancing the consumer interest. In these 118 activities, 65,000 full time Federal workers were involved, and the projects cost around $953 million a year. There were an additional 135 programs being carried on by these agencies which were felt to indirectly protect or help consumer interests, and there were another 43 additional activities identified as protecting the general public but not specifically billed as consumer programs.

In all, there were 296 Federal programs listed to help the consumer.

To these must be added the state programs, the county programs, and the programs of many of our major cities.

All states, according to a 1963 report by the Committee on Government Operations, spent nearly $34 million annually on regulation of food, drugs, cosmetics and related products.

In addition, there is the work of colleges, universities, and extension bureaus, of better business bureaus, chambers of commerce, labor unions, consumer organizations, and business—which has a wide-ranging and diversified consumer information program all of its own.

A great deal is being done and has been done for years to protect and inform the consumer. Whether it is well done, or properly organized, well planned or well received is another question. It exists. People who ignore it or talk about the need for consumer help are betting in part that their listeners don't know what's going on. This is fairly elaborate machinery.

So much for current consumer protection.

Let's talk about the consumer herself. In the first place, the consumer can be discussed in the aggregate, but it's a great mistake. Consumers are all different. They are people. Guy de Maupassant once said, "All men are alike but every woman is different."

I have resorted to statistics only because it makes the consumer comprehensible, and measurable.

Most consumers shop as if they had something more important to do.

As the latest Du Pont study shows, the average supermarket customer makes about 50 per cent of her purchases on an unplanned basis. Only about 31 per cent are specifically planned. The rest are either "generally planned—about 17 per cent" or substitute items—about 1.8 per cent. Depending on how one reads the statistics, at least half and perhaps as much as 69 per cent of supermarket purchases are made as a result of a decision made in the store.

The supermarket shopper moves on impulse. How much impulse depends on the kind of product she buys. For instance, about 65 per cent of the eggs are bought as a planned purchase; she had them on her list. But marshmallows, or heat-and-serve frozen dinners, or sponges or sponge cloths are unplanned decisions in about 75 per cent of the cases.

Progressive Grocer studies consumers so that grocery store owners can lay out their stores to conform to consumer shopper patterns. Here's part of the findings about supermarket shoppers:

1. They don't spend much time in the store—somewhere between 20 and 24 minutes.

2. They visit a lot of locations—around 50 in the store.

3. They buy from 24 to 40 items.

4. They spend from $11 to $16 on the average.

5. About two thirds of the shoppers don't use shopping lists, although half of upper-income shoppers do.

6. Men shop faster than women. They tend to spend less.

7. A major part of the time in the store—18 to 28 per cent, perhaps averaging around 25 per cent—is spent in waiting or talking.

This all means that the average supermarket shopper probably buys 32 items from 50 locations and spends $13.50 in 15 to 18 minutes.

People shop in food stores because they need to shop, and because their families like food. They don't linger around. They are quite critical of the 5 to 10 minutes they may be held up at the checkout counter.

Surveys have shown, for example, that the average shopper in the supermarket spends 12 seconds in the detergents section.

What we know about shopper behavior in supermarkets is important because it suggests that the future of consumer protection is severely limited by the inability of the consumer to be interested in the subject.

There are something like 6,000 items in a supermarket. But the evidence says that the shopper buys 32 from 50 locations in 15 minutes of actual shopping.

A major department gets ten seconds' consideration. At least half the items are impulse items. And only a third of the shoppers use lists.

This is the picture of a *confident* consumer. If she were worried about the values and prices and quantities being offered to her, she would certainly spend more time.

She can shop fast because she feels safe in what she's doing.

Parenthetically, the stores might well wish she spent more time. The more time the shopper spends in the store, the higher is her total buying.

I left out one important item. A number of years ago a research company found a significantly high proportion of women who needed glasses, but would not wear them in supermarkets when shopping. Vanity is an important element in all personality, and in this case it works in favor of the recognizable package, for those myopic ladies who can't read the fine print.

The evidence seems to suggest that shoppers are quite well equipped to get their shopping done rapidly; that there is a minimum of confusion about what they're buying; and that most of it is not carefully planned.

The evidence doesn't square very well with the consumer protection cult. They really believe that consumers need far more protection in labeling and packaging than is now provided.

As a practical matter, this is often difficult. Let me illustrate from *What's New in Home Economics*. A can of chunk-style tuna weighs 7 ounces; the same can of grated tuna weighs 6 3/4 ounces. Density of product makes the difference. Take pudding mix. The mixes are designed to be used with 2 cups of milk to yield 4 average servings. Chocolate pudding mix, of greater density, is in 4-ounce boxes; vanilla is in 3 1/4-ounce boxes. If the vanilla had to be packaged at 4 ounces, you'd have to add extra tablespoons of milk to the 2 cups, and the yield would be 4.9 servings. *Question*: Is this any less confusing or troublesome to the consumer?

After all, most consumer-goods manufacturers have made a career out of trying to be as simple and carefree as possible where the consumer is concerned.

If the consumer shops rapidly and casually and confidently in the supermarket, that most influence-free and democratic of commercial institutions, then what is the problem of consumer protection?

First, there is considerable evidence that most consumers consider themselves adequately protected. Last fall, in a survey in Seattle, 63 per cent of a consumer sample said they did not want more protective legislation.

Second, people who work closely with consumers don't sense any demand for consumer legislation.

Glenna McGinnis, food and equipment editor for *Woman's Day*, told the National Food Marketing Commission that "I can count on my fingers the complaints we have had from readers on the subject of food products, packaging, etc. in the more than twenty-five years I have been in my present job. Readers often telephone and ask for information or help, but not to complain about products."

Willie Mae Rogers, director of the Good Housekeeping Institute, says the great problem about consumer education is not the lack of educational material, but the difficulty in getting it disseminated and used. She told the Food Marketing Commission that "there is more consumer informational and educational material available today then ever . . . there is no excuse for any woman who can read and wants to be informed, not being informed."

A Good Housekeeping survey turned up four conclusions: (1) women do read labels; (2) they think they get the information they need from labels and packaging; (3) they would like more information on clothing labels; and (4) they have special complaints about packaging and labeling, but they apply to specific products. For instance, they complain about how hard some packages are to open.

Laura Lane, associate editor of *Farmer's Wife,* says farm wives want the same thing—packages which are easier to open.

It seems to me that these editors, whose particular job it is to know women and their needs, reinforce the idea that legislation is not the answer to the problem of consumer protection.

They are, by the way, far better informed than most people in Government. The Good Housekeeping Institute will get between eight and ten thousand letters a month from readers. A former chairman of the Federal Trade Commission regarded eleven hundred letters a month as a rolling wave of reaction.

What is the problem of consumer protection?

Perhaps part of it is to realize the truth of Miss Rogers' argument that people who want information get it.

A second part is to realize that people ignore information. Even very important information. For example, in a poll published last summer, 28 per cent didn't know that China was a Communist country. And two years ago, in a public opinion survey, 43 per cent didn't know that Vietnam was in Asia.

It's hard to imagine, with every newspaper and television station and radio station, and nearly every national magazine, flooded with stories about China and Vietnam, that this could be true. But many people are untouched by events, and relatively immune to information.

A third part is to realize that people have a way of responding which is very different from what is expected. People change more slowly than products. People don't necessarily keep pace with technology.

Let me tell you about the manufacturer of instant mashed potatoes whose package had detailed directions and a specific technique for best results: use cold milk, and beat the potatoes for just so many minutes—beat them any more and they got sticky.

Unfortunately, every housewife *knew* you could only use hot milk in mashing potatoes and that the more you beat them the better they were. She could not be told differently. The product failed because housewives failed, and the product was withdrawn from the market.

Charlotte Montgomery, a columnist for *Good Housekeeping*, says packages are often thoughtlessly designed, by men who don't realize housewives will need bifocals to read the package, or by an engineer whose language is incomprehensible to her. She wonders how many manufacturers are victimized by consumer habits, where housewives go cheerfully along, ignoring the new directions, and by not reading lose the benefits of additional conveniences.

Dr. Irene Oppenheim is assistant professor of home economics at Montclair State College in New Jersey. She is interested in consumer education. She says manufacturers have done an outstanding job of producing convenience foods to fit the needs of today's families but that the problem of intelligent choice is difficult. Because of "the wide variety of practices prevalent in indicating the net contents. Often the net contents are printed in a place where it's hard to find, or in small print, or in a color which contrasts poorly with the contents, if it's in a cellophane bag, or the background of the package or label."

She reported an interesting experiment. They showed sixty-eight women a well-known cake flour, in the $1\frac{1}{4}$-pound size. They were asked to tell the net weight of the contents. Half the women didn't look at the package for the net weight, which appears in front. They looked at the package, weighed it in their hands, and guessed. Four said they couldn't find it on the box, and three more said they could not see it. The remaining twenty-six stated the quantity they said they had read. But three of them were incorrect.

That's a somewhat puzzling—or frightening—story.

A fourth part of the problem is to recognize that particular emphasis will be placed on the under-equipped portions of our population. The poor and the illiterate will get special attention, as part of the war on poverty. It is the belief in some Government circles that "the poor pay more." There is quite a lot of support for this belief; in many cities unscrupulous dealers have swindled poor and ignorant people. This is indefensible and must stop. The forces of legitimate business ought to be in the forefront of getting it stopped.

It is also true, as Burleigh Gardner learned, that the poor avoid some bargain centers, like supermarkets, in favor of small but friendlier neighborhood stores.

This brings me to a summing up. I don't happen to believe that legislation is the solution to consumer protection. Consumer protection itself may be a misnomer; we may all be talking about consumer information and how to improve it.

Our changing population may have a lot to do with the choices we make. Zoe Coulson, food and nutrition editor of *What's New in Home Economics,* was remarking that American women marry younger and younger. About half the first married brides are under twenty, and eighteen is now the peak year for marriage. This year half the nation's population is twenty-five years of age or under. More wives have their first child at nineteen than in any other year, and one out of six teen-age wives has two or more children.

This substantial young family bloc probably needs more and better consumer information than any other group. They are very receptive to new ideas, and they are eager to learn new, quicker, and easier ways of doing essential household chores.

It seems completely logical to me for all business—and for the advertising business most of all—to interest itself in the problem of the consumer and informing her better.

If it is a matter of getting the sizes and weights clearly printed on packages, let's do it.

If it is a matter of clear and simple instruction, let's see if we can improve our language.

If it's a matter of understanding the consumer's needs better, let's do the research. Sometimes it isn't even necessary to do research. Mrs. Montgomery points out that if a housewife buys a new home with appliances already installed she often has a terrible time trying to get the original direction and installation booklets for the equipment from the manufacturer. Why should this be hard for her?

Or, Mrs. Montgomery again, in textiles and fibers the instruction label in the garment is usually not permanent. The only permanent label that stays with the fabric is the union label—which only proves to the housewife that some labels can be put on to stay.

Incidentally, in one of Mrs. Petersen's industry conferences it became clear that in the textile and fabric business, the main problem is not composition or thread count, but care and cleaning and maintenance. An industry conference—textile men, cutters, retailers, cleaners and launderers—is at work on the problem. From it will come some consumer information consumers will read, and be glad to read.

One more important part, it seems to me, is to make up our minds that if there are crooks and cheats in business we will use the best available means to get them out. If the Better Business Bureau can do it, fine. If not, then whatever legal action is necessary to make sure the honest don't suffer for the dishonest.

Finally, a change in our mental set. It's probably true that much of the professional consumer movement is mired in the 1930's. It is also probably true that much of today's business community does not see in the present consumer unrest the opportunity to do something for consumers which clearly needs to be done.

The emergence of a new young market, needing guidance and information and purchasing standards is a great opportunity for advertisers. And the agency business, with its long tradition of interpreting the advertiser to the public and the public to the advertiser, ought to play a considerable part in it.

If we study her needs, we will know what and why Johanna won't read. If we fulfill those needs, we will have come a long way to supplying that demand for consumer information which may be the heart of the "consumer protection" movement. And well-developed information will probably be far more useful to Johanna than legislation.

But Johanna has another responsibility, and it must be borne by her as an individual, the consumer. Our whole political system rests on informed people, making rational choices.

There's a great deal of consumer information, and if Johanna wants to be better informed, she must make the effort required of all consumers.

The need for the thinking citizen is implicit in our kind of government. Johanna has to work at it, and she probably has to work at consumer information or consumer protection as well. In a crude analogy, you can advertise seat belts. You can get gasoline companies to offer them at bargain prices. You can get seat belts made obligatory by law. You can have a National Safety Council campaign through the Advertising Council urging the consumer to buckle up. But only the consumer can reach down and snap her seat belt, and insist that her children do the same. If she won't do it, the advertising, information, and legislation are of no value. It is her peculiar responsibility. She has to exercise it.

STUDENT INVOLVEMENT IN EDUCATIONAL POLICY [7]

Edward D. Eddy, Jr.[8]

Fred M. Hechinger, education editor of the New York *Times*, commented recently on the ironic twist that "just at the moment when faculty members are often accused of trying to get off . . . [educational policies] committees, students are clamoring to get on." If the institutions yield to the entreaty, they may conceivably find student involvement a partial antidote to alienation. While unrest on the campus has generated from several sources, the students' sense of anonymity and separation from the planning and decision-making centers of the institution have often been prime irritants. This condition is not necessarily confined to the giant institutions. A student can feel unidentified with the educational process at the smallest college.

The uneasy and at times fatuously unruly conditions on college campuses during the past two years doubtless reflected the social stress under which modern man, with mixed success, must shape his experience. Students are not alone in the search for identity. While their responses to alleged or real frustrations may have been more demonstrative, vocal, or tumultuous than those of their elders, the latter may simply have used more sophisticated ways of venting their spleen. After all, time has been their ally for a longer period; and time has a way of refining techniques for the expression of displeasure.

At any rate, the campus experiences of the recent past have convinced students, as Joseph Katz and Nevitt Sanford remarked recently in *Phi Delta Kappan,* that educational reforms are possible. "Things will never be the same, and the colleges will be wise if they anticipate big changes."

Giving students a more responsible voice in the management of the enterprise of learning will not, of course, automatically restore peace to the troubled campus. Life is not that simple. But, according to Edward D. Eddy, president of Chatham College in Pittsburgh, "genuine student involvement in the formation of educational policy offers our best hope of regaining the lost concept of an academic community."

Mr. Eddy delivered this speech in Washington, D.C., on October 7, 1965, at the annual meeting of the American Council on Education.

[7] Text furnished by the American Council on Education. Reprinted by permission of the Council and Edward D. Eddy, Jr. This speech appears in *The College and the Student,* edited by Lawrence E. Dennis and Joseph F. Kauffman (Washington, D.C.: American Council on Education, Copyright 1966), pages 169-72.

[8] For biographical note, see Appendix.

I suppose that it is almost unnecessary to state the obvious: The once highly respected house of intellect has become a divided house, beset by internal dissension and external doubting. American higher education is currently suffering from an acute case of dyspepsia brought on by our inability to acknowledge our own digestive problems, a condition that does little to enhance general public acceptance of colleges and universities as infallible social necessities. We need to move fast to put the house of intellect in good order before it becomes a slum.

The complaint is at least threefold: Faculty members are accused of being devoid of any genuine sense of concern for the entire fabric of education, including student responsibility and morality. Students are said to be more interested in being heard than in hearing. And administrators are labeled as being pre-occupied with preserving form rather than with extending substance.

One answer to this predicament is, I believe, simple and clear: Genuine student involvement in the formation of educational policy offers the best hope of regaining the lost concept of an academic community. The time is right and ripe for *all* American colleges and universities to allow students a strongly contributing role in the shaping of educational policy. The "crazy colleges" of the past, such as Antioch and Reed, may well become the sensible pattern of the future. Every college and university committee ought to include *voting* student members. I would make an exception only of those committees which are engaged in personal discussion of individual faculty members in matters of promotion and tenure. It is too much to ask individual students in this case to pass on the qualifications of individual teachers.

I do not believe that students should have an *equal* role on all committees. I do believe that this generation of students in particular is deeply concerned with *meaningful* areas of human endeavor; functional trivia has no attraction for them. What, then, could or should mean more to a student than educational policy as it is shaped by thousands of decisions which, when taken together, determine the posture and policy of an institution?

Students have already proved themselves capable of assisting substantially in their own education through independent study. We all know how much they help to educate other students also. They are full participants, not just receiving but continually giving. They can be encouraged to give in a much deeper dimension. Student participation, with the fresh point of view it brings, is highly desirable in such areas as curriculum planning, evaluation of teaching and teachers, and academic administration including degree requirements, grading systems, and calendars.

Our neglect of student opinion in faculty evaluation is one good example of our failure to make proper use of students' insights. Most of us are scared to death of such evaluation. In the great majority of colleges and universities, we have nervously laughed it off for years. And in the process we have lost valuable time which could have been used to fashion some fairly reliable ways of obtaining trustworthy student reaction.

Certain conditions and guidelines are important to the discussion of student involvement. Here are some which occur to me:

First, involving students is no simple, snap-of-the-finger activity. As Henry May observed, the student protest movements "express vague wishes for immediate and simple solutions to complex problems." Student involvement *is* a complex problem. We are foolish to dismiss it as insoluble. We are equally foolish to attempt it by presidential decree.

Second, it is neither possible nor desirable for colleges to abdicate to the student the primary responsibility for policy. We cannot and we should not turn over our campuses to student rule. We would thereby negate the rationale for education: colleges exist because some people know more than other people. Nevertheless, we can take the cue from business and industry that it isn't reasonable to market what the consumer doesn't want to buy. Controlled consumer reaction never hurt any business and certainly won't destroy the integrity of any educational institution.

Third, student involvement must be more than the usual token indulgence. I suppose we ought to be realistic in recognizing that a minority of students today will never be satisfied with whatever role they play. But the presence of this minority should not dissuade us from attempting to achieve a genuine interchange among faculty, students, and administrators. Let us also be realistic in recognizing that the teaching faculty will be least anxious to involve students in educational policy making. And so:

Any steps must be a reflection of deep educational commitment and certainly not mere response to pressure. Merely raising the question of student involvement on most American campuses is a good exercise these days if only to straighten out campus thought regarding the effective role of the student. If the rationale proves to include "education for leadership," then our campuses can serve as splendid laboratories involving something more than the presidency of the Chess Club. We can begin to capitalize on the new student interest in educational matters as against the old student concern for trivia. For years, we have wanted a fire to burn; let's not throw water on the first flames.

Finally, valuable student involvement won't just happen. Most of us do not expect the younger, new faculty members to serve on key policy committees. We give them at least a year to get to know what is expected and to gain a perspective which experience alone can bring. If, therefore, we want genuine student involvement, we must provide a system which encourages them to acquire both experience and perspective. We must not make the mistake of blaming students for being transients on a college campus. The perspective gained should include what Charles Frankel urged when he wrote: "[The college] must find a way to communicate to [the student] that learning has its own imperative standards and demands, and its own schedules and routines, and that these cannot be modified for reasons of personal self-expression or convenience." Give one student one year of apprentice observation on one faculty committee and he'll know that lesson for years to come!

The result of student involvement in the formation of educational policy may well be the emergence of a new sense of academic community, possibly something quite different from what we have known before. For years we have been thirsty for student responsibility; we pontificated and then seeded the clouds of despair. The resulting hurricane has brought us wind and fury. Out of it can still come a new and brighter day.

The presence of students on every major committee surely could help us also to overcome a prevailing tendency to belittle undergraduate teaching. We are going to have to learn to accept and welcome criticism, to go on working under its severe eye, to maintain our sense of humor, and to be even prouder of the results because they were achieved as a community undertaking.

Involvement means caring. Students today *do* care and care deeply. Involving them in the total work of the academic community is one important way for the American college to prove its faith in a generation in which, frankly, we had damn well better believe.

ORATORY LOSES AN EXEMPLAR

EULOGY ON ADLAI E. STEVENSON [1]

CARL McGOWAN [2]

Adlai E. Stevenson died in London on July 14, 1965. Beyond reasonable doubt, he was America's most gifted speaker of the past two decades, and among the best in her entire history. His intelligence, versatility, and felicity of expression will not soon be forgotten. His performances were deft, graceful, and if the occasion demanded, movingly eloquent. He could deliver a eulogy on Winston Churchill and match, word for word, the power of England's greatest orator in his best days. But if the circumstance demanded, he could stand up to Valerian Zorin of the Soviet Union, as he did in the Security Council of the United Nations during the Cuban crisis, and meet charge and countercharge with withering rhetoric, but with unfailing compassion and civility. His words gave shape to the best in America's vision and ultimate purpose in the community of men. We contemporaries have, indeed, as the New York *Times* observed editorially, "been companions of greatness."

Since this series of selected speeches began in 1937, Mr. Stevenson has been represented eleven times, oftener than any other orator except Franklin D. Roosevelt. Future editions of REPRESENTATIVE AMERICAN SPEECHES will be more than a little impoverished by his absence. This final word in his praise comes from Judge Carl McGowan of the United States Court of Appeals, District of Columbia Circuit. Long-time friend and associate of Mr. Stevenson, he delivered the eulogy at the Washington National Cathedral on July 16, 1965.

We are a vast company—we friends of Adlai Stevenson. Only a few of our total number are met here in Washington today to mourn him. More will come together for the same sad purpose in his homeland of Illinois. But all taken together will be but a very small part of the whole.

This is because, in his case, the word *friend* has a staggering sweep. It comprehends those who have had the benison of his personal presence to delight as well as to inspire. But it also in-

[1] Text furnished by Carl McGowan, with permission for this reprint.
[2] For biographical note, see Appendix.

cludes literally millions, in this country and abroad, to whom he is only a voice.

It is a voice, however, to which they have listened since he began speaking in the accents of reason to the American people, and as he has continued to do to the peoples of the entire world in the United Nations. These people have, in all their sorts and conditions of life, of high and low degree, of varying color and religion, listened to that voice with unabated interest and with undiminished respect. They have heard in it the unmistakable intonations of friendship. They have responded with the gift of their affection to a man most of them have never seen.

They are of our company of friends today—as much as any one of us here. We have all heard the same voice.

That voice is stilled now. But its echoes are likely to be sounding down the corridors of history for a long time. For it is the essence of faith to believe that the world in its advancing age will set no less store than have we upon reason, upon intelligence, upon gaiety, upon charity and compassion and grace— all these things, and more, of and with which this voice has spoken to us so often and so clearly in the past.

We do not need now to be reminded of what we have lost. That hurt is deep—and no one of us is too old to cry. We may better, then, give thanks for what we have had, and rejoice in our recollections of how our good fortune came to be.

Many have asked how it was that a man of Governor Stevenson's sensibilities could have intruded himself into the dust and heat of politics. We may think, I believe, that it was simply his joyous response to one of his deepest instincts—that for public service. He knew that the greatest opportunities for effective public service lie in elective office. The shattering disappointments that beset that way of life can also dissolve in the satisfactions of feeling the reins of political power in one's hands harnessed to good and just ends.

The disappointments were his in cruel measure. But the satisfactions were his as well. We need not fear that he ever looked back with despairing regret at the way the final balance was struck.

There was a strong family bent for politics. And Adlai Stevenson was of a generation of Princeton students who thrilled to the saga of Woodrow Wilson—that figure in our history in whom the contrasting worlds of the university and the precinct have had their most dramatic conjunction.

In this Cathedral the spirit of Woodrow Wilson is always very close. Surely it has never been more so than at this moment. The youthful admirer has completed the course with honor, and is at rest with the admired.

The two have often been compared. Although there are obvious disparities in temperament, there are many similarities in political style. Above all, they had a common vision of a just society at home and a peaceful one abroad.

Both were agreed that the mobilization and direction of political power was a pursuit from which no man should turn away, or of which he should be ashamed. And who can say that the dream of the youthful Stevenson, in terms of a world made safe for democracy, did not include a happier ending, if only the rocky road to political power could be traversed once more by a man with the same vision?

Adlai Stevenson enjoyed politics. He relished the infinite variety of the people he met there. He found them to be, as in other walks of life, of all descriptions—good *and* bad, and, more frequently, partly good and partly bad. He had a particular liking for these last, for he knew that most of us, including himself, are in that group.

He sensed that strain of sentimentality which is always just under the surface of political relationships, and which binds together in a tacit brotherhood all those who live and die by the ballot box. He brought to this highly emotional environment his own warm responses, shaped by those qualities which, beneath all the surface toughness and cynicism, it valued the highest—a cheerful lightness of spirit, a gift for undemanding friendship, a sympathetic understanding that most politicians have creditable reasons for worrying about the day after election day. He had the expert political leader's sure instinct for trying to identify the

other fellow's problems and pressures before passing judgment
upon him.

The Stevenson story has now become a legend. The glories
of it are many, but none shines more brightly than the sight of
him putting to work at the United Nations these very qualities
which rocketed him to the foreground of domestic politics. It was
as if he were fated to move through personal disappointment to
the very center of the problems that assail all people, and upon
which depend the survival of civilization itself.

His whole life had been a preparation for events of this scale
of importance. And our sense of the fitness of things must be
touched by this completely civilized man doing battle for the
persistence of the very idea of civilization. For our biggest stake,
we put forward our best. And he met the challenge, to our, and
his, eternal honor.

If there is reason to be despairing on this day, it is because
this man has been removed from the important work of war and
peace. But he, who knew the perils ahead better than most, was
undaunted by them. In virtually the last of the magnificent
speeches he gave to the world, he said:

> For all our desperate dangers, I do not believe, in the words of
> Winston Churchill, "that God has despaired of His children."

Wherefore, then, are we now to falter and be faint of heart?
We have lost a friend, but all the world has lost one. And that
friend has left us in the fullness of his powers, and secure in
what he must have known to be a far-flung respect and affection.

He died as he would have wished, engaged in his country's
business, and mankind's.

APPENDIX

BIOGRAPHICAL NOTES

BALL, GEORGE W. (1909-   ). Born, Des Moines, Iowa; graduated Township high school, Evanston, Illinois, 1926; A.B., Northwestern University, 1930; J.D., 1933; admitted to Illinois bar, 1934; associated with General Counsel's office, Treasury Department, 1933-35; private law practice, Chicago, 1935-42; Washington, 1946-61; member of staff, General Counsel's office, Lend-Lease Administration, 1942-43; associate general counsel, Foreign Economic Administration, 1943-44; director, United States Strategic Bombing Survey, London, 1944-45; general counsel, French Supply Council, Washington, 1945-46; Under Secretary of State for Economic Affairs, 1961; Under Secretary of State, 1961-   ; executive chairman, committee to administer certain nonmilitary agencies abroad, 1966-   ; decorated, Legion of Honor (France); Medal for Freedom (United States); member, Phi Delta Phi fraternity. (See also *Current Biography: 1962.*)

BENNETT, JOHN C. (1902-   ). Born, Kingston, Ontario, Canada (parents United States citizens); student, Phillips Exeter Academy, 1918-20; A.B., Williams College, 1924; B.A., Oxford University, 1926; M.A., 1930; B.D., *magna cum laude,* Union Theological Seminary, 1927; S.T.M., 1929; D.D., Church Divinity School of the Pacific, 1940; Pacific School of Religion, 1943; Williams College, 1947; instructor in theology, Union Theological Seminary, 1930-31; assistant professor of Christian theology, Auburn Theological Seminary, 1931-35; associate professor, 1935-38; professor of Christian theology and philosophy of religion, Pacific School of Religion, 1938-43; professor of Christian theology and ethics, Union Theological Seminary, 1943-   ; dean of faculty, 1955-64; president, 1964-   ; ordained to ministry, Congregational Church, 1939; foundation lecturer at Chicago Theological Seminary, Yale University, Garrett Biblical Institute, and elsewhere; Phi Beta Kappa; author, *Social Salvation*, 1935; *Christianity and Our World*, 1936; *Christian Realism*, 1941; *Christian Ethics and Social Policy*, 1946; *Christians and the State*, 1958; *Christianity and Communism Today*, 1960; editor, *Nuclear Weapons and the Conflict of Conscience*, 1962; and other works; chairman, editorial board, *Christianity and Crisis*. (See also *Current Biography: 1961*.)

BOSLEY, HAROLD A. (1907-   ). Born, Burchard, Nebraska; A.B., Nebraska Wesleyan College, 1930; B.D., University of Chicago, 1932; Ph.D., 1933; honorary degrees, including D.D., Nebraska Wesleyan College, 1943; Northwestern University, 1950; L.H.D., Cornell College, 1953; entered Methodist ministry, 1924; director, religious activities, Iowa State Teachers College, 1934-38; minister, Mt. Vernon Place Methodist Church, Baltimore, 1938-47; dean, Divinity School, Duke University, 1947-50; minister, First Methodist Church, Evanston, Illinois, 1950-62; senior minister, Christ Church Methodist, New York City, 1962-   ; various assignments as lecturer at conferences and seminars; member, American Philosophical Association; named one of the fifty distinguished alumni, Pi Kappa Delta, 1963; author of many books, including *The Quest for Religious Certainty*, 1939; *Christian Faith*, 1945; *On Final Ground*, 1946; *Main Issues Confronting Christendom*, 1948; *Preaching on Controversial Issues*, 1953; *Sermons on the Psalms*, 1956; *Sermons on Genesis*, 1958; *Doing What Is Christian*, 1960.

BROOKE, EDWARD (1919-   ). Born, Washington, D.C.; B.S., Howard University, 1940; LL.B., Boston University, 1948; J.D., Portia Law School, Boston, 1963; admitted to Massachusetts bar, 1948; attorney general, Commonwealth of Massachusetts, 1962-   ; Republican candidate for secretary of state of Massachusetts, 1960; officer, infantry, World War II; decorated, combat infantry badge; selected as one of the ten outstanding young men, Boston, 1952; member, National Association of Attorneys General; Trial Lawyers Association; Boston Bar Association; author, *The Challenge of Change*, 1966.

CHAMPION, GEORGE (1904-). Born, Normal, Illinois; spent youth on farm; B.S., Dartmouth College, 1926, with major in history and political science; started career with National Bank of Commerce, New York City, 1926; assistant secretary, Equitable Trust Company, 1930; vice president, Canal Bank and Trust Company, 1931; second vice president, Chase National Bank, 1933; vice president, 1939; senior vice president, 1949-55; executive vice president, Chase Manhattan Bank, 1955-57; president, 1957-61; chairman, board of directors, 1961- ; director, American Smelting and Refining Company; Travelers Insurance Companies; Southern Railway System; Chase International Investment Corporation; treasurer, Freedoms Foundation; member, board of managers, New York Botanical Garden; president, New York City Chamber of Commerce, 1964. (See also *Current Biography: 1961*.)

CRICHTON, JOHN (1919-). Born, Padroni, Colorado; B.J., University of Missouri, 1940; served on newspapers in Colorado and Montana; joined *Advertising Age*, 1941; Washington editor, 1943; member, New York editorial staff, 1946-49; executive editor, 1949-57; editor, 1958; president, American Association of Advertising Agencies, 1962- ; secretary and director, Advertising Council; director, Advertising Research Foundation; Traffic Audit Bureau; Advertising Federation of America; Brand Names Foundation; member, Advertising Committee Advisory to the Secretary of Commerce; Advertising Committee of United States Council of International Chamber of Commerce; National Panel of Arbitrators of American Arbitration Association; Advertising Club of New York.

EDDY, EDWARD DANFORTH, JR. (1921-). Born, Saratoga Springs, New York; B.A., Cornell University, 1944; B.D., Yale University, 1946; Ph.D., Cornell University, 1956; associate director, Cornell Inter-Faith Program, 1946-49; assistant to the president, instructor in English, director of development, University of New Hampshire, 1949-54; acting president, 1954-55; vice president and provost, 1955-60; president, Chatham College,

1960- ; director, national study of character development in higher education, American Council on Education, 1957-58; selected one of ten outstanding young men, United States Junior Chamber of Commerce, 1955; trustee, Ellis School; author, *Colleges for Our Land and Time,* 1957; *The College Influence on Student Character,* 1959; contributor to magazines and journals.

FULBRIGHT, JAMES WILLIAM (1905-). Born, Sumner, Missouri; A.B., University of Arkansas, 1925; B.A. Oxford University, 1928; M.A., 1931; LL.B. with distinction, George Washington University, 1934; many honorary degrees; admitted to District of Columbia bar, 1934; special attorney, Antitrust Division, Department of Justice, 1934-35; instructor in law, George Washington University, 1935-36; lecturer in law, University of Arkansas, 1936-39; president, University of Arkansas, 1939-41; United States House of Representatives (Democrat, Arkansas), 1943-45; United States Senate, 1945- ; chairman, United States delegation to London Conference of Allied Ministers of Education, 1944; instrumental in establishing program for American scholars to study abroad; chairman, Foreign Relations Committee, United States Senate; Rhodes scholar; Phi Beta Kappa; author, *Old Myths and New Realities, and Other Commentaries,* 1964. (See also *Current Biography: 1955.*)

GRUENING, ERNEST (1887-). Born, New York City; Hotchkiss School, 1903; A.B., Harvard University, 1907; M.D., 1912; LL.D., University of Alberta, 1950; University of Alaska, 1955; managing editor, *Nation,* 1920-23; editor, 1933-34; founder, Portland *Evening News,* 1927; editor, until 1932; director, Division of Territories and Island Possessions, Department of Interior, 1934-39; administrator, Puerto Rico Reconstruction Administration, 1935-37; governor of Alaska, 1939-53; elected senator from Alaska to work for statehood in Washington, 1956; United States Senate (Democrat, Alaska), 1959- ; member, Committee on Governmental Operations, Committee on Interior and Insular Affairs, Committee on Public Works, United States Senate; author, *Mexico and Its Heritage,* 1928; *The Public Pays,* 1931; *The State of Alaska,* 1954. (See also *Current Biography: 1946.*)

HANNAH, JOHN (1902-). Born, Grand Rapids, Michigan; B.S., Michigan State University, 1923; D.Agr., 1941; many honorary degrees, including LL.D., University of Michigan, 1944; HH.D., University of Ryukus, 1952; L.H.D., University of Florida, 1953; D.Sc., University of Nigeria, 1961; president, Michigan State University, 1941- ; assistant secretary of defense for manpower and personnel, Department of Defense, 1953-54; member of boards of directors of several corporations and banks; member, National Committee for International Economic Growth; American Council on Education; president, Association of State Universities and Land-Grant Colleges, 1948-49; chairman, United States Commission on Civil Rights, 1957- ; member of many civic organizations; Pi Kappa Delta. (See also *Current Biography: 1952.*)

JACKSON, ESTHER MERLE (1922-). Born, Pine Bluff, Arkansas; B.S., Hampton Institute, 1942; M.A., Ohio State University, 1946; Ph.D., 1958; teacher of speech and drama, Clark College, 1949-56, 1961-64; specialist in theatre education, United States Office of Education, 1964-65; director of education, New York Shakespeare Festival, 1965-66; John Hay Whitney Opportunity fellow, 1956-57; fellow, Ohio State University, 1957-58; senior Fulbright research fellow and lecturer, 1960-61; professor of speech and theatre, Adelphi University, 1966- ; author, *The Broken World of Tennessee Williams,* 1965.

JOHNSON, LYNDON BAINES (1908-). Born near Stonewall, Texas; graduate, Johnson City (Texas) high school, 1924; B.S., Southwest State Teachers College, San Marcos, 1930; student, Georgetown University Law School, 1935-36; teacher, public schools, Houston, Texas, 1930-32; secretary to Representative Richard M. Kleberg, 1932-35; state director, National Youth Administration for Texas, 1935-37; member, United States House of Representatives (Democrat, Texas), 1937-49; United States Senate, 1949-61; minority leader, 83d Congress; majority leader, 84th-86th Congresses; resigned from United States Senate, January 3, 1961; Vice President of the United States, 1961-63; became

President of the United States upon the assassination of President Kennedy, November 22, 1963; elected President of the United States, 1964; author, *My Hope for America*, 1964. (See also *Current Biography: 1964*.)

KENNAN, GEORGE FROST (1904-   ). Born, Milwaukee, Wisconsin; A.B., Princeton University, 1925; vice consul, Hamburg, Germany, 1927; Tallinn, Estonia, 1928; consul, Vienna, 1935; Prague, 1939; first secretary, Berlin, 1940; counselor of Legation, Lisbon, 1941-43; minister-counselor, Moscow, 1945; department counselor and chief long-range adviser to Secretary of State, 1949-50; member, Institute for Advanced Study, Princeton, 1950-52, 1953, 1956, and at other times; ambassador to Soviet Union, 1952; ambassador to Yugoslavia, 1961-63; visiting professor, Oxford University, 1957-58; named University Fellow in History and Slavic Civilization, Harvard University, 1966; member, American Philosophical Society; American Academy of Political and Social Science; American Academy of Arts and Sciences; National Institute of Arts and Letters; recipient, Pulitzer Prize, Bancroft Prize, National Book Award; author of many books, including *Realities of American Foreign Policy*, 1954; *Russia Leaves the War*, 1956; *Decision to Intervene*, 1958; *Russia, the Atom and the West*, 1958; *Russia and the West under Lenin and Stalin*, 1961. (See also *Current Biography: 1959*.)

McGOWAN, CARL (1911-   ). Born, Hymera, Indiana; A.B., Dartmouth College, 1932; LL.B., Columbia University, 1936; admitted to bar, New York, 1936; Illinois, 1940; District of Columbia, 1948; private practice, New York City, 1936-39; Washington, 1946-48; Chicago, 1953-63; United States Naval Reserve, 1942-45; counsel to Governor of Illinois, 1949-52; member of faculty, Northwestern University Law School, 1939-42, 1948-49; member, Council of the American Law Institute; American Bar Association; Chicago Bar Association; member, United States Court of Appeals for the District of Columbia Circuit.

MARBURY, WILLIAM LUKE (1901-   ). Born, Baltimore county, Maryland; student, Boys' Latin School, Baltimore, 1910-16; Episcopal high school, Alexandria, Virginia, 1916-18; Virginia Military Institute, 1918-19; A.B., University of Virginia, 1921; LL.B., Harvard University, 1924; admitted to Maryland state bar, 1925; associated in firm Piper & Marbury, 1931-   ; president, Peabody Institute of Baltimore, 1948-57; chairman, board of trustees, 1957-   ; assistant attorney general, State of Maryland, 1930-31; consultant to Secretary of War, 1940-41; member, Harvard Corporation, 1947-   ; chancellor, Episcopal Diocese of Maryland, 1962-   ; fellow, American College of Trial Lawyers; member, American Law Institute; American Academy of Arts and Sciences; president, Maryland State Bar Association, 1966; Phi Beta Kappa.

PAUL VI, POPE (Giovanni Battista Montini) (1897-   ). Born, Concesio, Brescia, Italy; student, Arici Institute; Lombard Seminary; Ecclesiastical Academy; Gregorian University; Apollinare Juridical Faculty, Rome; distinguished scholar and linguist; ordained priest in the Roman Catholic Church, 1920; attaché, Apostolic Nunciature, Warsaw, 1923; on staff of Secretariat of State, Vatican, 1924; professor of history of pontifical diplomacy, 1931-37; pro-secretary of state, 1952; consecrated Archbishop of Milan, 1954; created Cardinal, 1958; elected Pope, June 21, 1963 (the 262d Supreme Pontiff of the Roman Catholic Church). (See also *Current Biography: 1963.*)

PERCY, CHARLES H. (1919-   ). Born, Pensacola, Florida; A.B., University of Chicago, 1941; honorary degrees, including LL.D., Roosevelt University, 1961; Illinois College, 1961; Lake Forest College, 1962; HH.D., Willamette University, 1962; began career with Bell and Howell Company, 1938; assistant secretary, 1943-46; corporation secretary, 1946-49; president, 1949-61; chairman, chief executive officer, 1961-66; director, Burroughs Corporation; Harris Trust and Savings Bank of Chicago; co-chairman, National Conference of Christians and Jews, 1954; chairman, Fund for Adult Education, Ford Foundation, 1958-61; vice chairman, Republican National Finance Committee, 1957-59; chairman, committee on Platform and Resolutions, Republican National Convention, 1960; lieutenant, USNR, 1943-45; named one of the ten outstanding young men, United States Junior Chamber of Commerce, 1949; recipient, World Trade Award, 1955; Republican candidate for governor of Illinois, 1964. (See also *Current Biography: 1959.*)

CUMULATIVE AUTHOR INDEX

1960-1961—1965-1966

A cumulative author index to the volumes of REPRESENTATIVE AMERICAN SPEECHES for the years 1937-1938 through 1959-1960 appears in the 1959-1960 volume.